The Role
of Central Banking
in China's
Economic Reforms

The Role
of Central Banking
in China's
Economic Reforms

Carsten Holz

East Asia Program
Cornell University
Ithaca, New York 14853

The *Cornell East Asia Series* publishes manuscripts on a wide variety of scholarly topics pertaining to East Asia. Manuscripts are published on the basis of camera-ready copy provided by the volume author or editor.

Inquiries should be addressed to Editorial Board, Cornell East Asia Series, East Asia Program, Cornell University, 140 Uris Hall, Ithaca, New York 14853.

ISSN 1050-2955
ISBN 0-939657-59-7

CONTENTS

PART I THE PEOPLE'S BANK OF CHINA

Part II MONETARY POLICY AND THE ECONOMY

FIGURES AND TABLES

Figures

Tables

ABBREVIATIONS

b   billion
CCP   Chinese Communist Party
GIOV   Gross Industrial Output Value
GNP   Gross National Product
m   million
PBC   People's Bank of China
PRC   People's Republic of China
SU   Soviet Union
TOVS   Total Output Value of Society

STATISTICAL NOTATION

-       the numerical value is exactly zero;
0   the numerical value is zero or less than half the final digit shown;
X   item does not exist;
.   no figure given.

PREFACE

The economy of the People's Republic of China (PRC) has moved from a high economic growth rate and increasing inflation in the early 1980s to a centrally imposed freezing of economic reforms with lower growth and inflation rates in 1989 and 1990. In 1991 the economy entered a new boom phase with, as of mid-1992, no end in sight. Is the circle of *fang luan shou si* (setting the economy free — chaos — reimposition of central control — recession) bound to repeat itself? Is overheating and subsequent clamp-down an inevitable phenomenon in the Chinese economy? What are the underlying causes and mechanisms that determine such macroeconomic variables as the growth rate of national income and the inflation rate?

This book attempts to provide one explanation of how macroeconomic variables in the PRC are determined and how their interaction led to the economic events of the past few years. It does not attempt to provide a detailed discussion of all the economic reform measures since 1978 but rather makes, implicitly, two simplifying assumptions: (1) all transfers of commodities and labor are reflected in monetary counterflows; and (2) all monetary flows are to some degree subject to monetary policy. This book, then, treats the real economy (the non-monetary sectors) as a mirror image of the monetary sphere.

Central banking — the core of the banking system — and implementation of monetary policy provide a very structured and direct approach to understanding how an economy "with Chinese characteristics" functions. Proceeding from central banking and monetary policy illuminates the key mechanisms upon which the economic system hinges. Clear relationships between economic variables can then be established, showing how the overheating of the Chinese economy in the late 1980s came about, what the effects of the clamp-down were, and why a renewed turnabout is taking place in 1991/1992.

The introduction explains the close interrelationship between reforms in the real economy and developments in the monetary sphere. With the reforms in the real economy the scope of one function of money — as a medium of choice — was enlarged. This change necessitated a new set-up of the banking system, with a central bank at its core.

xi

Part I first analyzes the organization of the newly created central bank (Chapter 1). What is its formal position? What are its objectives? How is decision-making power on monetary policy distributed within — and partly outside — the central bank? It then examines individual instruments of monetary policy from two angles: Liquidity policy and interest rate policy (Chapter 2,3, and 4). The implementation of both the old instruments of "administrative management" and the new instruments of "economic control" is covered qualitatively and, as much as possible, quantitatively. How are the instruments supposed to work? Do they work? If not, why not? Can the central bank achieve its objectives? What are the major problems it faces? Finally, Part I considers the influence of state budget deficits and financial institutions on the central bank's monetary policy and control over the monetary system (Chapter 5).

This detailed discussion of the PRC's central bank could be seen as an end in itself, providing insight into the making and implementation of monetary policy and the functioning of the banking system as a whole. But it also serves as the key to one explanation of the behavior of (and the interrelationship between) various macroeconomic aggregates in the second part of the book.

Part II starts with a discussion of the intermediate objectives of monetary policy in the PRC and examines the degree to which they have been achieved since the transformation of the People's Bank of China (PBC) into a central bank in 1983 (Chapter 6). It then applies the theory of monetary overinvestment to the case of the PRC (Chapter 7). A circular flow model, representing a modified version of this theory, establishes causal chains between various macroeconomic variables, with monetary variables at the core. Economic events in the PRC in the years from 1984 until today are well explained within this model. The business-cycle framework (i.e., monetary overinvestment) together with the insights into the monetary sphere gained in Part I finally reveal the basic defect of the Chinese economy and allow conjectures as to what could happen if certain exogenous variables in the monetary sphere were changed (Conclusions). In particular, what might happen if the status of the central bank were redefined?

Throughout this book an attempt has been made to give the reader as much access to the original material as possible by including the romanization of the Chinese characters (in *hanyu pinyin*) in the text. At times the inclusion of *hanyu pinyin* expressions and definitions of Chinese terms may seem somewhat cumbersome, yet the potential gain in accuracy outweighs the inconvenience. A short Chinese-English glossary is provided at the back of the book.

Chinese regulations on the monetary system (and a few other official Chinese-language sources) are quoted at various places in this book. Many times the set-up envisaged in these regulations proves inconsistent in itself — apart from the fact that, as is shown subsequently, reality does not always correspond to the letter of the law (or to leadership's wishes).

Present tense has been used when referring to what seem permanent features of the Chinese economic system. Expressions such as "today" or "now" denote the period from late 1989 to 1991, a period with no significant changes in the monetary system.

Three figures could serve as an overview of the book: Figure 1 for the introduction, Figure 13 (together with the conclusions on the page preceding it) for Part I and Figure 14 for Part II.

I am very grateful to Loren Fessler, Macau, who was the first to go over the early drafts to correct my American English usage. I am deeply indebted to Tom Lyons, director of the East Asia Program at Cornell University, for tremendous help in preparing the manuscript for publication. All errors and shortcomings are, of course, mine.

Introduction: The Monetary System
in the Context of Economic Reform

Due to reforms in China's real economy (i.e., the non-monetary sectors), in the early 1980s the role of money changed. For the first time in the history of the PRC, money began to matter. Subsequently the institutional set-up of the banking system had to be altered, and ultimately new monetary instruments had to be established.

This introduction first describes the change in the role of money and its implications. The second section then presents the historical framework for central banking in the PRC today, showing how monetary reforms came about, and outlines the structure of the banking system within which the central bank operates at the present point of time.

1. Change in the Role of Money

Inter-Enterprise and Consumption Circuits

In socialist economies a strict distinction has been made between enterprises and consumers. The PRC has not abandoned this concept.

In the inter-enterprise circuit (that is, in money flows between enterprises), cash payments play only a negligible role. All payments are supposed to be carried out through earmarked bank accounts without involving any cash. External sources of enterprises' funds are allocations from the state budget and bank loans. Before the beginning of the economic reforms in 1978, banks were supposed to provide only part of the working

1

capital needed by enterprises in accordance with the "commodity inventory system" (or "real bills principle"): money created through credit backed by the purchase of (material) goods used in production is supposed to have no inflationary effects; once the finished products leave the enterprise and are paid for, the credit is repaid.[1] In the inter-enterprise circuit a surplus of money cannot arise, as money is centrally controlled through a monetary plan corresponding to a real plan. Transfer payments in the inter-enterprise circuit are easily monitored, and any purchase of commodities contrary to the real plan prevented. Money is a unit of account and a medium of exchange, ensuring the smooth functioning of the real economy. It stores value in so far as it guarantees the transfer of commodities at a point of time as outlined in the plan. Money is not a medium of choice.[2]

Consumers, however, receive wages and salaries in cash and have a choice of both time and object of their purchase. This choice implies the danger of a discrepancy between, on the one hand, salaries and wages, the main sources of cash, and, on the other hand, the supply of consumption goods, the main channel for withdrawal of cash from the economy. Increasing salaries and wages have enabled consumers not only to demand basic necessities of everyday life, of which the quantity demanded can be reliably estimated, but also to demand "luxury" goods, for which the demand fluctuates in directions and magnitudes not always predictable. The discrepancy can exist both in overall quantity (amount of cash to be spent by consumers in a certain period of time vs. supply of commodities in that period) and in particular commodity markets (type of goods demanded vs. type of goods supplied). The danger of this discrepancy manifests itself in the latent possibility of inflation if (i) prices are flexible and (ii) the demand for goods made possible by the amount of cash held by the public exceeds the supply of goods in a certain period.

Planning authorities have several measures at their disposal to defuse this discrepancy:

— limit the cash flow to individuals, and/or withdraw excess cash from individuals;

— change the prices of goods;

---

[1] Wulf 6/86, 213.

[2] Dembinski 1988, 284ff.

— change the structure and volume of production (and improve product quality);

— keep the two circuits of monetary circulation separate in order to prevent leakage, which can only further endanger the implementation of monetary and real plans.[3]

The authorities are extremely reluctant to limit the cash flow to individuals or to raise the prices of goods as would be required in order to eliminate the gap, which so far has more often than not arisen from too high a supply of money (cash) rather than from a lack of demand for commodities. With inflexible commodity production by mainly state-owned enterprises, the emergency solution therefore has been to siphon off an excess supply of cash through voluntary or involuntary increases in savings (*huobi huilong*).

Real and Monetary Spheres

Figure 1 suggests why division into two separate circuits and control of each circuit has become less and less practicable since the beginning of the economic reforms in 1978. First, reforms in the real economy may directly affect the monetary sphere, e.g., if local enterprises or governments are allowed to make their own independent decisions on whether or not to take out loans abroad. Second, reforms in the real economy may indirectly affect the monetary sphere, e.g., if material inputs have to be bought on the free market at market prices and possibly be paid for in cash. As a result of such reforms purchase decisions of enterprises are no longer completely under control and may vary from the real plan; extensive cash usage by enterprises then violates the separation into two circuits.

Both themes have in common that to enterprises, as well as households, money becomes a medium of choice. In a changed real economy (less real plan, less centrally controlled prices) enterprises must be able to determine time, object and volume of their purchase acts themselves. This requires the freedom to possess and dispose of a certain amount of money kept in accounts or in cash. The administrative control of cash is confronted with increased consumption by enterprises (e.g., business lunches with suppliers) and the purchase, with payment in cash, of investment goods listed in the

---

[3] Dembinski 1988, 288f.

Figure 1. Economic Reforms in the Real Economy and Their Influence on the Monetary System

AN INCREASE IN ...	LEADS TO THE CREATION OF / AN INCREASE IN ...

Opening to the Outside World
 	
Decentralized decisions on foreign trade
Direct investment by foreigners and joint ventures
Foreign debt of the PRC (use and repayment)
 	
Domestic Reforms and Revival of the Economy
 	
Different types of ownership
  — agriculture: responsibility system
    (decentralized decision-making authority, individual income, specialization)
  — industry and commerce:
    issuing of stocks and bonds
    collective and individual-owned enterprises
    (decentralized decision-making authority, individual income,
    specialization, independent investment)
    horizontal, deregulated enterprise mergers across regional boundaries
Local and regional economic independence, central cities, and state administration
    according to rules
 	
Responsibility system in enterprises
  — independence and possibility of bankruptcy
  — tax payments instead of handing over profits (own funds, tax evasion)
  — investment financing through own funds/bank loans (instead of state funds)
  — unplanned working capital requirements
  — deregulation of the labor market and salaries/wages
Deregulation of the commodity market (entry, marketing, quantity, prices)
	decentralized, mainly individual unplanned decisions on
	
	  monetary variables (directly) and
	
	  real variables (with serious consequences for the monetary sector)
	
	requiring
	
	a fundamental reform of the financial system.

real plan and intended for purchase with payment through transfers between bank accounts only.

Accumulation of large amounts of cash by the population and the newly-found freedom of enterprises, together with a range of commodity prices now determined by the market instead of administratively, introduce the phenomenon of inflation. If the monetary system is not to obstruct the reforms in the real economy, administrative management of credit according to plan and the separation into two circuits begins to falter. The supply of money starts to matter.

The administration, already deprived of a large part of its former influence on the real economy, would like to continue to exercise control over the real economy via the monetary system using the banking sector as "macro-control" authority *(hongguan kongzhi jigou)*. Monetary policy is supposed to replace much of the real plan. Vested interests, however, obstruct its implementation. Local governments try to use the banking sector to accelerate local development outside the real plan, enterprises demand more rights over the usage of their funds, and consumers have at their disposal large amounts of cash and savings deposits easily convertible into cash. The exercise of control on the amount of money supplied (credit and cash) and limitations on its usage have become central to the economic reforms.

2.   Institutional Reform of the Banking System

Development of Central Banking

Early history. The People's Bank of China (PBC), founded on 1 December 1948 before the proclamation of the PRC, has always been responsible for the implementation of monetary policy. After "liberation" in 1949, a large number of special banks were founded to promote the socialization of the economy and to take over private banks through state-individual ownership. These various "special" banks have at times become part of the PBC only to be re-established as independent units. The PBC itself was at times reduced to being the paymaster of the Finance Ministry. (See Figure 2.)

During the First Five-Year Plan (1953-1957) the principle of monetary administration was "unified state control over revenues and expenditures, savings and credit" *(tongshou tongzhi, tongcun tongdai)*. Banks simply fulfilled state orders without making any independent decisions. (One

Figure 2. Development of Financial Institutions

Institution	1948	1949	1950	....	1954	1955	....	1978	1979	1980	1981	1982	1983	....	1986	1987	1988	Notes
"Central Bank Shanghai"	0————	?																since 1928
People' Bank of China (PBC)	0———X————————																	central banks in soviets; PBC since 1 Dec. 1948; 1970–78 subordinated to the Finance Ministry; since 17 Sept. 1983 solely central bank
State Administration of Exchange Control			0————————————————————————————————															
Industrial and Commercial Bank of China													0————					since 17 Sept. 1983
Bank of China								X————————————————										split from PBC
Construction Bank of China					0——													1958 – 1962 part of Finance Ministry
Agricultural Bank of China					X———		X————————————————											53-57/63-65; split from PBC
Rural Credit Co-op.													0————					
Urban Credit Co-op.												0—————						
Investment Bank	partly since 1930s 0—————————————————————————————————									0————								
Bank of Communications	founded in 1908, 0———														X———			1954-86 in HongKong only
CITIC								X————————————————										

exception was that they could supplement "planned working capital" by short-term working capital loans.)

In order to finance the multitude of new industrial projects during the Great Leap (1958-1960), monetary policy turned very flexible: "as much credit as needed, where needed and when needed" (*xuyao duoshao dai duoshao, nali xuyao nali dai, shenmo shihou xuyao shenmo shihou dai*) with corresponding price increases, especially in 1961. Due to the ensuing policy of economic readjustment in the 1960s, the PBC again took over control of credit and cash in circulation. But all attempts at using "economic levers" (the price mechanism) and increasing the decision-making powers of the PBC were cut short by the Cultural Revolution beginning in 1966. The PBC was incorporated into the Finance Ministry in 1970.[4]

Emergence of the People's Bank of China as a Western-type central bank. Decisive changes in the monetary system were made by the Third Plenum of the Eleventh CCP Central Committee in December 1978. Most importantly, in order to do justice to the diverse needs of different economic sectors and branches, several special banks were split from the PBC, which remained both a commercial and central bank.[5]

It soon became obvious, however, that the overlapping areas of responsibility of the various special banks and the double function of the PBC were impractical.[6] Again and again the areas of responsibility and the positions of the individual special banks had to be delimited.[7] Even the final conversion of the PBC into a solely central bank through a State Council resolution on 17 September 1983 (hereafter: PBC Constitution of 1983) and the creation of the Industrial and Commercial Bank of China, consisting of the former commercial section of the PBC, did not end discussion of the functional differences between the central bank and the

---

[4] Liu Hongru 1987, 6-10; Shevel 3/85, 78-80; Zhang Guile 10/83, 23f.

[5] For the Agricultural Bank of China the decision was made on 30 Nov. 1979. For the Bank of China see State Council 22 Sept. 1980, and for the People's Insurance Company of China see State Council 27 Dec. 1982.

[6] According to Liu Hongru, then vice-governor of the PBC, the establishment of a two-tiered banking system had originally not been intended (Liu Hongru 1987, 129-137). A two-tiered banking system might not have been intended, yet this possibility always existed and officials of the caliber of Liu Hongru must have well known the range of possibilities. "To seek truth from facts" (trial and error) then facilitated further changes.

[7] E.g., in State Council 14 July 82.

special banks. Nor did the reform decisions of the Central Committee of the CCP in October 1984.

Shortly after the October 1984 decision Premier Zhao Ziyang created a "work group," consisting of representatives of the PBC, the State Commission for Reform of the Economic System, the Economic Research Center of the State Council and the Finance Ministry, as well as some "younger comrades," to propose reforms of the banking system. The proposal designed by this group included three objectives:

(1) establishment of a centralized administrative system in which the central bank can act flexibly in stimulating the economy and implementing macroeconomic control;

(2) establishment of a banking system consisting of the central bank as the head and a large number of different financial institutions; creation of financial centers of different sizes based in "central cities;"

(3) development of different types of credit and "circulation channels" (*rongzi qudao*); professional management, as well as modern leadership and administration of financial institutions.[8]

Although this proposal went to the State Council as early as December 1984, it was not translated into action.

It was only in the following years that the status of banks in the economic reforms was enhanced, although banks never received as much attention as, for example, price reform. A second milestone, after the decision in 1983 to convert the PBC into a central bank, was set with the "Provisional Regulations on the Administration of Banks in the PRC" (hereafter: Bank Regulations of 1986),[9] passed by the State Council on 7 January 1986. In 1983 a vague two-tiered banking system had been created; now the first comprehensive and systematic banking regulations were passed which "provisionally" regulated (i) the position and objectives of the central bank, the special banks and the other financial institutions, and (ii) the administration of money, credit, savings, and interest rates.[10]

---

[8] Liu Hongru 1987, 39-42.

[9] State Council 7 Jan. 1986.

[10] Besides the 1983 constitution and 1986 regulations more than 600 laws and regulations on the monetary system were passed by the State Council and the PBC between 1979 and 1988 (of which 40 by the State Council). (Zhang Xiumin 6/88, 13.)

The introduction and reintroduction of special banks necessitated by reforms in the real economy did not inevitably lead to the creation of a two-tiered banking system. Rather, separation of central banking from commercial banking came to be seen as the solution for two problems. First, the PBC, acting both as central bank and itself a competing special bank, discriminated against the other special banks. Second, control over the money supply was left to the PBC, partly a special and thus commercial bank, at a time when the separation into inter-enterprise and consumption circuits could only become more difficult to enforce.

The then prevalent enthusiasm for reform and adoption of Western administrative structures and methods facilitated the initial changes envisaged in 1983. The ultimate position of the central bank in the banking and economic system did not have to be decided upon immediately. Indeed its position might purposely have been left undecided until the further emergence of a new economic system; the reforms in the industrial sector did not start until 1984.[11]

Banking trial cities. As with all economic reforms, the reforms of the banking sector were conducted through the proven trial-and-error process as much as possible. This meant the introduction of banking trial cities (*jinrong gaige shidian chengshi*) and joint conferences of all cities of this type.

The first "work conference of banking trial cities" took place in January 1986. The second conference, in Beijing in August 1986, saw reports on experiments with interbank money markets, discounting of bills, establishment of non-rural financial institutions in collective ownership and of "financial institutions without banking-character," different types of contractual responsibility systems, and the professional management of banks. Additional cities were accepted as banking trial cities. After the third

---

[11] This point of view can be supported by several articles in ZGJR (*China Finance*), the monthly magazine published by the PBC. Furthermore, starting in 1983, the nature of a central bank was expounded in ZGJR over a period of 26 months, giving due consideration to the experiences of western countries, among them the USA, Great Britain and West Germany. This series is in no way inferior to western textbooks on banking and money; its author is Liu Hongru, then vice-governor of the PBC.

Sheng Mujie 1989, 39, lists as the only reason for the transformation into a solely central bank the necessity to control and regulate the increasing number of financial institutions working more and more under market conditions.

and fourth conferences (Wuhan in December 1986 and Dalian in September 1987), the number of trial cities and areas reached 27.[12]

One characteristic feature of all these conferences is the participation not only of representatives from the PBC and the special banks but also of representatives from central and local governments as well as of other individuals.[13] A reform of the monetary system cannot be determined and implemented by the PBC and special banks alone, but requires the consent of decision-makers in governments, government agencies and the odd individual not further specified.[14]

Structure of the Present Banking System[15]

The present banking system is characterized by a core of four traditional special banks and a large and changing constellation of other banks and financial institutions. The four traditional special banks are the Industrial and Commercial Bank of China, the Agricultural Bank of China, the Bank of China, and the People's Construction Bank of China. (See Table 1 and Figure 3.)

— The Industrial and Commercial Bank of China, established in September 1983, contains the former "special bank section" of the PBC. The Industrial and Commercial Bank of China provides short- and medium-term credit to industrial and commercial enterprises and obtains deposits from enterprises of the same sectors and from individuals.

---

[12] Chen Muhua 2/87, 7; Liu Hongru 1987, 45f; Ren Junyin 11/87, 14.

Trial cities in January 1986 were Guangzhou, Shenyang, Wuhan, Chongqing and Changzhou; in August 1986, Nanjing, Wuxi, Suzhou, Dandong, Wenzhou, and Ningbo, (among others) and all of Guangdong province were added.

[13] Ren Junyin 11/87, 12.

[14] With 27 cities being named banking trial cities the question arises as to whether the regulations in the monetary system and the authority of the PBC are not being undermined by a host of special rights. It is furthermore doubtful whether restricted experiments conducted for a limited period of time under special rights allow generalization and whether a possible massive influx of money (because, e.g., of higher interest rates offered) from surrounding, non-reformed areas does not distort the results. (Zhang Huaqiao 11/87, 20-22.)

[15] Barnham 15 March 1988; FEER 5 May 1988; Vetter 9/85; Obersteller 1987, 46-65; Huang Min 1988, 105-112; ZGJR, FEER, and C.a. in general.

— The Agricultural Bank of China, re-established in 1979, is the counterpart in the countryside to the Industrial and Commercial Bank of China in urban areas. Rural credit co-operatives are subordinated to the Agricultural Bank of China.

— The Bank of China finances all foreign trade, takes out loans abroad and issues bonds abroad. The State Administration of Exchange Control, although part of the PBC, works in close co-operation with the Bank of China and its offices are usually located within branches of the Bank of China.

— The People's Construction Bank of China channels earmarked funds from the state budget to investment projects in the form of loans to enterprises. It can also independently give loans financed through the repayment of former state budget allocations to enterprises. The China Investment Bank, subordinated to the People's Construction Bank of China, was founded in 1981 with the sole purpose of channeling World Bank loans to projects in the PRC. Today its scope of operations includes the distribution of credit received from other foreign financial organizations.

Apart from the four special banks, other important financial institutions include the Bank of Communications, the China International Trust and Investment Corporation, rural and urban credit co-operatives, "People's Banks," and post offices.

— The Bank of Communications was re-established in 1987; 50 percent of its capital was paid in by the state, 45 percent by local governments, state-owned and collective enterprises, and 5 percent by individuals. In contrast to the four banks above, whose areas of responsibilities are clear-cut, the Bank of Communications is a competitor to both the Industrial and Commercial Bank of China and the Bank of China. In addition to its headquarters in Shanghai it has branches in all major cities of the PRC. The Bank of Communications could serve as a model for the foundation of new banks.

— China International Trust and Investment Corporation (CITIC), founded in 1979 in connection with the passing of the joint venture law, is the most important of the trust and investment companies. Its objective is to raise investment funds domestically and abroad. The scope of business has been more and more enlarged, so that CITIC today is a competitor to most of the above banks. CITIC itself is also a partner to joint ventures and owns the (CITIC) Industrial Bank.

— Rural credit co-operatives first went into business in the 1930s and 1940s. After 1949 they were deployed by the state to eradicate usury in the villages and to support rural development. Credit co-operatives are privately owned by shareholders and are not directly controlled by the PBC but rather through the Agricultural Bank of China, where a "minimum reserve" is to be kept. The State Council, in a resolution of 17 July 1986, stopped the expansion of rural credit co-operatives into cities by legalizing urban credit co-operatives supervised directly by the PBC. Besides credit co-operatives, credit departments of supply and marketing co-operatives existed for a long time in the countryside. These credit departments, however, have either ceased to exist or their impact has become insignificant.

— The "credit group" or "People's Bank" is another form of rural financial institution. It consists of a small number of people who lend money to each other in an informal, agreed-upon way. The extent of such people's banks is difficult to estimate. In the banking trial city of Wenzhou they are said to provide one third of all credit.

— Post office savings deposits have become possible only within the last two to three years. No loans are given.

Besides these firmly established financial institutions, a host of small — and to a high degree independent — financial institutions have sprung up since the beginning of the economic reforms. Some of them are included in Figure 3.

Figure 3. Banking System

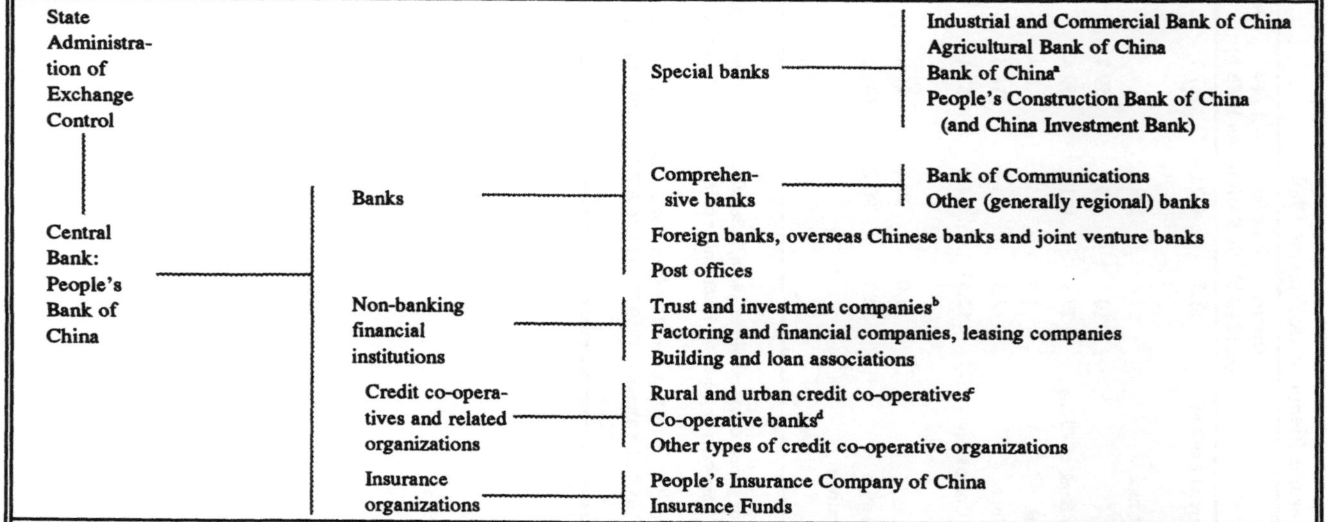

State Administration of Exchange Control

Central Bank: People's Bank of China

Banks
- Special banks
  - Industrial and Commercial Bank of China
  - Agricultural Bank of China[a]
  - Bank of China[a]
  - People's Construction Bank of China (and China Investment Bank)
- Comprehensive banks
  - Bank of Communications
  - Other (generally regional) banks
- Post offices
  - Foreign banks, overseas Chinese banks and joint venture banks

Non-banking financial institutions
- Trust and investment companies[b]
- Factoring and financial companies, leasing companies
- Building and loan associations

Credit co-operatives and related organizations
- Rural and urban credit co-operatives[c]
- Co-operative banks[d]
- Other types of credit co-operative organizations

Insurance organizations
- People's Insurance Company of China
- Insurance Funds

Notes:

a. Including 13 "sister banks" in Hong Kong.

b. One trust and investment company is the China International Trust and Investment Corporation, CITIC, with its CITIC Industrial Bank.

c. Rural credit co-operatives are administered not directly by the People's Bank of China but by the Agricultural Bank of China.

d. A co-operative bank consists of several rural or urban credit co-operatives.

Sources: Liu Hongru 1987, 136; others.

Table 1. Size of Various Financial Institutions 1988

Financial institution	Capital[a] (in RMB b)	Loans[b] (in RMB b)	Assets (in RMB b)	Branches
Industrial and Commercial Bank of China	13.7	497.0	561.7	29,998
Agricultural Bank of China	22	263.2	.	50,777
Bank of China	10	183.7	559.7	959
People's Construction Bank of China	27.9	121.3	339.4	13,815
China Investment Bank	1.5	.	6.7	.
Bank of Communications	2.5	18.5	111.6	45
Trust and Investment Companies (1987)	12.53	44.0	57.1	745
CITIC	3.0	10.1	21.8	.
Rural Credit Co-operatives	13.3	90.8	191.1	60,897
Urban Credit Co-operatives	.	.	.	3,265
Post Offices	.	X	>7.0	13,651

Notes:
  a. Capital consists of *guben* or *ziben* where given, otherwise of *ziyou zijin* or *jingzhi*.
  b. Loans consist of *fangkuan* or *daikuan*, loans under other names have not been included.

Sources: FEER 5 May 1988, 64f; Barnham 15 March 1988; China Financial Statistics (1952-1987), 136f,165,168f; Almanac 1989, 86-111,169; ZGJR 1/89; WEH 3 April 1989, 12.

PART I

THE PEOPLE'S BANK OF CHINA

Chapter 1

Organization

Before analyzing the various monetary policy instruments in the following chapters — that is, the channels through which the PBC interacts with the rest of the economy — it is necessary to gain an understanding of the People's Bank of China itself. What authority does it possess compared to financial and other institutions in the economy? What are its objectives? What are the implications of its organizational structure?

1. Legal Position

The PBC Constitution of 1983 for the first time in the history of the PRC established a two-tiered banking system:

The People's Bank of China is the state organ of the State Council that exercises leadership and control over the financial and monetary affairs throughout the country.[1]

The Industrial and Commercial Bank of China, the Agricultural Bank of China, the Bank of China, the People's Construction Bank of China, and the People's Insurance Company of China, acting as economic entities at the bureau level directly under the State Council, shall independently

---

[1] PBC Constitution of 1983, 1.

exercise their functions and powers and fully discharge their respective authorized functions in conformity with the state laws, decrees, policies and plans.[2]

The People's Bank of China will control[3] the activities and operations of the specialized banks and other financial institutions, including the Insurance Company, chiefly by economic means. These institutions have the obligation to carry out the decisions of the PBC and its Council [Board of Directors]; the PBC is authorized to impose administrative or economic sanctions on any violator. The China International Trust and Investment Corporation shall put its activities and operations under the control and supervision of the PBC. The People's Construction Bank of China, while remaining under the leadership of the Ministry of Finance in its operations related to public finance, shall carry out the decisions made by the PBC and its Council regarding credit principles, policies and plans.[4]

Both the PBC and the special banks (as well as other financial institutions) are thus in close contact with the State Council. Whereas the PBC is part of the State Council, the special, solely state-owned banks, are "economic entities at the bureau level [*juji*] directly under the State Council." To avoid a monobank with special banks as departments, the special banks have been subordinated directly to the State Council rather than the PBC. The special banks, however, are not completely independent of the PBC. The PBC "will control their activities and operations ... chiefly by economic means," but not *only* by economic means. The presence of the PBC's governor on the State Council can ensure that the PBC's orders are obeyed — if the other members of the State Council such as, e.g., the Finance Minister, agree.

"Economic means" stands for the use of "economic levers" (*jingji ganggan*) — that is, the price mechanism (commodity prices, interest rates and wages) — to achieve one's objectives. Differing from economic means are the administrative means such as credit plans and state decrees. The

---

[2] PBC Constitution of 1983, 4.

[3] The definition of *guanli*, in the English version of the PBC Constitution of 1983 rendered as "to control," is given in Chinese-Chinese dictionaries as "to be responsible for the smooth realization of a job assigned." (Xiandai hanyu cidian 1985.)

Below *guanli* will be translated as "to administer."

[4] PBC Constitution of 1983, 4.

PBC thus does not only "control" the special banks in the sense of "supervise" whether the PBC's rules are obeyed, but also intervenes in the management of the special banks whenever necessary. In everyday business this means that monetary policy is enforced by economic means. If the economic means do not meet with success, the PBC is free to ensure the "smooth" functioning of the monetary system by any means.

The latent conflict between PBC and State Council is most obvious in the case of the People's Construction Bank of China, which remains under the "leadership" of the Finance Ministry. How much influence can the Finance Ministry exert on the PBC? What happens if "credit guidelines" published by the PBC cannot be reconciled with requests by the Finance Ministry? Officially the PBC and the Finance Ministry are on the same hierarchical level, since the Finance Ministry is one of 31 ministries and the PBC is one of two "other state organs on the level of a ministry"[5] (the other being the Auditor-General's Office). An explicit mechanism for decision-making either does not exist or is not published.

2. Objectives

The Bank Regulations of 1986 specify three objectives of equal weight for all financial institutions:

The central bank, the special banks and the other financial institutions shall conscientiously realize the general and special monetary policies of the state;[6] their monetary activities shall have as objectives development of the economy, currency stability, and increase in economic efficiency.[7]

The above sentence contains two important statements.

First, there is a state monetary policy which is not necessarily decided upon by the PBC.[8] If state monetary policy is not decided upon by the PBC, which institution is responsible for monetary policy? And if the PBC

---

[5] There are also eight commissions on the ministerial level.

[6] *Fangzhen zhengce* is (here and below) rendered as "general and special policies;" another translation would be "guidelines and policies."

[7] Bank Regulations of 1986, Art. 3.

[8] Although the phrasing allows for the meaning that the PBC's monetary policy is the state monetary policy this is probably not intended.

is not responsible for monetary policy, then how is it supposed to implement economically necessary monetary measures in the case when they run contrary to state monetary policy? Can the PBC influence state monetary policy, or is its sole task to execute orders? Neither the Bank Regulations of 1986 nor other published regulations provide any answer to these questions. Second, both the PBC and special banks shall attain the three objectives.[9] Formally, insofar as the PBC is concerned, three possible conflicts exist between the different objectives. The PBC avoids these conflicts in practice by dropping the third objective, the increase in economic efficiency; it only talks of currency stability and development of the economy. Special banks, on the other hand, are to strive towards an increase in economic efficiency through their credit policy. What is left to Chinese economists to discuss in the case of the central bank is the conflict between currency stability and development of the economy. Depending on one's point of view either development of the economy is stressed and inflation accepted ("Sino-Keynesians") or currency stability is seen as prerequisite to economic growth ("Sino-Monetarists"). Most Chinese economists tend towards the second position, because the PRC hardly ever suffers from a lack of aggregate demand. At the same time inflation is unacceptable to Chinese still aware of the hyperinflation during the Guomindang Regime up through 1949.[10] There is a very practical reason for the PBC to support the Sino-Monetarist school: in the case of inflation the PBC will inevitably be blamed, but if economic development is regarded as insufficient the PBC does not immediately come under attack.

What influence do special banks (and other financial institutions) exert on the stability of the currency? That special bank which, with almost unlimited possibilities of refinancing by the PBC, does not excessively increase loans to its customers will, compared to other banks, experience a relatively declining volume of business and thus a decrease in influence over the local economy. If bonus payments to employees are linked to the volume of

---

[9] According to Chen Muhua, then Governor of the PBC: "The points of view [of the PBC and special banks] are different, yet the objectives are the same." (Chen Muhua 2/88, 7.) Chen Muhua offers no further explanation.

[10] Xue Muqiao 1/88, 18.

The PBC Constitution of 1983 only required the PBC to "... concentrate its forces on the maintenance of currency stability and on the discussion of macroeconomic decisions on the monetary system of the nation." (PBC Constitution of 1983, 2.)

business, then every special bank striving for stability of the currency would limit the income level of its employees unnecessarily.[11]

The Bank Regulations of 1986, in addition to the three general objectives, also mentions various "duties" of the PBC and the special banks,[12] which are taken up below.

3. Structure

Board of Directors

According to the Bank Regulations of 1986, the PBC shall establish a Board of Directors as the "decision-making body of the PBC Head Office"[13] — not as decision-making body for state monetary policy. The PBC Head Office is an executive organ with its governor and vice-governors in charge of routine matters and implementation of decisions made by the Board of Directors.[14]

Duties. The duties of the Board of Directors (Bank Regulations of 1986) are to discuss general and special policies for the monetary system; to discuss important relevant questions of the annual state credit plan, the cash plan and the foreign exchange plan; to determine the principles of establishment and dissolution of special banks and other financial institutions as well as their division of labor; and to discuss other important matters of the monetary system.[15]

The Board of Directors is thus at complete liberty in choosing the subjects of its discussions ("other important matters"), but the emphasis is on "discuss" and not on "decide." The PBC Constitution of 1983 states that in case no agreement can be reached by the Board of Directors, the governor has the final say; however, in all important questions the State

---

[11] As to the objectives of banks in trial cities see Zhang Shaojie 11/87, 13, rendered below.

[12] Bank Regulations of 1986, Art.5.

[13] Bank Regulations of 1986, Art.7.

[14] Liu Hongru 1987, 160; Lu Peijian 3/84, 5.

[15] Bank Regulations of 1986, Art.7.

Council shall be asked to make the final decision.[16] This is simply a continuation of the previously noted vague wording when it comes to decision-making power. What decision-making power does the Board of Directors actually have? The Board can, but need not, feel responsible for a specific problem. If it thinks itself responsible yet cannot reach an agreement, the State Council shall be asked for a decision.[17] What happens if the Board of Directors does not think itself responsible or is not convened? Again, the published regulations do not provide any answer.

The first one-day meeting of the Board of Directors took place on 18 January 1984,[18] and the third meeting of the year 1985 was on 24 August 1985.[19] Later on such meetings either went out of fashion or were no longer announced. It is not certain whether the Board was (or is) convened regularly, but at the most it has been (or is) convened once every quarter.[20] At the two meetings mentioned above, the Board of Directors had the sole purpose of promulgating general policies through a speech by the head of the Board of Directors who, according to the regulations, is at the same time governor of the PBC. This would suggest that de facto decision-making power rests with either the governor of the PBC or some outside institution giving orders to the governor.

As to the way meetings of the Board of Directors are conducted, Lu Peijian, then governor of the PBC, said on 18 January 1984:

With regard to the problems which are to be discussed by the Board of Directors, the PBC shall, before the meeting is convened, hold discussions with the ministries, commissions and special banks concerned as well as with the insurance company [i.e., with all members of the Board of Directors].

If all participants in these discussions adhere to the guidelines, general and special policies of the Party and the decisions of the State Council,

---

[16]   PBC Constitution of 1983, 3.

[17]   King 1965, 128ff, cites Alfred Kuo-liang Ho: "The Grand Council in the Ching Dynasty," *Far Eastern Quarterly* 11, 167-182 (Feb. 1952), on the monetary policy in China 1845-1895: "The Board of Revenue was in charge of financial affairs of the Empire [Qing Dynasty], but extraordinary, emergency or policy measures were often brought directly to the attention of the Emperor by the central and provincial officials."

[18]   PBC 3/84.

[19]   Chen Muhua 10/85, 2.

[20]   Lu Peijian 3/84, 5, speaks of one quarterly meeting.

and if they take into consideration the general situation and only act after coordinated consultations, in many questions unanimity will be achieved.[21]

This means that there can be no confrontation of different opinions, but rather only a prior agreement based on leadership by the governor of the PBC and on a host of Party and State Council resolutions and decisions, which cannot be questioned.

Membership. According to the PBC Constitution of 1983, the Board of Directors includes the governor and vice-governors of the PBC; various advisors and experts of the PBC; one vice-minister each from the State Planning Commission, the State Economic Commission[22] and the Finance Ministry; presidents of the special banks; and the managing director of the People's Insurance Company of China.[23] (See Figure 4.) The governor of the PBC is at the same time chairman of the Board of Directors; the vice-chairmen are to be chosen from among the members of the Board of Directors.[24] The Board of Directors "appoints" a secretary from among its members.

Altogether three different interest groups are represented in the Board of Directors: the PBC, the ministries and commissions (of the same level), and the special banks. Suppose the representatives of the PBC are interested in decisions of the Board of Directors safeguarding the stability of the currency and guaranteeing economic growth. What are the objectives of the ministries? The ministries will first strive to achieve their own objectives, which for the Planning Commission is realization of its real plan, for the State Economic Commission (or its successor) economic growth, and for the Finance Ministry a balanced state budget. All these objectives have little in common with currency stability. Neither do the objectives of the special banks, as shown above. As the PBC's representatives in the Board of Directors are outnumbered by members inimical to currency stability, the PBC would seem to be forced to rely on prior diplomatic negotiations and

---

[21]   Lu Peijian 3/84, 5.

[22]   This commission does not exist any more; a likely replacement candidate as a member of the PBC Board of Directors is a vice-minister of the State Commission for the Reform of the Economic System.

[23]   PBC Constitution of 1983, 2f.

[24]   No information at all is available on how the chairman and the vice-chairmen are to be chosen.

Figure 4. People's Bank of China: Members of the Board of Directors

Institutional line-up	Personnel				Further information
	1984	24 Aug. 85	Early 1989	Late 1990	(on personnel, late 1990 or latest available)
Governor of the PBC (chairman of the Board of Directors)	Lu Peijian	Chen Muhua	Li Guixian	Li Guixian	Member of the 13th Central Committee, State Councillor, member of the State Planning Commission, Chairman of the Board of Directors of the Asian Development Bank
Vice-governor of the PBC (vice-chairman of the Board of Directors)	Liu Hongru	Liu Hongru	Liu Hongru		Candidate of the 12th and 13th Central Committee, Vice-minister of the Commission for the Reform of the Economic System
Further vice-governors of the PBC (members of the Board of Directors)	Qiu Qing	Qiu Qing	Qiu Qing	Qiu Qing	Director of CITIC
	Li Fei				
	Zhu Tianshun	Zhu Tianshun			
			Zhou Zhengqing	Zhou Zhengqing	Chairman of the Board of Directors of the China Finance Institute
			Tong Zengyin	Tong Zengyin	
				Guo Zhenqian	Member of the 13th Central Committee, Deputy Secretary of Hubei Province CCP, Deputy for Hubei Province to the 7th National People's Congress
				Chen Yuan	Son of Chen Yun, member of the State Commission for Science and Technology
				Bai Wenqing	
General Secretary	Wang Weicai	Yin Jieyan			Head of the Foreign Affairs Bureau of the PBC (1990)

PBC advisors/experts					
	Shang Ming	Shang Ming			Chairman of the Board of Directors of the People's Insurance Company of China (1988)
Vice-ministers of the					
Finance Ministry	Chi Haibing				Vice-chairman of the State Council Leading Group for the Investigation of the Chinese Industry
State Planning Commission	Fang Weizhong				Candidate of the 12th and 13th Central Committee
State Economic Commission	Yan Ying				
Presidents of special banks					
Ind. and Commercial Bank of China	Chen Li	Zhang Xiao	Zhang Xiao	Zhang Xiao	
Agricultural Bank of Ch.	Han Lei	Ma Yongwei	Ma Yongwei	Ma Yongwei	
Bank of China	Jin Deqin	Jin Deqin	Wang Deyan	Wang Deyan	
People's Construction Bank of China	Wu Boshan	Zhou Daojiong	Zhou Daojiong	Zhou Daojiong	Chairman of the Board of Directors of the China Investment Bank
Others	Qin Daofu	Qin Daofu	Qin Daofu	Qin Daofu	Manag. Director of the People's Insurance Co. of China
	Tang Gengyao	Tang Gengyao	Tang Gengyao	Tang Gengyao	Director of the State Administration of Exchange Control
	Che Peiruan				Head of the Foreign Affairs Bureau of the PBC (1989)

Sources: (1) Institutional line-up: State Council, 17 Sept. 1983, 2. (2) Personnel: 1984: State Council, 17 Sept. 1983, English version; PBC 3/84, 2. 24 Aug. 1985: Chen Muhua 10/85, 3. Early 1989 and late 1990: various articles (e.g., Jinrong yaowen 7/90, 56; ZGJR 2/90, 16; Almanac 1989, 593ff; Almanac 1990, 509ff; entry according to personnel. (3) Further information: Bartke 1987; Bartke 1991; C.a. 10/87, 799–803; ZGJR 4/90, 60; South China Morning Post 7 March 1990; CCP Annual Report 1990.

coordination. A Board of Directors making major monetary policy decisions would amount to financial institutions and ministries helping themselves freely to the money printing press instead of being monitored by the central bank.

Not only are the interests of the Board of Directors detrimental to a sound monetary policy, but furthermore the institutional set-up does not favor qualified decisions. Both the large number of members and their possible lack of qualification impede efficient and correct (from the point of view of the PBC's objectives) decision-making. It is therefore very reasonable to convene meetings of the Board of Directors only once a quarter for one day after extensive prior consultation. And it would not be surprising if the Board of Directors after a few meetings has been abandoned.

Head Office

The PBC is headed by one governor and several vice-governors. The appointment procedures are not published. The PBC Constitution of 1983 mentions that during the transformation of the PBC into a solely central bank, highly qualified professionals from the special banks and the People's Insurance Company of China were to be moved to the central bank. If it is assumed that at the PBC appointment procedures similar to those used at other financial institutions are in effect, then at least the governor and the vice-governors are appointed by the State Council.[25]

When the first governor of the PBC, Lu Peijian, was replaced by Ms. Chen Muhua on 21 March 1985,[26] the appointment was made by the Standing Committee of the National People's Congress upon the proposal

---

[25]   Of the special banks only the Constitution of the Bank of China of 22 September 1980 is available. The Board of Directors of the Bank of China is appointed by the State Council and meets once annually. The chairman proposes a president and several vice-presidents who have to be approved by the Board of Directors. The State Council is asked to appoint those chosen.

For the People's Insurance Company of China the state departments "concerned" appoint a Board of Directors which then elects the Standing Committee. The Standing Committee nominates a chairman and several vice-chairmen and asks the State Council to appoint those chosen. The chairman of the Board of Directors nominates the managing director and several deputies, who are then all appointed by the Board of Directors.

In both procedures the main positions are filled either directly or indirectly by the State Council or by state departments.

[26]   C.a. 3/85, 152.

of the then Premier (and thus head of the State Council) Zhao Ziyang. The reason for asking the National People's Congress for the appointment might have been the intention to give Chen Muhua a firmer foothold than her predecessor. No information could be found on who appointed Li Guixian[27] in April 1988 and Lu Peijian in 1983. The appointment of Chen Muhua was clearly aimed at strengthening the PBC: Chen Muhua, previously head of the Ministry of Foreign Economic Relations and Trade, was a member of the CCP Central Committee and a candidate (alternate member) to the Politburo,[28] as well as a member of the State Council's Standing Committee, the most important decision-making body of the state.[29] She resigned in April 1988 ostensibly due to old age (but probably because of disagreements with the then Premier, Zhao Ziyang). Li Guixian, her successor, holds the same positions, except that he is not a candidate to the Politburo.

The State Council is the focal point of the state decision-making structure. Economic decisions as important as monetary policy should not be expected to be made by an institution at the ministerial level, such as the PBC, but by the State Council Standing Committee (upon orders from, or in agreement with, the Party leadership). The State Council Standing Committee has 14 members, among whom are the head of the Finance Ministry and the head of the State Planning Commission.[30]

Decision-making power is not ascribed by law to certain independent institutions responsible for their part of the economy, but is exercised by an elite in the state organization (State Council Standing Committee) and Party (Central Committee and Politburo) consisting of officials who know each other well. The monetary policy the professional body of the PBC can push through depends decisively on its influence on the more often than not financially illiterate governor and the governor's standing in the State

---

[27] FAZ 8 April 1988.

[28] Euromoney 9/86, 48.

[29] The State Council Standing Committee consists of (in October 1990):
(1) Premier (who, at the same time, is a CCP Politburo and Central Committee member);
(2) 3 vice-premiers (all Politbureau and Central Committee members);
(3) 9 State Councilors (2 of which Politbureau members; 8 of which Central Committee members);
(4) 1 Secretary General (also Central Committee member).
(C.a. 10/90, 790/4.)

[30] As of late 1990 the head of the Commission for the Reform of the Economic System was not a member of the State Council (C.a. 10/90, 790/4). However, Li Peng, the former head, was a member by virtue of his being Premier.

Council. What decision-making power can the "decision-making" body of the PBC, the Board of Directors (with the vice-ministers of other ministries and the presidents of the special banks), possess in such a system?

While sharing monetary decision-making power with the State Council and, to a lesser degree, the representatives of special banks and ministries, the PBC also maintains a close relationship with various financial and other institutions as well as with the Party. The PBC is represented on the Board of Directors of the People's Insurance Company of China.[31] As to special banks, the Bank of China is the only special bank for which a constitution is published. No mention is made of the PBC being represented on its Board of Directors. It is, however, likely that officials of the PBC are either part of the decision-making structure of all special banks, or are asked for their opinion or approval before major decisions are made. The PBC is also represented in state commissions and ministries. Liu Hongru, former vice-governor of the PBC has, for example, been vice-minister of the Commission for the Reform of the Economic System all along. Lower-level institutions are not excluded. The PBC is, for example, represented on the Special Committee for the Promotion of the Fast Developing Tourism Industry.[32]

Although in the PBC as a whole there does not exist any CCP organization parallel to the administrative organization,[33] the governor of the PBC is a member of the CCP Central Committee. Chen Muhua, the former governor of the PBC, also served as Secretary of the Leading Party Group (*dangzu shuji*) in the PBC. With the highest state official in the PBC also being the highest Party official in the PBC a source of friction is eliminated. The governor thus is in a very strong position.

The PBC Head Office itself is supported by a large (and changing) configuration of departments. (See Figure 5.) In the following chapters, analysis of monetary instruments is undertaken without reference to particular departments. An exception is the State Administration of Exchange Control, which is covered in more detail in the section on the Foreign Exchange Plan.

---

[31]   State Council 27 Dec. 1982.

[32]   C.a. 6/88, 450f.

[33]   Li Guixian 3/90, 4.

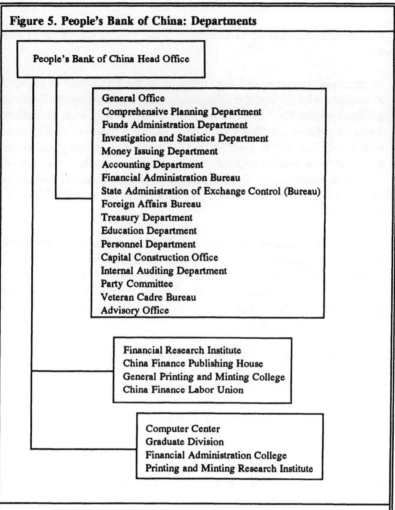

Figure 5. People's Bank of China: Departments

People's Bank of China Head Office

General Office
Comprehensive Planning Department
Funds Administration Department
Investigation and Statistics Department
Money Issuing Department
Accounting Department
Financial Administration Bureau
State Administration of Exchange Control (Bureau)
Foreign Affairs Bureau
Treasury Department
Education Department
Personnel Department
Capital Construction Office
Internal Auditing Department
Party Committee
Veteran Cadre Bureau
Advisory Office

Financial Research Institute
China Finance Publishing House
General Printing and Minting College
China Finance Labor Union

Computer Center
Graduate Division
Financial Administration College
Printing and Minting Research Institute

Notes: The Financial Research Institute and the China Finance Publishing House publish ZGJR, a monthly publication.

Almanac 1990, 509, does not list the Party Committee, the China Finance Labor Union and the Financial Administration College, but adds an Administrative Department, a Policy Research Office, a Regulations and Law Department, a Control Bureau and the Daily Finance Publishing House.

Sources: Jin Jiandong 1986, 40; State Council 17 Sept. 1983, English version.

Branches

On the establishment of PBC branches, the PBC Constitution of 1983 states:

In principle, branches and sub-branches of the PBC shall be set up in accordance with the division of economic zones of the country. Under the guidance of the PBC Head Office, and in conformity with the national financial policies and State Credit Plan, the main functions of the branch offices will be: (a) to regulate credit funds and currency circulation within their respective regions; (b) to coordinate, guide, supervise and inspect the operations of the special banks and other financial institutions; and (c) to undertake other activities as instructed by PBC offices at a higher level.

The PBC will exercise vertical leadership and centralized control over banking management and personnel administration of all its branches and sub-branches. Local governments at all levels shall facilitate and supervise the implementation by the PBC of the guiding principles and policies of the State, but they shall not interfere with the routine operations of the Bank.[34]

The Bank Regulations of 1986 are very brief:

The PBC establishes branches in accordance with the needs of economic development. The branches of the PBC fulfill the duties of the central bank in the regions under their control and head and administer the monetary system in these regions.[35]

The transformation of the PBC into a solely central bank was characterized by the conversion of the PBC's commercial departments into the Industrial and Commercial Bank of China in September 1983.[36] After the foundation of the Industrial and Commercial Bank of China, only about one thousand of the PBC's 23,166 branches remained in 1985. Their

---

[34]   PBC Constitution of 1983, 3.

[35]   Bank Regulations of 1986, Art.8.

[36]   Although this separation should have been accomplished by 1984, it dragged on until at least 1986. (PBC 2/86.)

number reached 2,431 in 1988, with a branch in almost every county.[37] (See Table 2.) Since the process of transformation took far longer and was more painful than expected, the redirection of the PBC towards "economic regions" or "central cities" (in an attempt to escape the traditional state administrative strongholds) did not receive the priority it was supposed to obtain.[38]

Table 2. Branches of the People's Bank of China				
Branches	1985	1986	1987	1988
Provincial level[a]	29	29	29	29
Municipalities directly under provincial governments	136	146	146	158
Cities on provincial level	.	7	10	12
Districts (prefectures)	164	159	159	155
Cities on county level	50	114	159	204
Counties	559	1749	1775	1760
Banking Schools	.	31	33	38

Notes:
  a. Including the three municipalities directly under the central government and the five autonomous regions.
  For comparison: there were 1986 counties in 1987.
  Not listed are various institutions (not further specified), the number of which was 78 in 1987 and 75 in 1988.
Sources:
  Statistical Yearbook 1988, 3,765; Statistical Yearbook 1989, 58. China Financial Statistics (1952-1987), 168, speaks of 1934 branches on the county level in 1987 (no information on other years). Almanac 1989, 169, gives different figures for the hierarchical divisions, but the same total of 2,431 branches besides the Head Office.

For the establishment of branches on the county level the criterion is "according to need." The 559 branches of the PBC on the county level in 1985 covered only one fourth of all counties. Originally it was planned to

---

[37] Although the PBC already in 1983 was transformed into a central bank, the official statistics did not list the Industrial and Commercial Bank of China as a separate entity before 1985. (Statistical Yearbook 1988, 3,765; Almanac 1989.)

[38] Liu Hongru 1987, 158, states that presently the PBC cannot but keep the old branches and wait and see whether the economic regions deserve more attention in the future.

maintain no PBC branches at all on the county level. But friction arising from (i) special banks not obeying the orders of the local Industrial and Commercial Bank of China, which, besides being a special bank, also represented the PBC, and (ii) the conflicting interests of the two parts (commercial vs. central bank departments) of the Industrial and Commercial Bank of China itself led to a change of plans.[39] In February 1986 the PBC and the Industrial and Commercial Bank of China announced that PBC branches on county level could be retained if the PBC provincial branch and the provincial government so decided. The Industrial and Commercial Bank of China on the county level was to transfer 15% of its personnel to the local PBC branch; one of its (or another special bank's) vice-directors was to be appointed head of the local PBC branch. PBC and special banks were to have separate money vaults. The process of transformation was to be completed by mid-1986.[40]

The close relationship between the PBC and special banks as well as possible relationships involving the provincial government are obvious. It can only be in the interest of a provincial government to retain PBC branches in its province, since having a larger share of the central banking administration implies more power and more chances to influence the money supply. Personnel from the PBC and the special banks know each other well, and the head of the PBC branch will not forget the former superior who might have been responsible for his transfer. As to the quality of the PBC staff, it is doubtful whether the special banks transferred their best personnel. The procedure used to establish county level PBC branches thus does not favor the monitoring of the special banks by the PBC.[41]

Both the PBC Constitution of 1983 and the Bank Regulations of 1986 contain very little information on the decision-making powers of the PBC branches. Within the PBC, organization is strictly hierarchical (see Figure 6) with occasional special rights for certain branches. Some form of local monetary policy exists, which, as on the national level, is formulated not by the PBC alone but by a local PBC Board of Directors through a "joint conference" (*lianxi huiyi*) under the leadership of the PBC, consisting of the PBC, special banks, and other institutions "concerned." The joint conference can be further split into (i) "horizontal and vertical" joint conferences (*zongheng lianxi huiyi*) under the direction of the local planning commission and the PBC, with financial institutions, commissions and other

---

[39] Liu Hongru 3/86, 9; Gongzuo yanjiu 7/85, 33.

[40] PBC 2/86, 24.

[41] Also see Wei Zhenguang 12/85, 8f.

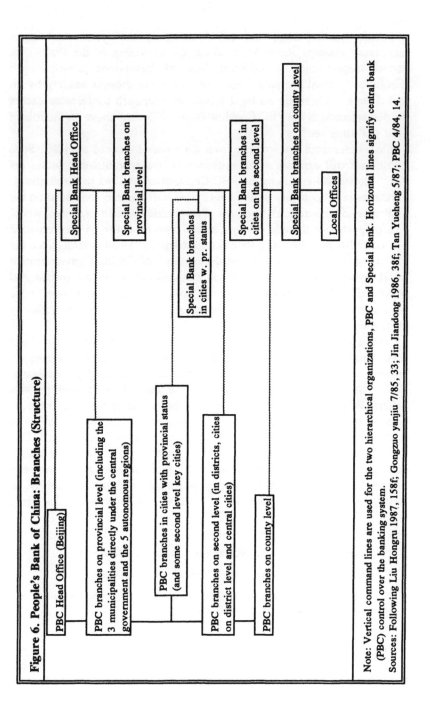

Figure 6. People's Bank of China: Branches (Structure)

PBC Head Office (Beijing)

PBC branches on provincial level (including the 3 municipalities directly under the central government and the 5 autonomous regions)

PBC branches in cities with provincial status (and some second level key cities)

PBC branches on second level (in districts, cities on district level and central cities)

PBC branches on county level

Special Bank Head Office

Special Bank branches on provincial level

Special Bank branches in cities w. pr. status

Special Bank branches in cities on the second level

Special Bank branches on county level

Local Offices

Note: Vertical command lines are used for the two hierarchical organizations, PBC and Special Bank. Horizontal lines signify central bank (PBC) control over the banking system.

Sources: Following Liu Hongru 1987, 158f; Gongzuo yanjiu 7/85, 33; Jin Jiandong 1986, 38f; Tan Yuecheng 5/87; PBC 4/84, 14.

authorities participating, and (ii) "vertical special" joint conferences (*zongxiang zhuanye lianxi huiyi*) under the leadership of the PBC, with various departments of different financial institutions participating.[42] Resolutions passed by such joint conferences are deemed binding by all participants.[43] There are no legal foundations for such conferences except the one sentence in the PBC Constitution of 1983 cited above on the role of local governments.[44]

Joint conferences are sensible from the point of view of the PBC. State institutions still exercise some influence on the appointments within the PBC, despite statements in the PBC Constitution of 1983 to the contrary. Furthermore, a monetary policy which does not take into consideration the local state administration (the owner of local state-owned enterprises) would be a preposterous thought to any Chinese central banker. A confrontation between PBC and the local state administration is inconceivable since the PBC is regarded as a "functional department" of the local government.[45] Local governments which decide on state allocations to enterprises and which still might directly or through local ministries administer some enterprises, cannot be allowed to be subordinate to, or without authority over, the local PBC.

Central monetary plans give enough leeway to "suit measures to local conditions" (*yindi zhiyi*). The PBC branch has to perform a balancing act between orders from the PBC Head Office and from local governments. Either the stability of the currency or the realization of state projects suffers. When a local government presses for the realization of its projects, perhaps the implementation of a certain investment not reconcilable with central monetary plans, the CCP is supposed to act as a mediator.[46] Due to the economic reforms, however, Party directives do not carry the weight they once did. Instead, local interests, without having to bear any responsibility, endanger a monetary policy aimed at currency stability. In early 1990, Li Guixian, governor of the PBC, stated explicitly that every

---

[42] Yang Changzeng 6/86, 24; PBC Shanghai 2/86, 16; PBC Taiyuan 2/86.

[43] Chen Xigu 5/84, 26; Gongzuo yanjiu 7/85, 33; Herrmann-Pillath 1/87, 15.

[44] In the past "leaders" from the administration have occasionally been appointed head of the joint conference. (Song Yingwei 4/87, 26.)

[45] Mo Ran 3/88, 53.

[46] Walters 1982, 11-36.

The Chinese expression *tiaotiao kuaikuai* ("central and regional") stands for the dual leadership: Strict, functional vertical leadership (*lingdao*) by superior institutions and horizontal guidance (*zhidao*) by local governments and the Party.

bank branch had to "consciously accept the leadership of the local CCP committee."[47]

Counterweights to the local joint conferences are provided by the regular, possibly monthly, meetings of PBC branch directors (*quanguo fenhang hangzhang huiyi*), generally held in Beijing. Participants represent all provincial PBC branches and the PBC branches in municipalities on a provincial level and in the Special Economic Zones. The large number of participants (probably more than 50) with widely diverging interests, depending on the location of their PBC branches, impedes decision-making. Yet the purpose of these conferences might well only be to promote central monetary policy and to obtain immediate feedback.[48]

After his appointment as governor of the PBC, Li Guixian immediately called a conference of PBC branch directors.[49] Even the Premier, Li Peng, did not think it beneath his dignity to participate in the first conference of the year 1988.[50] The PBC branch directors serve as transmission mechanisms for state monetary policy. As such they are to be taken seriously, even though they are not decision-makers of monetary policy.[51]

Monetary policy in the PRC thus is determined and implemented not by an independent and strong central bank. Decision-making power in the monetary sphere has to be shared with the State Council and, to a lesser degree, with financial and other institutions, while the implementation of monetary policy leaves much room for participation by other institutions on the local level.

---

[47]   Li Guixian 3/90, 4.

[48]   The course of such a conference in Beijing on 17 to 19 August 1988, was as follows: First a vice-governor of the PBC, Zhou Zhengqing, held an introductory speech on the monetary policies to be adopted. After a discussion of implementation, another vice-governor of the PBC, Liu Hongru, summed up the results (including an admonition to bank cadres not to accept presents). No decisions were made. (Jin zuida 10/88; no complete account of the introductory speech and the discussion is given.)

[49]   ZGJR 7/88, 9f.

[50]   Zhan Wu 3/88, 43.

[51]   More information on these conferences is in FEER 20 Oct. 1988, 100f; Chen Muhua 2/88, 4; Kongzhi 3/88; Zhang Yongyu 4/88; Jianding 12/88; Li Guixian 2/90.

PBC branch directors not only meet with representatives of local governments or with staff from PBC headquarters but also participate in symposia on various monetary affairs. A symposium in the Special Economic Zone Shenzhen in late 1987, for example, dealt with medium- and long-term developments in the banking system. (Shenhua 2/88; Hong Yuncheng 3/88, 39.)

Chapter 2

Monetary Policy Instruments:
Traditional Liquidity Policy

The PBC describes itself as being in a period of transformation from administrative management of the monetary sphere (that is, the traditional planning system) towards macroeconomic control by economic means (that is, Western-type monetary policy). Going over the details and intricacies of monetary plans and their changes is at times tedious. It is nevertheless necessary in order to show what goes wrong with central banking in the PRC, and for what reasons. A summary of all monetary instruments is rendered in Figure 13 ("Monetary Instruments") at the beginning of Part II.

This chapter will cover liquidity policy within the traditional administrative planning system whereas "modern," Western-type liquidity policy is discussed in the following chapter. Those instruments used for interest rate policy — where the differentiation between traditional and modern monetary policy is not as clear-cut — will be reviewed in Chapter 4.

Despite difficulties in maintaining strict separation between checking accounts and cash (i.e., the inter-enterprise and consumption circuits), the PBC still clings to the old planning system in which credit, cash circulation and foreign exchange are centrally planned. Each of the three plans, with the credit plan itself consisting of a number of sub-plans, will be discussed in detail in this chapter.

1. Credit Plan[1]

An introduction to the three main credit plans and to the general planning process in the monetary system permits discussion of administrative management of credit later in this section. A summary of problems associated with the credit plan system concludes the section.

Particular Credit Plans

The system of credit plans consists of three main plans:

(1)   State Comprehensive Credit Plan (*guojia zonghe xindai jihua*);

(2)   PBC Credit Plan (*renmin yinhang xindai jihua*);

(3)   Special Bank Credit Plans (*zhuanye yinhang xindai jihua*).[2]

A special bank branch on the lowest level draws up its credit plan and submits it to both the PBC branch on the same level and the superior special bank branch. The superior special bank branch, taking into consideration the credit plans of all subordinate branches, draws up its own credit plan and submits it to the PBC branch on the same level and to its immediate superior branch in the special bank hierarchy. This process is continued up to the highest hierarchical level. The PBC branches on all levels combine their own credit plans (the PBC Credit Plan, which includes loans to

---

[1]   Sources cited below include several regulations, some of which are listed here for an overview:

(1) Credit Administration 1985 (PBC 8 Oct. 1984 (a));

(2) PBC Credit Administration 1985 (PBC 8 Oct. 1984 (b));

(3) Industrial and Commercial Bank of China Credit Administration 1985 (ICBC 8 Oct. 1984);

(4) Credit Administration 1987 (PBC 1/87 (a));

(5) Special Banks Credit Administration (PBC 1/87 (b)).

[2]   While the State Comprehensive Credit Plan encompasses both the PBC Credit Plan and the Special Bank Credit Plans, the Social Comprehensive Credit Outline (*shehui zonghe xinyong guihua*) consists of the State Comprehensive Credit Plan and other monetary activities, (for example, by foreign institutions and "other financial institutions"). Drawn up by the PBC, the plan serves only a supplementary purpose. (Jin Jiandong 11/86, 17.)

The latest addition is a credit plan solely for non-bank financial institutions (*fei yinhang jinrong jigou xindai jihua*). (Buduan 3/88, 25; Zhou Zhengqing 5/88, 23.)

financial institutions) with the credit plans received from local special bank branches into a Comprehensive Credit Plan. The PBC Head Office finally receives PBC Credit Plans and Comprehensive Credit Plans from its provincial branches (including autonomous regions, municipalities directly under the central government and, since 1987, cities on a provincial level and the Special Economic Zone Shenzhen) as well as the credit plans from each special bank on the national level. The final product of the PBC Head Office is a State Comprehensive Credit Plan, including both the PBC Credit Plan and the Special Bank Credit Plans.

As none of the credit plans is published,[3] three balance sheets are included here (as Figures 7, 8, and 9): (i) Consolidated Balance Sheet of All (State) Banks reflecting fulfillment of the State Comprehensive Credit Plan, since it is frequently referred to below; (ii) Balance Sheet of the PBC reflecting fulfillment of the PBC Credit Plan, since it offers valuable insight into the entanglement between central bank and special banks/state; and (iii) Balance Sheet of the Industrial and Commercial Bank of China reflecting fulfillment of one individual Special Bank Credit Plan, since it shows both the dependence of special banks on loans from the central bank and the role of special banks in funding enterprises. All Chinese bank balance sheets have some characteristics in common: Certain quarterly changes in cash in circulation and credit volume. Both decrease during the first quarter of each year and show the largest increase in the fourth quarter due to the state purchase of agricultural products and increased efforts to fulfill the real plans towards the end of the year.

The PBC Balance Sheets for 1985 and 1986 were regularly published,[4] but those for later years were not. (See Figure 8.) Occasional individual figures published for the years 1987 to 1989, however, allow the conclusion that the basic structure of the PBC Balance Sheet did not change in later years.

Among the deposits at the PBC are interest-free deposits of all state organs (including offices and organizations), which are partly held at special banks, plus deposits of the special banks, consisting of minimum and excess reserves.[5] Part of the increase in deposits by state organs may be used by local PBC branches, which can give loans to non-banking institutions either

---

[3] Their outlines are given in textbooks on the banking system. For example, for an outline of the State Comprehensive Credit Plan see Huang Min 1988, 125.

[4] For example, in Almanac 1987.

[5] PBC Constitution of 1983, 5; Bank Regulations of 1986, Art.36f.

Figure 7. Consolidated Balance Sheet of All Banks

(1985 and 1986; including People's Bank of China, Industrial and Commercial Bank of China, Agricultural Bank of China, Bank of China, People's Construction Bank of China and Rural Credit Co-operatives; in RMB b)

ASSETS	1985	1986	LIABILITIES	1985	1986
All loans	627.173	811.651	All deposits	458.760	584.087
Loans to industrial enterprises	(116.508)	(165.311)	Enterprise deposits	(207.153)	(264.301)
Loans to industrial supply and marketing enterprises and goods and material departments	(38.083)	(47.705)	Deposits by the state	(36.837)	(31.145)
			Deposits for capital construction	(-)	(-)
Loans to commercial enterprises	(264.930)	(308.941)	Deposits by offices and organizations	(32.576)	(39.597)
Loans to construction enterprises	(26.707)	(36.941)	Urban savings deposits	(105.781)	(147.145)
Loans to urban collective-owned enterprises and individual industrial and commercial households	(32.128)	(42.554)	Rural savings deposits	(56.481)	(76.612)
			Rural deposits by collectives	(19.932)	(25.287)
Loans to agriculture	(78.285)	(109.605)			
Loans for investment in fixed assets	(70.532)	(100.594)	Liabilities to international financial institutions	7.818	12.423
Gold	1.204	1.204	Cash in circulation	98.783	121.836
Foreign Exchange	9.310	7.712			
Assets at international financial institutions	8.869	10.043	Bank capital	77.782	86.165
Loans to the state	27.505	37.005	Profit of current year	7.030	7.937
Others	5.648	5.593	Others	29.536	60.760
Total use of funds	679.709	873.208	Total sources of funds	679.709	873.208

Note: With PBC Balance Sheets only available for 1985 and 1986, the Consolidated Balance Sheet of All Banks is rendered here for the same years only, although later figures are available, too.

Sources: Financial Statistics of China (1989-1985), 1; Almanac 1987, II-9.

Figure 8. Balance Sheet of the People's Bank of China
(1985 and 1986; in RMB b)

ASSETS	1985	1986	LIABILITIES	1985	1986
All loans	261.193	319.845	All deposits	70.254	71.929
Loans to the state	(27.505)	(37.005)	State deposits	(36.837)	(31.145)
Loans to financial institutions	(224.859)	(267.593)	Deposits by offices and organizations	(33.417)	(39.597)
Rediscounting	(.)	(1.798)	Other deposits	(.)	(1.187)
Other Loans	(8.829)	(1.645)			
State allocation of special loans	(.)	(11.804)	Cash in circulation	98.783	121.836
Gold	1.204	1.204	Minimum reserves	42.046	56.531
Foreign Exchange	9.310	7.712	Excess reserves	45.992	55.783
Assets at international financial institutions	8.694	10.043	Liabilities to international financial institutions	7.818	12.423
Others	5.593	5.593	Others	21.101	25.895
			of which capital	(17.705)	(.)
Total use of funds	285.994	344.397	Total sources of funds	285.994	344.397

Sources: Financial Statistics of China (1989-1985), 1; Almanac 1987, II-9.

directly or indirectly via special banks.[6] The minimum reserve rate since September 1988 is 13% for special banks and CITIC. In 1985/86 the excess reserves were about as large as the minimum reserves and thus constituted, if they could be withdrawn any time, a correspondingly large potential for the creation of money. While the minimum reserves increased continuously from 1985 to 1988, excess reserves fell to a level of approximately 3% of all lending by financial institutions.[7] All reserves of special banks at the PBC yield interest.

More than 80% of all PBC assets in 1985/86 consisted of loans to special banks. The multiplier effect of these loans, which amounted to approximately half of all deposits at special banks, was limited by the strict enforcement of the credit plan. A special bank could only exceed the limits on loans laid down in the credit plan if its deposits exceeded its planned amount of deposits (*duocun duodai*). The PBC, despite its role as a central bank, also provides direct loans to certain (non-banking) target groups. These loans are made under special conditions and are supposed to serve economic development. According to the Bank Regulations of 1986, Art. 30, the state is not allowed to overdraw its account at the PBC. Yet loans have been given by the PBC to the state for many years.

Neither a credit plan for the special banks (abstract or with figures) nor a balance sheet for all special banks (without PBC) is published. By way of example the balance sheet of the Industrial and Commercial Bank of China (1986) is reproduced here (Figure 9). About one third of all deposits at the Industrial and Commercial Bank of China in 1986 were loans obtained from the PBC. These loans were not balanced by any securities or treasury bonds deposited with the central bank. The main purpose of loans by special banks was to supply working capital exceeding planned working capital furnished by the state. Today, with greatly reduced state budget allocations, banks supply all working capital[8] and almost all of the investment funds that

---

[6]   PBC 8 Oct. 1984 (a).

[7]   Li Yuping 6/90, 30; Almanac 1989; according to the sum of the relevant entries in the balance sheets of Individual Banks.

[8]   State Council 25 June 1983.

Figure 9. Balance Sheet of the Industrial and Commercial Bank of China
(1986; in RMB b)

ASSETS	1986	LIABILITIES	1986
All loans	384.895	All deposits	255.374
Loans to industrial enterprises	(185.035)	Enterprise deposits	(115.525)
Loans to commercial enterprises	(104.484)	Urban savings deposits	(119.666)
Loans to urban collective-owned enterprises and individual industrial and commercial households	(32.081)	of which:	
		time savings deposits	[(97.339)]
		demand savings deposits	[(22.327)]
Special loans	(1.568)	Issues of financial bonds	(1.659)
Other loans	(13.597)	Other deposits	(18.524)
Loans for investment in fixed assets	(48.130)		
Minimum reserves	24.293	Capital	18.435
		Others	39.233
Deposits at PBC	13.713		
		Loans from PBC	112.686
Cash	2.827		
Total use of funds	425.728	Total sources of funds	425.728

Note: Figures for 1985 are not available, probably due to the fact that the separation of PBC and Industrial and Commercial Bank of China was achieved only in 1986.
Source: Almanac 1987, II-9.

enterprises obtain from external sources.[9] The amount of loans to private enterprises is negligible.[10]

Administrative Management of Credit

Principles. Between 1979 and 1984 administrative management of credit followed the principle of "unified planning, administration on different levels, linking deposits and loans, and control of the balance" (*tongyi jihua, fenji guanli, cundai guagou, cha'e kongzhi*).[11] Linking deposits and loans meant that the volume of credit depended on the amount of deposits attracted. At the beginning of the year the (planned) balance between deposits and loans at a special bank provincial branch was calculated on the basis of deposits planned for the end of the year, plus funds to be obtained from the special bank's head office, minus the volume of credit planned for the end of the year. If the balance was positive, it had to be handed over to the special bank's head office; if it was negative, the special bank's head office assigned the provincial branch an additional amount of money, financed, if necessary, by loans from the PBC Head Office. Any amount of deposits obtained above the planned amount could be used by the provincial branch. The provincial branch used the same procedure with lower-level branches.

---

[9]   Funds for investment are generally obtained from the People's Construction Bank of China which has built up its own resources through the accumulation of state budget allocations to enterprises it has turned into repayable loans. (State Council 30 May 1981.)

In 1985 all loans to construction enterprises and 39% of all loans for investment in fixed assets were given by the People's Construction Bank of China. Since 1984 the loans for capital construction investment (investment in new projects, including construction of a completely new facility, or an addition to an existing facility) are supposed to come exclusively from the People's Construction Bank of China; the Industrial and Commercial Bank of China, the Agricultural Bank of China and the Bank of China should only give loans for investment in technical updating and transformation (investment in projects to renew, modernize or replace existing assets). (State Council 30 May 1984, definitions of investment types are from Statistical Yearbook 1989, XXXV.)

Investment in fixed assets is classified as (i) capital construction, (ii) technical updating and transformation, and (iii) others.

[10]   Individual enterprises are required to have a business license, a certain amount of own capital and a repayment guarantee.

[11]   Huang Min 1988, 132-134; Peng Songjian 1987, 396f.

In January 1985[12] the credit plans of special banks were renamed "Annual Credit Funds Income and Expenditure Plans" (*niandu xindai zijin shouzhi jihua*),[13] each consisting of

— a "Concise Credit Funds Income and Expenditure Plan" (*fenxiang xindai zijin shouzhi jihua*) and

— a "PBC Refinancing Plan" (*xiang renmin yinhang jiekuan jihua*) for loans from the PBC to the special banks.

Since 1985 the head office of each special bank distributes the amount of new loans from the PBC among its provincial branches and reports the distribution to the PBC Head Office. The PBC Head Office then forwards "credit notifications" to its provincial branches with instructions on how much can be loaned to the respective provincial special bank branch. The principle in force is "unified planning, division of funds, deposit of credit funds, and mutual money flow" (*tongyi jihua, huafen zijin, shidai shicun, xianghu rongtong*).[14] While planning is still centralized, the funds are now divided in that each special bank head office has a certain amount of funds at its own disposal and loans can be obtained (in accordance with the plan) at local levels from the PBC. "Deposit of credit funds" means that a special bank branch on the provincial level takes out a loan from the local PBC in accordance with the PBC Refinancing Plan and channels these funds further down its hierarchy.[15] On every level the funds obtained from PBC loans must be held at the local PBC branch until used. The account at the local PBC cannot be overdrawn.[16] "Mutual money flow" means the permission to establish a local/regional "horizontal" (on the same administrative level) interbank money market. The changes in the administration of credit have three implications. First, central control is reduced with the increased autonomy of provincial-level bank branches within the PBC Refinancing Plan and with the creation of an interbank money market. Second, special bank branches on every level

---

[12] PBC 8 Oct. 1984 (a), Art.7.

[13] According to ICBC 8 Oct. 1984 approval is given by the State Planning Commission.

[14] PBC 8 Oct. 1984 (a), Art.3.

[15] There have been discussions on whether or not to locate these loans from the PBC to special banks on an even lower level. (PBC 6/86, 27f.)

[16] Huang Min 1988, 132-134.

strive to retain as much money as possible instead of handing it back to the higher-level special bank and ultimately to the provincial PBC branch. Third, if those funds deposited at local PBC branches can be freely withdrawn, a correspondingly large increase in money supply out of the PBC's control can result.

While the PBC Refinancing Plan is imperative in that it cannot be exceeded, the Special Bank Credit Plans are, with the exception of capital construction investment loans, indicative. (Capital construction investment loans are imperative.) Loans for technical updating and transformation may not exceed the planned annual volume but can be flexibly allocated by the special banks. Thus the policy of "wearing a hat" (*dai mao*), that is, of giving all loans according to instructions from economic departments, is, at least de jure, abandoned. Since special banks are supposed to allocate loans for technical updating and transformation according to the "economic efficiency" of projects, the departments concerned only enjoy the right of proposal. Loans for working capital, as long as they remain within the PBC Refinancing Plan, depend only on the amount of deposits attracted.[17]

Changes in the PBC Refinancing Plan are possible in well-founded cases. A formal request must be made to the PBC before a deadline towards the end of the year.[18]

Since 1987 the PBC, when drawing up the State Comprehensive Credit Plan, is supposed to also take into consideration the "rational" economic growth rate (*jingji heli zengzhanglu*), planned increases in the price level (*wujia jihua shangshenglu*) and changes in the velocity of money (*huobi liutong sudu bianhua*). The first step is to determine the increase in money supply and the amount of funds presently available; the volume of loans will then be increased as necessary. The credit volume and structure, however, will continue to be the main intermediate monetary objective (achieved through direct administrative management), since control via the money supply is not yet feasible. The State Council retains the final say on all

---

[17]   PBC 8 Oct. 1984 (a), Art.8; ICBC 8 Oct. 1984, Art.5; Qiu Qing 12/84.

For the "central supply and marketing of goods and materials" some special regulations still exist at the Industrial and Commercial Bank of China.

As to working capital: A survey conducted in the second half of 1986 at Industrial and Commercial Banks and Agricultural Banks in 9 banking trial cities revealed that in 1985 only 18.5 % of all new working capital loans were for projects specifically designated in the plan. For January to September 1986 the figure was 14.0 %. (Zhang Shaojie 11/87, 11.)

[18]   PBC 12/84, 22-24.

In 1985 the deadline was in October.

important monetary variables such as the overall credit volume.[19] In the past, the PBC had to take into account different production reference numbers (*kongzhi shuzi*)[20] in combination with empirical values such as the relationship between currency in circulation and output, and the general and special policies of the Party.[21] Such reference numbers proved to be very useful as long as the real economy was centrally planned. With the reforms in the real economy, however, the rules in the monetary sphere had to be changed; the empirical values of the past are no longer reliable.[22]

The Special Bank Credit Plans and the use of credit funds are to be "separated." The PBC Refinancing Plan no longer guarantees the supply of a certain amount of funds to a special bank but only states the maximum amount possible. There is a difference between (i) annual loans of the PBC Head Office to special bank head offices and of PBC branches above the county level to special bank branches of the same level, and (ii) short-term loans by local PBC branches to local special bank branches according to local needs (but still within the PBC Refinancing Plan).[23]

This new distinction has been further elaborated as follows:

(i)   Annual loans (*nianduxing daikuan*) to meet the needs of "rational" economic development.
    Source: State deposits at the PBC, minimum reserves of special banks, and issuing of cash.
    Duration: One year or, at most, two years.

(ii)   Short-term loans (*duanqi daikuan*).
    Source: Excess reserves of special banks at the PBC.

  - Seasonal loans (*jijiexing daikuan*) to reconcile short-term scarcity of funds.
    Duration: Two to four months.

---

[19]   Jin Jiandong 11/86, 16f.

In 1988 for the first time a projection of the development of the money supply was supposed to be drawn up and published. It has not been published.

[20]   Reference numbers (control figures) are the main targets or norms formulated in plans. These numbers constitute the cornerstones of the planned economy.

[21]   Peng Songjian 1987, 383.

[22]   PBC 8 Oct. 1984 (a); PBC 1/87 (a).

[23]   In early 1988 (Buduan 3/88, 25f) there were complaints that the annual loans to special banks all went to the special banks' head offices.

- Bridging loans/call money (*richaixing daikuan*) to bridge a shortage of funds due to transfer payments not yet arrived.[24]
  Duration: Ten to twenty days.

- Rediscounting of bills (*zaitiexian*).
  Duration: Generally six months.[25]

The two types of loans are characterized by the familiar *tiaokuai* system: *tiao* stands for loans given by the PBC Head office to the special banks' head offices, which then channel them further down their hierarchies; *kuai* stands for loans by PBC branches down to the second (the district) level to corresponding special bank branches. Despite new flexibility in the allocation of loans, the credit plans of special banks remain as a "cage" (*longzi*), loans for capital construction investment being imperatively planned and all other loans being indicatively planned.

The principle for the types of loans described above is "rational supply of loans, fixed duration, guaranteed repayment and favoring circulation" (*heli gongei, guiding qixian, youjie youhuan, zhouzhuan bianyong*). Nevertheless repayment is a permanent problem, especially with bridging loans, since special banks are afraid that once the loan is repaid it will be difficult for them to obtain a new loan in the future. Spare liquidity can always be used on the interbank money market.

Under the procedures promulgated, the PBC is explicitly no longer responsible for the supply of funds to the special banks on the various levels. Special bank branches are asked to use the money market, to increase deposits, and to issue bonds. Yet in practice the PBC can only effectively control the credit ceiling for annual loans; short-term loans given by local PBC branches have increased by a large amount in past years. The total sum of refinancing of financial institutions by the PBC dropped from 38% of all credit in 1986 to 31% in 1988, but then increased again to 34% in 1989. (See Table 3.)

With the introduction of the "control of the balance" in 1979, loans from all banks to non-banking institutions increased at a steady rate from 1980 to 1983. In late 1984 it was announced that the new regulations in 1985

---

[24] Bridging loans are also used for the purchase of an unexpectedly large harvest of agricultural and sideline products. The amount is negotiated between PBC and special bank branches on the provincial level and then lent by local PBC branches to local special bank branches. (PBC 8 Oct. 1984 (a).)

[25] PBC 1/87 (a); PBC 1/87 (b).

would use the credit volume at the end of 1984 as the basis for the 1985 monetary plans. This led to an immediate increase in loans in 1984. Growth rates of credit remained high in 1985 and 1986. Only in 1987, with the PBC no longer responsible for the refinancing of special banks, did the growth rates return to their former level. The regulations in 1987 could thus be seen as reimposing stricter control on the refinancing of special banks by the PBC and thereby limiting the growth in the volume of credit.

Apart from the changing regulations on refinancing of special banks by the PBC, the PBC, enjoying far-reaching powers, employs a host of special regulations as it deems necessary. Among these regulations are the following. (i) PBC branches in the 14 open coastal cities, the four Special Economic Zones (plus Hainan) and in designated areas[26] enjoy larger decision-making powers on development loans and special loans, plan fulfillment, and the purchase of foreign exchange than PBC branches elsewhere.[27] (ii) Local PBC branches may retain part of the yearly increase in deposits by state organs and use these to hand out loans for purposes decided upon by the branch; these loans are given either directly by the PBC branch or indirectly via special banks.[28] (iii) Special requests by the state for additional loans to capital construction projects are met by the PBC Head Office, which either designates the relevant special bank or asks its provincial branch to provide the loans.[29] (iv) Since 1987 the rural credit co-operatives have to make special deposits at the PBC during the first half of the year besides keeping regular minimum reserves at the Agricultural Bank of China; these funds are then released during fall for the purchase of agricultural and sideline products.[30] (v) If the PBC is in danger of loosing control over the total credit volume, it may introduce a credit ceiling[31] or

---

[26] Specifically, the *lao-shao-bian-qiong* ("old-minor-border-poor") areas, i.e., the "liberated" areas (Chinese soviets before 1949), the areas heavily populated by minorities, border areas, and poor areas.

The Industrial and Commercial Bank of China accepts a special status for 8 provinces: Inner Mongolia, Guangxi, Guizhou, Yunnan, Gansu, Qinghai, Ningxia and Xinjiang.

[27] PBC 8 Oct. 1984 (a), Art.19-21; ICBC 8 Oct. 1984, Art.4.3.

[28] PBC 8 Oct. 1984 (b), Art.3.1.

[29] PBC 8 Oct. 1984 (a), Art.3.4.

[30] C.a. 11/87, 852f; FEER 24 March 1988, 61-63; FEER 5 Jan. 1989, 54f.

[31] Such ceilings are particularly damaging since both efficient and inefficient enterprises are affected.

Table 3. Development of Loans by State Banks and of Refinancing by the People's Bank of China (in RMB b)

	1978	1979	1980	1981ᵃ	1982	1983	1984	1985	1986	1987	1988ᵃ	1989
Consolidated Balance Sheet												
Assets	187.65	216.26	262.43	317.07	361.84	412.49	537.03	637.45	811.14	987.04	1,148.53	1,361.79
All credit (except to state)	185.00	203.96	241.43	286.02	318.06	358.99	476.61	590.56	759.08	903.25	1,055.13	1,240.93
yearly change (in %)	X	10	18	15	11	13	33	24	29	19	17	18
PBC Balance Sheet												
Assets	.	.	.	.	.	.	.	285.99	344.40	.	.	.
Financial institutions												
Minimum reserves	.	.	.	.	.	.	.	42.05	56.53	.	(76)ᵇ	.
Excess reserves	.	.	.	.	.	.	.	45.99	55.78	.	(30)ᵇ	.
Loans to special banksᶜ	.	.	.	.	.	.	.	225.49	267.59	.	.	.
Loans to special banksᵈ	.	.	.	.	.	.	.	225.49	272	279	324	428
of which (in %): annual	.	.	.	.	.	.	.	.	82	80	68	53
short-term	.	.	.	.	.	.	.	.	18	20	32	47

Notes:

a. Since 1981 including the People's Construction Bank of China, since 1988 including the Bank of Communications and the Zhongxin Industrial and Commercial Bank.

b. Figures are derived by adding up the relevant entries in the balance sheets of all special banks and several other financial institutions as given in Almanac 1989.

c. According to Almanac 1987, II-9.

d. The total for 1985 has been taken from Almanac 1987, II-0; for the calculation of annual increases the relative increases given by Li Yuping 6/90, 30 are used. The "of which" lines are taken from the same source. The latter source also offers absolute increases, which, however, do not match completely with the official 1985 figures and the relative increases, probably due to rounding.

Sources: Consolidated Balance Sheet: Almanac 1989, 56f; ZGJR 5/90, 61. PBC Balance Sheet: Almanac 1987, II-9; Li Yuping 6/90, 30.

freeze deposits.[32]

Monitoring the implementation of administrative credit management. On account of the increasing slackness in central credit planning the need arose for the PBC to monitor the behavior of financial institutions more attentively. The "PBC Temporary Regulations on Internal Auditing"[33] of 5 July 1985 were a first attempt by the PBC to keep special banks' activities under control. PBC branches on all levels (including the head office) established a department for internal auditing under the leadership of the head of the branch. Special banks as well as the PBC branch itself are to be audited.

Internal auditing, as exercised by the PBC, covers all business activities of all financial institutions. Auditors examine implementation of state economic policies including monetary policies; implementation of relevant state laws, decrees, and regulations as well as of all regulations stipulated by the PBC; implementation of credit, cash, and foreign exchange plans and management of financial affairs; economic efficiency; and other matters that the PBC thinks need auditing.[34] In a final auditing report suggestions for improvement are made. With approval of the PBC branch concerned, loans (by the PBC) to a special bank may be stopped and deposits (at the PBC) frozen. If "economic and financial discipline" is seriously violated, the PBC suggests punishment to the "relevant departments." The relationship between the PBC and the special banks thus is not one of control but one of co-operation: Suggestions are made, the special bank branch might be admonished or praised, but the PBC does not have much direct leverage on the behavior of special banks. Chinese economists therefore request more rules and regulations for the monetary system, better preparation of auditors and more rights for the PBC.[35]

---

[32] For example, in Hangzhou in 1989 institutions had to wait for two months before they could withdraw their new deposits. (FEER 5 Jan. 1989, 54f.)

[33] PBC 5 July 1985.

These regulations were examined, discussed and passed by the Board of Directors of the PBC.

Although the translation offered by Chinese-English dictionaries for *jihe* is "auditing," Chinese-Chinese dictionaries (e.g., Caizhengjuan 1987, 591) show that "internal auditing" is a more appropriate translation. Reality in 1985 confirms the latter translation.

[34] PBC 5 July, Art.3.

[35] Ji Jun 3/88.

Three months after passing the Regulations on Internal Auditing, the State Council in October 1985 approved the "PBC Report on the Development of Credit Investigation." The Credit Examination Bureau at the PBC under the nominal leadership (*lingdao*) of the local government and the de facto leadership (*qiantou*) of the PBC together with the special banks examined various financial institutions, especially with regard to the situation in September 1985 and the fourth quarter of 1984. A general lack of law enforcement was revealed.[36]

Since the transformation of the PBC into a central bank and the beginning of the use of "economic" instruments, special banks are to report — monthly, quarterly and annually — to both superior special bank branches and the local PBC branch, on the volume of loans and cash payments and on the general situation (e.g., industrial output, market changes). Such reports include an analysis of the current situation, and, if possible, suggestions for improvement, which are then passed on to the leadership and to the relevant departments outside the banking system.[37]

A different approach is moral suasion, which ranges from State Council decrees and PBC circulars to pledges to work "in the spirit of" this or that Party resolution. At the beginning of each year the governor of the PBC in his New Year speech summarizes the high points of the last year and announces the slogan for the present year, which is then engraved in bankers' minds by constant repetition.

Propaganda work is not restricted to the PBC, but is continued by the governments on different levels. In some cases a PBC branch might ask the local government for propaganda support. The local government then passes a resolution addressed to the target group. For example, in mid-1988 a request by the State Council to increase the velocity of money went to enterprises via the PBC, State Planning Commission, Finance Ministry, and local governments. The problem was that once an enterprise had secured a loan for the purchase of material inputs (or even equipment) it would try

---

[36] State Council 12 Oct. 1985.

The Credit Examination Bureau at the PBC deplored six problems: The credit examination by banks in general was too lenient, in that of the loans for technical updating and transformation only about 50% were paid back on time and many loans were re-allocated for capital construction or for bonus payments; there were problems with briefcase enterprises and individual households; trust and investment companies gave loans for capital construction outside the plan; there was a black market for foreign exchange; granting loans was often linked to personal favors; banks used various tricks to attract more deposits. (State Council 12 Oct. 1985.)

[37] Zhang Dun 9/87; Jin Jiandong 11/86, 18f; Liu Hongru 11/86, 14f.

hard to avoid repayment of the loan. This could be achieved by keeping large stocks or storing faulty products. Pressure on the enterprise to repay loans was then exerted from all sides, by the bank, the government and, occasionally, the Party.[38]

Problems Arising from Administrative Credit Management

With the economic reforms administrative credit management has proven to be inadequate. First, since the principle of strict central planning no longer holds, the concept of administrative credit management meets with problems it was not intended to cope with originally. Second, state interference on all levels thwarts the PBC's efforts to control the monetary system. Some examples are listed below.

Problems arising within the banking system. The actual increase in investment in fixed assets exceeds the planned increase in most years. Special banks switch funds restricted for use in the second half to the first half of the year, give loans to institutions they are not supposed to, or do not monitor closely the use of working capital loans. Once the capital construction projects are completed, working capital loans are required, even if the original projects were not contained in any plan. If special banks cannot provide these loans because of a shortage of funds, pressure will be brought to bear on the local PBC branch to make extra funds available. Special bank branches can only profit from a larger volume of credit, and there is no inherent mechanism to stop their ignoring limits set by the PBC.[39]

During harvest, special banks have to provide funds for the state purchase of agricultural and sideline products. Special banks, especially the Agricultural Bank of China, have to keep a high reserve during the other months of the year, arrange for a large volume of loans to be repaid during fall, or request new loans from the PBC. Reserves are de facto limited, and the repayment of loans hardly ever works out as planned. Therefore every fall the PBC is asked to increase its refinancing of the special banks. Furthermore, peasants want to be paid in cash. The large increase in cash

[38] On various other measures see PBC 9/87; Chen Muhua 2/88; Zhou Zhengqing 8/88.

[39] According to a survey, increasing the credit volume, together with increasing deposits, ranked first among the objectives of special banks in nine banking trial cities. (Zhang Shaojie 11/87, 14.)

in circulation has severe consequences for cash management and plans. In a banking system using economic levers, the special banks would have to recall an incomparably larger volume of loans to make the cash available. The result invariably is the issuing of IOUs ("pieces of white paper," *baitiao*) by the special banks — although IOUs are much despised by peasants — together with new funds from the PBC.[40]

Fierce competition among all financial institutions to increase deposits has led to premiums on new savings. An example is the "purchase entitlement for a color-TV/refrigerator linked to new savings" at a time when these goods were scarce.[41]

Obvious violations of state and PBC regulations on the part of the special banks include the delay of transfer payments to other financial institutions[42] and the retaining and use of deposits by state organs when the PBC should be notified and those deposits be transferred to the PBC.[43]

The money market renders attempts by PBC branches to control the credit volume of local special banks impossible. On the other hand, a general scarcity of funds and thus a de facto suspension of the money market brings about the danger of special bank branches not being able to meet their obligations to other banks. In order to avoid chain reactions, the PBC has to step in.

Various new types of financial institutions have emerged with as their main purpose, it seems, evasion of state and PBC regulations. Special banks have set up trust and investment companies to circumvent the credit plan.[44] State organs establish "covert (financial) firms" (*bianxiang gongsi*). Some enterprises create "enterprise banks" with the help of special banks.[45]

A large selection of special loans (e.g., for infrastructure projects) is subject to misuse by PBC and special bank branches. Local governments try to convert special loans into budget revenues.[46]

---

[40] Lin Guobao 26 Dec. 1988; FEER 1 Dec. 1988, 71.

[41] Financial institutions obtain these "purchase entitlements" from department stores and use them as an incentive to increase savings. (Lin Guobao 26 Dec. 1988.)

[42] Tong Zengyin 1/89; Huang Min 1988, 154-159; Cheng Chuyuan 1959, 87-107.

[43] Huang Gangming 2/86, 22.

[44] Since April 1986 (PBC 26 April 1986) trust and investment companies' loans, if they are given for investment in fixed assets, are supposed to be included in the credit plan, especially if the loans are used for capital construction, or for leasing business.

[45] Tang Yongyi 2/88.

[46] Chang Gong 3/88, 31.

Monetary plans have to take into consideration price changes. If prices change more than expected, (planned) monetary variables might have to be adjusted.

Problems arising from state intervention. An annually recurring problem is the sale of various state bonds. In some cases the PBC has to advance the money[47] and to coerce the special banks into fulfilling their duties in selling the bonds. Since these bonds are not popular and are sold mainly to enterprises by force and to individuals as deductions from salaries and wages, the PBC threatens special banks with refusal to permit the special banks' own issuing of bonds or with a cut in refinancing.[48] Some newer types of state bonds even have to be purchased by the special banks themselves.

Despite a scarcity of loanable funds, financial institutions are to support all key projects and projects involved in the supply of raw materials and energy, communications, export production, or purchase of agricultural and sideline products.[49] Guidelines exist by which other industries enjoy some kind of priority. If total investment in capital construction turns out to be higher than desired, the State Council may pass a concise list of which projects are to be cut. Banks simply have to follow suit.[50]

Governments at all levels can use extra-budgetary funds (*yusuanwai zijin*)[51] by channelling them through less controlled trust and investment companies into, for example, unplanned capital construction. Once these

---

[47] Bank Regulations of 1986, Art.30, prohibits the purchase of state bonds by the PBC.

[48] PBC 9/87, 4.

[49] Nuli 1/88, 5.
Not to mention special requests by the state which then are satisfied by a "shifting" (*tiaoji*) of funds. An example is the financing of investment in technical updating and transformation in 1985. (State Council 7 Oct. 1985.)

[50] C.a. 12/88, 893; FEER 8 Dec. 1988, 60f.
The success of such cuts in 1988 is to be doubted since they were generally anticipated and the projects concerned completed ahead of time. Furthermore enterprises can use non-declared profits or obtain loans from financial institutions outside the credit plan. Enterprises in Guangdong Province can carry out their investment through a subsidiary in Hong Kong (since foreign projects are not cut).

[51] Extra-budgetary funds consist of: "Additional" income of local financial departments (e.g., from additional taxes), special funds of state enterprises (e.g., from depreciation funds), revenues of various central and local departments from enterprises, and income of state institutions and administrative units. (Caizhengjuan 1987, 230f.)

projects are completed banks are asked to provide the necessary working capital, although the project was originally not included in any plan.

There are a number of loans called "essential loans" (*bude budai daikuan*),[52] including "necessary loans" (*zeren daikuan*), "basic loans" (*jishu daikuan*), loans for "political projects" (*zhengzhi xiangmu daikuan*), and loans to "lifeblood enterprises" (*mingmai daikuan*). With local governments thus determining a special bank's assets, the PBC cannot but bail out special banks in need of further funds.[53]

The state is not allowed to overdraw its account at the PBC, yet it receives loans from the PBC.[54]

2. Cash Plan[55]

While the credit plan registers stocks (year-end amounts of credit), the cash plan registers flows (cash receipts and disbursements throughout the year). Imbalances in the cash plan are avoided by issuing or withdrawing cash. Since decisions on the demand for cash are to a large extent made outside the banking sector, the cash plan can never be precisely fulfilled. Large discrepancies between cash plan and actual cash flows, however, affect the State Comprehensive Credit Plan through the entry "cash in circulation" in the latter (Figure 7 above).

---

[52] Zhang Shaojie 11/87.

[53] In the survey mentioned above, in 1986 three fourths of all loans for technical upgrading and transformation provided by the special banks questioned were determined by the local government.

[54] Bank Regulations of 1986, Art.30.

In the third quarter of 1988 loans to the state amounted to 57 b yuan as compared to total loans (in the Consolidated Balance Sheet of All Banks, including the PBC) of 1,058 b yuan. (ZGJR 1/89.)

[55] If no other source is given all statistical material is from China Financial Statistics (1952-1987). This book for some time was the only source with material usable to reconstruct cash flows. Almanac 1989, 75-82, now contains the same information.

Issue Departments and Cash Administration Regulations[56]

Issue departments subordinated to the PBC exist on all levels down to the county level. In a county without a PBC branch, the issue department is administered by a special bank.[57] The maximum amount of cash a special bank can draw from the PBC is restricted by its excess reserves.[58]

The use of cash in the economy is strictly limited. Units (non-individuals — that is, mainly enterprises and state administrative organs) may use cash only for

— salaries, wages and allowances;
— payment of casual laborers;
— bonuses (in accordance with state regulations);
— labor insurance, welfare benefits and other payments to individuals as determined by the state;
— purchase of agricultural and sideline products as well as other materials from individuals;
— business travel;
— petty cash;
— other payments as ordered by the PBC.[59]

How much cash units need for petty expenses (*lingxing zhichu*) during no more than three to five days is determined and controlled by the special bank at which a unit has its account.[60] The cash administration of special banks is controlled by the PBC of the same level.

---

[56]   The Cash Administration Regulations were passed by the State Council in September 1988. (State Council 8 Sept. 1988.)

[57]   In this case the issuing vault (*faxingku*) and the business vault (*yewuku*) are to be kept strictly separate. The large increase in money in circulation in 1985 might partly be traced back to an inadequate separation of vaults within special banks. (In 1985 there were PBC branches in only about one third of all counties.)
The Bank Regulations of 1986 in Art. 31 state once more that no person or unit may violate the regulations and use the cash stored in the vaults of the issue department.

[58]   PBC 4/84, 14; Qiu Qing 12/84, 11; PBC 2/86.

[59]   State Council 8 Sept. 1988.

[60]   State Council 8 Sept. 1988, Art.5,9.
In remote areas enterprises may keep up to 15 days' cash.
In 1989 it seems to have been difficult for an enterprise to keep more than 200 yuan in cash. (Zhao Baowei 1/90, 31.)

Table 4. Cash, Retail Sales and Purchase of Agricultural and Sideline Products

Year	Cash in circulation (in RMB b)	As a multiple of cash in circulation:			
		Sale of commodities	Social retail sale of commodities	Purchase of agricultural and sideline products	Social purchase of agricultural and sideline products
1953	3.94	5.1	8.8	1.9	4.2
1954	4.12	5.6	9.3	2.4	4.6
1955	4.03	6.4	9.7	2.7	4.8
1956	5.73	5.6	8.0	1.5	3.4
1957	5.28	6.5	9.0	1.4	4.1
1958	6.78	5.3	8.1	0.9	3.4
1959	7.51	5.6	8.5	1.1	3.7
1960	9.59	4.5	7.3	0.5	2.3
1961	12.57	3.0	4.8	0.4	1.6
1962	10.65	3,9	5.7	4.6	2.0
1963	8.99	4.6	6.7	0.9	2.6
1964	8.00	5.5	8.0	1.2	3.4
1965	9.08	5.2	7.4	1.2	3.4
1966	10.85	4.7	6.8	1.2	3.2
1967	12.19	4.5	6.3	1.0	2.8
1968	13.41	3.9	5.5	0.8	2.5
1969	13.71	4.1	5.8	0.8	2.4
1970	12.36	4.7	6.9	0.8	2.8
1971	13.62	4.5	6.8	0.8	2.7
1972	15.12	4.5	6.8	0.8	2.5
1973	16.61	4.4	6.7	0.8	2.6
1974	17.66	4.3	6.6	0.7	2.5
1975	18.26	4.4	7.0	0.7	2.3
1976	20.40	4.2	6.6	0.6	2.3
1977	19.54	2.6	7.3	0.6	2.5
1978	21.20	4.5	7.4	0.6	2.6
1979	26.77	4.2	6.7	0.7	2.6
1980	34.62	3.9	6.2	0.8	2.4
1981	39.63	4.0	5.9	0.9	2.8
1982	43.91	4.0	5.9	1.0	2.5
1983	52.98	3.8	5.4	1.3	2.4
1984	79.21	3.0	4.3	1.0	1.8
1985	98.78	2.9	4.4	0.8	1.7
1986	121.84	2.7	4.1	0.8	1.6
1987	145.45	2.7	4.0	0.8	1.6

Note on terminology: Sale of commodities is the sale of commodities by state trading companies for cash; social retail sale of commodities, in contrast, consists of all transactions where retail commodities are involved, including those by non-state trading units. The same difference holds for the purchase of agricultural and sideline products.

Sources: China Financial Statistics (1952-1987), 3,5,80,82,84,86,188,190,196,198.

Disbursements and Receipts by State Banks

In the past the PBC used a simple rule of thumb to determine the increase in cash supply: 1 yuan in circulation equals purchase of agricultural and sideline products worth 4 yuan or retail sales worth 8 yuan.[61] This rule of thumb is no longer valid; more and more cash is in circulation as compared to a certain nominal amount of retail sales (or similarly of purchases of agricultural and sideline products).[62] (See Table 4.) There are two possible reasons for the decrease in the velocity of cash (measured as the ratio between nominal retail sales and cash in circulation or between nominal purchases of agricultural and sideline products and cash in circulation). Either the relative shares of the two items in all receipts/disbursements or the demand for cash ceteris paribus has changed. In any case, since the old rule of thumb no longer does justice to reality and furthermore does not offer any explanation of the underlying causes behind the change in ratios, a more sophisticated approach has become necessary. This second approach takes into consideration the relative shares of all different receipts and disbursements of cash in one year as measured by state banks. (See Table 5.)

Of all cash disbursements the relative importance of the purchase of agricultural and sideline products first increased from 1978 (10% of all cash disbursements) to 1983 (19%) and then decreased again until 1989 (10%). The importance of the largest item, salaries and wages, declined continuously over the same period (46% to 24%). The item which, in contrast, showed the highest increase is the withdrawal of savings (10% to 33%); every year a relatively larger share of all cash disbursements was brought about by the withdrawal of savings deposits. Of all cash receipts, on the other hand, the relative importance of retail sales was reduced by almost one half (71% to 36%). The item whose importance increased most is the receipt of savings, that is, new savings deposits (11% to 38%). (An analysis on a yearly basis reveals that the increase in withdrawal of savings is more than offset by the increase in the total volume of savings.) As an overall result, the importance of almost all channels which change the amount of cash in circulation was reduced, with the exception of savings

---

[61] C.a. 9/84, 525.

Peebles 6/84, 47, speaks of a relationship between cash and retail sales of 1 : 7.5 - 9.

[62] The downward trend of the (nominal) state purchase of agricultural and sideline products per RMB was temporarily reversed with the beginning of the agricultural reforms, when the state purchase price for agricultural products was increased.

Table 5. State Banks: Disbursements and Receipts of Cash[a]

Disbursements / Receipts	Total	(1) Salar./ wages	(2) Agr.	(3) Ent.	(4) Goods	(5) Serv.	(6) Tax	(7) Rural credit	(8) Towns. ent./ instit.	(9) Self-empl. units	(10) Savings	(11) Urban credit co-op.	(12) Remitt.	(13) Others	(14) Cash in circ.	(15) Disb. minus rec.
1978																
Dis. RMB b	135.26	61.7	12.8	8.8	X	X	X	29.7	.	.	13.0	.	3.8	5.4		
in %	100	45.6	9.5	6.5	X	X	X	21.9	X	X	9.6	X	2.8	4.0		
Rec. RMB b	133.60	X	X	X	95.3	10.5	0.5	5.4			14.3		2.6	5.0	21.20	1.66
in %	100	X	X	X	71.3	7.9	0.4	4.1	X	X	10.7	X	2.0	3.7		
1981																
Dis. RMB b	245.23	97.0	35.6	14.96	X	X	X	54.7	.	.	29.1	.	5.0	8.9		
in %	100	39.5	14.5	6.1	X	X	X	22.3	X	X	11.9	X	2.0	3.6		
Rec. RMB b	240.22	X	X	X	158.8	15.7	0.9	17.9	.		35.0		4.2	7.8	39.63	5.01
in %	100	X	X	X	66.1	0.4	0.4	7.4	X	X	14.6	X	1.7	3.2		
1983																
Dis. RMB b	351.94	115.8	67.0	19.6	X	X	X	70.6	13.0	.	48.1	.	5.9	12.0		
in %	100	32.9	19	5.6	X	X	X	20.1	3.7	X	13.7	X	1.7	3.4		
Rec. RMB b	342.87	X	X	X	202.8	19.4	1.8	37.7	5.22		59.8		5.1	11.1	52.98	9.02
in %	100	X	X	X	59.1	5.7	0.5	11.0	1.5	X	17.4	X	1.5	3.2		

1984																		
Dis.	RMB b	446.99	141.6	78.9	27.1	X	X	X	X	88.8	18.0	.	66.4	.	7.0	19.2	79.21	26.23
	in %	100	31.7	17.7	6.1	X	X	X	X	19.9	4.0	X	14.9	X	1.6	4.3		
Rec.	RMB b	420.76	X	X	X	X	234.6	23.9	2.4	45.7	8.0	.	84.6	.	6.2	15.5		
	in %	100	X	X	X	X	55.7	5.7	0.6	10.9	1.9	X	20.1	X	1.5	3.7		
1985																		
Dis.	RMB b	569.48	178.7	83.5	36.5	X	X	X	X	109.5	16.9	5.7	100.9	.	9.3	28.6	98.78	19.57
	in %	100	31.4	14.7	6.4	X	X	X	X	19.2	3.0	1.0	17.7	X	1.6	5.0		
Rec.	RMB b	549.91	X	X	X	X	286.4	32.2	3.6	58.0	8.4	3.6	124.2	.	8.3	25.3		
	in %	100	X	X	X	X	52.1	5.8	0.7	10.6	1.5	0.7	22.6	X	1.5	4.6		
1986																		
Dis.	RMB b	684.39	215.8	101.3	41.3	X	X	X	X	122.2	22.1	6.8	131.2	.	10.6	33.1	121.8	23.06
	in %	100	31.5	14.8	6.0	X	X	X	X	17.9	3.2	1.0	19.2	X	1.6	4.8		
Rec.	RMB b	661.33	X	X	X	X	327.9	38.6	4.4	69.7	10.0	4.2	165.8	.	9.6	31.0		
	in %	100	X	X	X	X	49.6	5.8	0.7	10.5	1.5	0.6	25.1	X	1.4	4.7		
1987																		
Dis.	RMB b	901.57	251.2	118.9	53.0	X	X	X	X	152.5	32.4	11.3	210.6	6.8	13.6	51.35	145.4	23.61
	in %	100	27.9	13.2	5.9	X	X	X	X	16.9	3.6	1.3	23.4	0.8	1.5	5.7		
Rec.	RMB b	877.96	X	X	X	X	389.6	49.1	5.9	89.6	15.2	7.1	256.7	7.3	12.9	44.7		
	in %	100	X	X	X	X	44.4	5.6	0.7	10.2	1.7	0.8	29.2	0.8	1.5	5.1		

1988	Unit	(1)	(2)	(3)	(4)	(5)	(6)	(7)	(8)	(9)	(10)	(11)	(12)	(13)	(14)/(15)
Dis.	RMB b	1,349	317.9	149.6	79.7	X	X	X	193.4	45.9	18.2	405.7	18.8	19.9	100.0	213.4
	in %	100	23.6	11.1	5.9	X	X	X	14.3	3.4	1.3	30.1	1.4	1.5	7.4	67.95
Rec.	RMB b	1,281	X	X	X	521.6	65.1	8.0	105.0	22.9	11.1	433.6	13.8	18.8	81.1	
	in %	100	X	X	X	40.7	5.1	0.6	8.2	1.8	0.9	33.8	1.1	1.5	6.3	

1989	Unit	(1)	(2)	(3)	(4)	(5)	(6)	(7)	(8)	(9)	(10)	(11)	(12)	(13)	(14)/(15)
Dis.	RMB b	1,527	368.0	153.5	92.5	X	X	X	180.5	46.0	19.2	502.6	22.7	23.2	118.6	234.4
	in %	100	24.1	10.1	6.1	X	X	X	11.8	3.0	1.3	32.9	1.5	1.5	7.8	21.00
Rec.	RMB b	1.505	X	X	X	548.3	78.7	11.0	111.3	23.7	11.5	572.7	20.7	22.5	105.4	
	in %	100	X	X	X	36.4	5.2	0.7	7.3	1.6	0.8	38.0	1.4	1.5	7.0	

Notes:

a. The headings stand for: (1) Salaries and wages (plus other disbursements to individuals); (2) Purchase of agricultural and sideline products; (3) Management expenses of (administrative) enterprises; (4) Sale of goods; (5) Services; (6) Tax revenue; (7) Rural credit; (8) Township enterprises and institutions; (9) Self-employed units; (10) Savings; (11) Urban credit co-operatives; (12) Remittances; (13) Others; (14) Cash in circulation (at year-end); (15) Total disbursements minus receipts.

For each year the first row contains the absolute amount of cash disbursed throughout the year by state banks through the various channels; the second row shows the amount of cash disbursed through any one channel as a share of all disbursements in that year (in %); the third and fourth row contain the same type of information for receipts. The last two columns contain the amount of cash in circulation at year-end and its change over the previous year. Example: In 1989 an amount of 572.7 b yuan was saved, corresponding to 38.0% of all cash receipts of state banks, while an amount of 502.6 b yuan in savings was withdrawn, corresponding to 32.9% of all cash disbursements by state banks. Cash in circulation was increased in 1989 by 21.0 b yuan (total disbursements minus total receipts) to, at year-end, 234.4 b yuan.

Sources: China Financial Statistics (1952-1987), 5,82f,86f,106f,110f; Almanac 1989, 57,78; Statistical Yearbook 1990, 666f.

receipts and disbursements, which greatly increased.[63] Since savings deposits are voluntary and can be withdrawn any time — the principle in effect is "voluntary savings, voluntary withdrawal, payment of interest and secrecy"[64] — this change reflects an increasing degree of choice in purchasing decisions by individuals and less state control over cash in circulation and thus over the real economy.

The difference between receipts and disbursements (receipts minus disbursements) of savings deposits at state banks as percentage of total receipts changed from 1% in 1979 to 5% in 1986 and 1987, 2% in 1988 and 5% in 1989.[65] In the years up to 1989 individuals not only increased their savings every year but also saved an ever higher share of their (cash) income. At the same time, however, they also increased their cash holdings by large amounts: The difference between the total of all cash disbursements and the total amount of all cash receipts remained positive and, in general, increasing. (The somewhat extraordinary year 1988 will be dealt with in more detail below.)

The shift in the relative importance of savings receipts and disbursements and the increase in cash holdings seem to balance each other as the ratio of the total amount of disbursements (or receipts) to cash in circulation has remained remarkably steady. For all disbursements the ratio has, in the period covered, varied between a high of 6.6 in 1983 and a low of 5.6 in 1984. Furthermore, activities not covered by disbursements and receipts of cash by state banks (for example, the sale of grain or vegetables by a peasant to a city dweller on a free market) have either not changed (relatively) by any significant degree during the course of economic reforms or these changes have been offset by other factors. An example for an offsetting factor would be inflation. Activities not covered by cash flows

---

[63] The item called "savings" is not defined by the source. Since only state banks are part of the cash plan, various savings (e.g., at trust and investment companies) remain unconsidered.

[64] Bank Regulations of 1986, Art.47.
"Savings campaigns" have been undertaken in the past [Cheng Chuyuan 1959, 46-48]. Although slogans on village walls promoting savings are still part of everyday life in 1989, coercion today is exercised through the reduction in salaries/wages in exchange for treasury bonds, and through the issuing of IOUs as payments to peasants for state purchases of grain.

[65] Another measure to assess the increase in savings is the amount of total (new) savings (receipts minus disbursements) as percentage of the total salaries and wages and the purchase of agricultural and sideline products ("urban and rural salaries and wages") during a year. This percentage share has increased from 1% in 1978 to 10% in 1987, 6% in 1988 and 13% in 1989.

into or out of state banks tend to require a larger amount of cash in circulation; yet inflation tends to reduce cash holdings. Given the high inflation rates in the years 1987 to 1989 one could have expected a reduction in the amount of cash demanded (cash in circulation). This was, except for 1989, not the case. (A closer analysis will have to wait until Part II.)

Problems Arising from Administrative Cash Management

The cash plan, as compared to the credit plan, has one striking disadvantage: The flow of cash owned by individuals cannot be controlled and that of cash held by enterprises can be controlled only with great difficulty.

Disbursements. Although many attempts have been made to limit the amount of salaries, wages and bonus payments[66] (i.e., disbursements), and to have all such transactions completed through separate accounts under the strict control of special banks, these efforts have met with little success.[67] The PBC cannot directly influence this variable. The cash disbursements of (administrative) enterprises[68] likewise are not under the direct control of the PBC. Although the Regulations on Cash Administration of 1988 explicitly list in eleven points actions considered as offenses, enterprises still find ways to circumvent the cash plan.

The absolute increase in disbursements for the purchase of agricultural and sideline products from 1978 to 1989 to 12.0 times the original value (Table 5) cannot be due to corresponding increases in agricultural and sideline production alone; total agricultural output value for that period increased 4.7 times, while the quantity of, for example, rice and wheat produced did not even double.[69] As purchases of agricultural and sideline products by the state during this period accounted for most such purchases, price increases must explain part of the total increase in disbursements. The PBC, however, is not the institution deciding upon administrative price

---

[66] In 1985 bonuses which exceeded the amount of four months' average salary (or wages) were taxed progressively. (C.a. 7/85, 453.)

[67] State Council 25 Nov. 1987.

[68] "Administrative enterprises" (*xingzheng qiye*) is not defined in the source but probably means all state units involved in the production of (material) goods.

[69] Statistical Yearbook 1988, 216,248; Statistical Yearbook 1990, 333,359.

changes. When the PBC in the fall of 1988 refused renewed refinancing to special banks, forcing the Agricultural Bank of China and other special banks to find solutions on their own (e.g., via the interbank money market), the shortage of loans and cash resulted in the issuing of IOUs on the scale of 2 to 3 b yuan. In November 1988 the PBC's refusal of refinancing was retracted.[70]

The PBC also has little control over "rural credit" except that it might try to refuse refinancing to special banks. From 1953 to 1989 there has not been a single year in which receipts in this category have been larger than disbursements; in general disbursements have exceeded receipts many times over. Only since the middle of the 1980s has this discrepancy been somewhat reduced. Rural loans in the past seem to have been interpreted as subsidies or rural salaries and wages (because of low state-administered prices for agricultural and sideline products).

Receipts. The PBC has hardly any more control over receipts than over disbursements. Retail sales (sales of goods), sales of services, and tax revenues (in cash) are beyond the PBC's reach. Only savings deposits can be influenced to some extent through interest rates and savings campaigns.

Fortunately, an increase in savings deposits is also in the interest of special banks in that all deposits exceeding the planned amount of deposits are at the special bank's own disposal. While in 1978 deposits by enterprises amounted to 1.7 times savings deposits (by individuals) this proportion was reduced to 0.6 in 1989. Savings deposits thus outweigh enterprise deposits in importance today.[71]

Limits of administrative cash management. With the reforms in the real economy the PBC can no longer correctly predict such items as retail sales: both quantities and prices may fluctuate widely. At the same time the

---

[70]   FEER 5 Jan. 1989, 55; FEER 2 March 1989, 83.

[71]   To arrive at these figures a combination of the Consolidated Balance Sheet of State Banks (including, since 1982, the People's Construction Bank of China and, since 1988, the Bank of Communications and the Zhongxin Industrial and Commercial Bank of China) and of the Balance Sheet of Rural Credit Cooperatives was necessary. This is the closest one can possibly get to a Consolidated Balance Sheet of the banking sector as a whole. (i) All deposits by state organs, deposits for capital construction (an item given up as a separate item in the statistics in 1981), "others" in the Consolidated Balance Sheet of State Banks, and (ii) "rural deposits" (not defined), "deposits by agricultural collectives," and "others" in the Balance Sheet of Rural Credit Co-operatives are ignored. The ignored items amounted to a figure equal to 72% of all enterprise deposits in 1989. (Almanac 1989, 56,65; ZGJR 5/90, 61.)

velocity of cash (in circulation) changes. If individuals use cash to pay for the purchase of investment goods (which are possibly produced outside the real plan) and the enterprise receiving the cash neither deposits it at a bank nor informs the bank of it, but uses the cash for the payment of bonuses to its employees or for the purchase of consumer goods, transfers of funds are outside any state plan or state control and the velocity of cash in circulation as measured by state bank figures underestimates the true velocity. If enterprises disregard cash administration regulations or if peasants sell their products on free markets,[72] the velocity of cash as measured by state banks becomes irrelevant. As a result of the economic reforms in the real economy, variables important to monetary policy become less predictable and the separation into two circuits falters: administration of cash flows so as to stabilize the currency becomes unrealistic.

The problem would be less severe if part of the increase in cash in circulation were offset by reduction of the special banks' excess reserves at the PBC — that is, if the PBC were to change to economic control, instead of continuing to rely on administrative management. Although special banks are generally asked to press for repayment of loans during the first half of each year in order to be prepared for the purchase of agricultural and sideline products during fall, these appeals always seem to fail. In fall special banks are reluctant to deplete their excess reserves at the PBC, and local governments bring the necessary pressure to bear on the local PBC.

The traditional concept of "withdrawing" the excessive amount of cash in circulation during the first months of the new year becomes more and more difficult every year. (See Table 6.) Although from 1983 to 1987 the amount of cash in circulation was in fact reduced during the first half of the year, the increase during the second half of the year always more than made up for the decrease. Finally, in 1988, the amount of money in circulation was not reduced during the first quarter, as planned, by 8 b yuan (6%), but only by 1.2 b yuan (1%), and started rising again in the second quarter — by 10.1 b yuan (7%). The overall change in the first half of 1988 was thus positive. The PBC should not be held responsible for such developments. How could it have prevented the salary and wage payments (cash disbursements of state banks) from reaching an unusually high 50% of all

---

[72] These sales reached 46 b yuan in 1987, 15 times the amount of 1978, corresponding to 11% of retail sales. (Statistical Yearbook 1988, 686.)

In Sichuan Province more than 25% of all cash in circulation was in the hands of enterprises. (FEER 5 Jan. 1989, 54f, according to *Economic Daily* 9 Nov. 1988.)

Table 6. Cash in Circulation

Year/Quarter		Cash in circulation (in RMB b)	Change over previous quarter (%)	Change over previous year (%)
1979		26.8	X	X
1980		34.6	X	29
1981		39.6	X	14
1982		43.9	X	11
1983	1	43.4	-1	
	2	42.2	-3	
	3	46.7	1	
	4	53.0	13	21
1984	1	51.1	-4	
	2	49.1	-4	
	3	58.7	20	
	4	79.2	37	49
1985	1	78.8	-1	
	2	75.8	-4	
	3	82.7	9	
	4	98.8	19	25
1986	1	89.9	-9	
	2	88.8	-1	
	3	97.8	10	
	4	121.8	25	23
1987	1	114.3	-6	
	2	113.5	-1	
	3	127.0	12	
	4	145.4	14	19
1988	1	144.2	-1	
	2	154.3	7	
	3	185.0	20	
	4	213.4	15	47
1989	1	209.9	-2	
	2	208.1	-1	
	3	208.2	0	
	4	234.4	13	10
1990	1	215.5	-8	

Sources: 1983-1985: Financial Statistics of China (1979-1985), 2,3,6,7,8. Since 1986: ZGJR 6/86 9/86 12/86 4/87 5/87 9/87 11/87 4/88 7/88 10/88 1/89 4/89 7/89 10/89 1/90 5/90 7/90.

annual salary and wage payments during the first half of the year[73] or the administrative disbursements of enterprises from increasing 60% compared to the same period of the year before?[74]

In August 1988 the State Council approved a change of 20 b yuan in the planned annual increase in cash in circulation, to a planned increase of 40 b yuan. The additional cash was supposed to be used for the purchase of agricultural and sideline products. Cash in circulation in the third quarter of 1988 reached 185.0 b yuan, an increase of 39.6 b yuan. The final increase for the whole of 1988 was 68 b yuan.[75]

Only in 1989 with an inflation rate of approximately 20% for the second year in succession,[76] was the amount of cash in circulation somewhat reduced in the first half of the year through drastic administrative measures and kept to its lowest level of increase for the whole year since the beginning of the reforms in 1978. The parallel movement of cash in circulation and the inflation rate suggests a strong correlation between the two variables. This question will be dealt with in Part II.

3. Foreign Exchange Plan

As a result of the open policy in the real economy, monetary flows between China and other countries have increased. With higher imports and exports, with the establishment of Special Economic Zones and joint venture enterprises, with the development of the tourism industry and with increased activities by Chinese enterprises abroad, the need for a strengthened administration of foreign exchange arose. In March 1979 the State Council approved the establishment of the State Administration of Exchange Control which in 1982 was subordinated to the PBC (instead of to the Bank of China).

[73] FEER 22 Sept. 1988, 70f.

[74] PBC 19 Aug. 1988.

[75] Ibid.

[76] Retail Price Index 1988: + 18.5%, 1989: + 17.8%; Living Cost Index 1988: + 20.7%, 1989: + 16.3%.
State Statistical Bureau 3/89, VI; State Statistical Bureau 2/90, V.

The State Administration for Exchange Control, together with its branch offices, will exercise unified control of foreign exchange[77] under the leadership of the People's Bank of China. The Bank of China's responsibility for unified management of foreign exchange remains unchanged.[78]

Branches of the State Administration of Exchange Control exist in all provinces, municipalities directly under the central government, autonomous regions and Special Economic Zones. While the State Administration of Exchange Control is located at all levels within the Bank of China, the extent to which their personnel overlap is not known.[79]

The State Administration of Exchange Control possesses extensive authority in all matters involving foreign exchange, ranging from the formulation of laws and regulations to the determination of the RMB exchange rate and central administration of all foreign exchange in the PRC.[80] Yet the PBC's control over foreign exchange through the State Administration of Exchange Control is not complete. The question therefore arises as to how strongly variations in foreign exchange holdings in the PRC affect the monetary sphere.

Foreign Exchange Administration

The (State) Foreign Exchange Plan (*guojia waihui shouzhi jihua*) is jointly drawn up by three institutions: the Ministry of Foreign Economic Relations and Trade, the Ministry of Finance, and the State Administration of Exchange Control. The Ministry of Foreign Economic Relations and Trade is generally responsible for all foreign trade and debt; the Ministry of Finance for the foreign exchange budgets of all state organs; and the State Administration of Exchange Control for foreign trade activities on the

---

[77] Foreign exchange consists of: foreign banknotes and coins, foreign bonds, transfer payments in foreign denominations, and "other foreign exchange funds." (Tang Gengyao 1986, 51.)

[78] PBC Constitution of 1983, 3.

The English version, in contrast to the original Chinese one, does not qualify the foreign exchange as "state" foreign exchange.

[79] Chu 1987, 353; International Monetary Fund 1986.

[80] For a list of the duties of the State Administration of Exchange Control see Tang Gengyao 1986, 57.

provincial level and below, for income received from overseas Chinese, and for foreign exchange income of individuals. The State Administration of Exchange Control submits an overall National Foreign Exchange Plan for approval to the State Council via the State Planning Commission. All responsibility for the Foreign Exchange Plan, including its implementation, rests with the State Administration of Exchange Control and the Bank of China.[81]

State organs have to sell all their foreign exchange revenues to the state and the purchase of foreign exchange from banks has to be approved by the plan (or special requirements have to be met).[82] In Special Economic Zones non-private organizations may retain 80% of all foreign exchange income. In the various provinces the percentage ranges from 25 to 80.[83] All retained foreign exchange has to be deposited at a bank and its utilization must be approved by the plan.[84] Banks dealing in foreign exchange are the Bank of China and a few other financial institutions. Approval from the State Administration of Exchange Control is required.[85]

Since 1988 the State Administration of Exchange Control has headed Foreign Exchange Adjustment Centers in Guangzhou, Shanghai, and in the Special Economic Zones, in which all enterprises at least partly foreign-

---

[81]   International Monetary Fund 1986.

[82]   Tang Gengyao 1986, 51,58.
Strict regulations also exist for gold and silver (State Council 15 June 1983; State Council 28 Dec. 1983). All gold and silver transactions are made through the PBC (not the State Administration of Foreign Exchange Control).
State gold reserves amounted to 12.67 m ounces for almost 10 years. Yet gold production has increased for years and all gold must be sold to the state. The actual state gold reserves are thought to be considerably higher than the figures published, and might be used for the repayment of foreign debts. (C.a. 5/88, 361.)

[83]   FEER 12 Jan. 1989, 45f.
Until the beginning of 1989 the Special Economic Zones could retain all (100 %) of their foreign exchange income.

[84]   Tang Gengyao 1986, 58f.
Enterprises wholly owned by foreigners or overseas-Chinese and equity joint ventures may retain all foreign exchange earnings and dispose of them within certain limits (Tang Gengyao 1986, 58f). Interest-free RMB loans are obtained by depositing foreign exchange (interest-free) at the Bank of China (C.a. 12/86, 761f). If further requirements are met, such as utilization of advanced technology or production of goods covered by state-planned import substitution, these enterprises enjoy further special rights such as the sale of products domestically with payment in foreign exchange (Tang Gengyao 1986, 60).

[85]   PBC 4/84; PBC 9/87, 4.
The Bank of China also uses the money market or co-operates with other special banks.

owned can exchange RMB and foreign exchange at market rates.[86] (In the Special Economic Zone Shenzhen, however, the ownership does not matter and all firms may participate.)[87]

All financial institutions taking out loans in foreign currencies abroad need approval from the State Administration of Exchange Control.[88] Enterprises may obtain approval directly from the PBC. Several regulations require all foreign debts to be registered at the State Administration of Exchange Control.[89]

PBC and State Administration of Exchange Control, however, are not up to the task. The State Administration of Exchange Control is regarded as subordinate by many Chinese institutions which want to take out loans abroad.[90] It lacks the authority necessary to enforce regulations. The sharing of responsibilities between the PBC and the State Administration of Exchange Control, although the latter is a department of the PBC, does nothing to improve the control of foreign debts.[91] The Ministry of Finance in March 1988 suggested the establishment of a department for the administration of foreign debts under its auspices. So far no decision seems to have been reached.[92] The Ministry of Finance has always been

---

[86]   FEER 5 May 1988, 64f.

The black market rate of foreign exchange in terms of RMB was double the official rate at the beginning of 1989. After another two depreciations of the RMB, the rate was almost on a par in early 1991.

[87]   Zhang Guanghua 6/90.

This source also includes a history of foreign exchange trading.

The foreign exchange traded in these centers amounted to US $ 6.3 b in 1988 and US $ 8.6 b in 1989.

[88]   China Business Guide 1986, 165-167, lists all institutions with such permission. Bank of China, CITIC and the other approved financial institutions may also serve as guarantors.

[89]   PBC 9/85; PBC 28 Sept. 1987; State Council 17 June 1987.

For the repayment of the debt neither the PBC nor the State Administration of Exchange Control is responsible.

[90]   FEER 28 March 1985; FEER 3 April 1986.

[91]   Apart from such organizational problems Chinese authorities face the challenging task of tracing down the activities of Chinese enterprises and financial institutions in Hong Kong. In October 1988 Chinese authorities launched an investigation into several hundred mainland Chinese offices in Hong Kong (C.a. 11/85, 844f). (Besides five large enterprise groups, there are more than 3,000 mainland Chinese offices in Hong Kong representing provincial governments, cities or enterprises. This figure does not take into account Hong Kong - PRC joint ventures. (C.a. 10/88, 773.))

[92]   According to C.a. 5/88, 361, this department has already been established.

responsible for World Bank loans, whereas the PBC has been responsible for loans from the International Monetary Fund and the Asian Development Bank, while the Ministry of Foreign Economic Relations and Trade has been in charge of loans from foreign governments.[93]

The PBC and the State Administration of Exchange Control are thus neither in charge of all foreign exchange administration nor capable of fully controlling all foreign exchange flows. What are the consequences for monetary policy?

Influence of the Foreign Exchange Sector on Liquidity Policy

Study of the foreign exchange sector suffers from a severe lack of statistics and explanations on the few foreign exchange figures published. Three assumptions have to be made in order to draw conclusions about the influence of the foreign sector on the PBC's liquidity policy. These technicalities have been relegated to the notes of Table 7.

If credit and cash plans in a centrally planned economy are strictly adhered to, changes in the amount of foreign exchange at the PBC have no consequences at all since the PBC guarantees the implementation of the plans and the special banks are bound by these plans. Due to reforms in the real economy, however, credit, cash and foreign exchange plans no longer accurately describe all monetary flows, and changes in PBC foreign exchange holdings do influence the monetary and real economy.

How large are these changes? The largest fluctuations in (PBC) foreign exchange involved an increase by US$ 6.191 b in 1982 over 1981, and a decrease by US$ 6.519 b in 1985 from 1984. In 1985, therefore, 17.046 b yuan (sale of US$ 6.519 b by the PBC) were withdrawn from the banking sector. (See Table 7.) For comparison: At the same time excess reserves of the special banks at the PBC amounted to 45.992 b yuan and cash in circulation to 98.78 b yuan (an increase by 19.57 b yuan over 1984).[94] Foreign exchange transactions thus can considerably influence the monetary base.[95] Yet it is not clear how big a change in the PBC foreign exchange

---

[93] Handelsblatt 13 Feb. 1989.

[94] China Financial Statistics (1979-1985), 1,9, and Table 7.

[95] According to International Monetary Fund 12/90, 168, until 1 January 1985 all foreign trade and related transactions were settled at a fixed internal settlement rate which covered 80% of all external transactions.

could be due to possible changes in the valuation of foreign currencies.[96]

What are the possible effects of changes in foreign exchange holdings at financial institutions other than the PBC on the liquidity policy of the PBC? In a planned economy these changes have no effect since the changes are planned, and the rest of the economy is completely isolated through its own plans. If changes in foreign exchange, however, are not covered by the plan and not reported to the State Administration of Exchange Control, they could, if sufficiently large, disturb the liquidity policy of the PBC and the real economy. For example, a local institution could increase its foreign debts without approval from the PBC. This foreign exchange could be used to purchase capital construction goods abroad. Once the investment is completed RMB working capital loans would be necessary (and, as seen above, could somehow be made available). If foreign exchange is used to purchase consumer goods abroad which then are sold inside China, the cash plan is affected.

Assuming that official statistics are correct and foreign exchange is deposited with the Bank of China or the PBC, changes in all foreign exchange in the PRC at the Bank of China or the PBC together with changes in foreign debt, should counterbalance the current account.[97] The developments in the years from 1982 to 1989 indirectly confirm the published figures for foreign exchange in the PRC. In 1982 and 1983 a current account surplus led to an increase in foreign exchange. In 1984, despite an increase in foreign debts and a surplus in the current account, the total amount of foreign exchange decreased. This discrepancy could, for example, be due to statistical difficulties or to a change in valuation. In 1985 and 1986 large current account deficits led to a rapid increase in foreign debt and a reduction in foreign exchange. The increase in foreign debt continued in the following years, with a small current account surplus and increases in foreign exchange in 1987, but current account deficits in 1988 and 1989 combined with a small reduction in foreign exchange in 1988 and a small increase in foreign exchange in 1989.

In 1985, the year of the largest expansion in the volume of credit, the state foreign exchange stock decreased from US$ 8.220 b to US$ 2.644 b and the current account deficit reached a maximum of US$ 11.417 b. This

---

[96] With the revaluation of the Japanese Yen, the PRC's foreign debt (to a large extent denominated in Japanese Yen) continuously increases. No information is available on the currency shares in the PBC's foreign exchange.

[97] On the differences in current account figures, due to different statistical concepts, see Hagemann 5/88, 35-40.

Table 7. Foreign Exchange and Foreign Debt

	1979	1980	1981	1982	1983	1984	1985	1986	1987	1988	1989
Exchange rate in Y RMB/US $	1.496	1.530	1.746	1.923	1.981	2.796	3.202	3.722	3.722	3.722	4.722
PBC foreign exchange:											
in RMB b	2.058	-0.847	8.957	21.769	26.607	26.356	9.310	7.712	18.208	15.844	26.454
change against previous year	X	-2.905	9.804	12.812	4.838	-0.251	-17.046	-1.598	10.496	-2.364	10.610
in US $ b at given exch. rate	1.375	-0.553	5.131	11.322	13.432	9.427	2.908	2.072	4.892	4.257	5.602
State foreign exchange stock (in US $ b)	0.840	-1.296	2.708	6.986	8.901	8.220	2.644	2.072	2.923	3.372	5.550
PBC foreign exchange without state foreign exchange stock (in US $ b)[a]	0.535	0.743	2.423	4.336	4.531	1.207	0.264	-	1.969	0.885	0.052
Foreign exchange balance (in US $ b); at Bank of China	1.314	3.558	2.065	4.139	5.441	6.200	9.269	8.442	12.313	14.176	11.472
All foreign exchange at PBC and Bank of China: (in US $ b)[b]	2.689	3.005	7.196	15.461	18.873	15.627	12.177	10.514	17.205	18.433	17.074
change against previous year	X	0.316	4.191	8.265	3.412	-3.246	-3.450	-1.663	6.691	1.228	-1.359
Current account (in US $ b)	.	.	.	5.674	4.240	2.030	-11.417	-7.034	0.300	-3.802	.
Change in foreign exchange reserves according to balance of payments (in US $ b)[c]	.	.	.	6.291	3.648	0.095	-2.353	-1.275	4.852	2.236	.
Total foreign debt (in US $ b):											
Chinese sources	.	.	.	6.058	6.397	7.234	15.825	.	.	.	43[d]
IMF estimates	.	.	.	.	9.608	12.085	19.884	25	33.6	.	.
Gold (m ounces)	12.80	12.80	12.67	12.67	12.67	12.67	12.67	12.67	12.67	12.67	12.67

Notes:

a. It might well be the case that this item is due only to changes in valuation.

b. Consisting of: State foreign exchange stock + PBC foreign exchange without state foreign exchange stock + foreign exchange balance (at Bank of China).

c. Errors and omissions in the period from 1982 to 1988 ranged from US $ b 0.092 to 1.450.

d. Of which 89.7% medium- and long-term.

The following translations are used: State foreign exchange stock (*guojia waihui kucun*), (PBC) foreign exchange (*waihui zhankuan*), foreign exchange balance (of the Bank of China at the end of the year from business transactions; *zhongguo yinhang waihui jiecun*), and foreign exchange reserves (*waihui chubei*, equals *guojia waihui kucun + zhongguo yinhang waihui jiecun*).

Assumptions made are: (1) The foreign exchange in the Consolidated Balance Sheet of all banks equals the foreign exchange in the PBC Balance Sheet. Evidence: The foreign exchange in the Consolidated Balance Sheet equaled the foreign exchange in the PBC Balance Sheet in 1985 and 1986 (the only years, for which a PBC Balance Sheet is available). (2) The foreign exchange of the PBC includes the state foreign exchange stock, but not the foreign exchange balance of the Bank of China. Evidence: One of the duties of the PBC is the administration of foreign exchange and of the state foreign exchange stock (Bank Regulations of 1986, Art.5). To judge by the amounts, the PBC foreign exchange can, at any point of time, have included the state foreign exchange stock; in 1986 the two figures correspond in all four digits. If the Bank of China's foreign exchange balance were included in the foreign exchange of the PBC, which is quantitatively impossible, it would not make sense to list the Bank of China foreign exchange balance separately from the state foreign exchange stock in Chinese statistics. (3) The amount of foreign exchange at the PBC at year-end, given in the statistics in RMB, has always been converted at the year-end exchange rate.

Sources:

Exchange rate and gold: Financial Statistics of China (1979-1985), 16; ZGJR 4/87 4/88 1/89.

State foreign exchange stock and foreign exchange balance: China Financial Statistics (1952-1979), 155; ZGJR 4/89.

PBC foreign exchange: Financial Statistics of China (1979-1985), 2f; ZGJR 4/87 4/88 4/89.

Current account: China Financial Statistics (1952-1987), 158; Almanac 1989, 119f; International Monetary Fund 12/90.

Total foreign debt: FEER, 26 March 1987, 53f; FEER, 7 Jan. 1988, 40f; Hu Xiaolian 7/90, 39.

was due to the attempt to reduce domestic purchasing power through the sale of imported consumer goods. Foreign exchange transactions thus cannot only cause disturbances if they are outside the plan, but may also be deliberately used for domestic economic policy purposes. Domestic economic policy, however, is not determined by the PBC.

Given the increasing difficulties in controlling the monetary sphere through credit, cash and foreign exchange plans, it may seem sensible to switch to a Western-type monetary policy. Modern (mainly Western-type) liquidity policy will therefore be discussed in the following chapter.

Chapter 3

Monetary Policy Instruments:
Modern Liquidity Policy

In contrast to administrative management through plans, liquidity is also affected by two "economic" means: a minimum reserve requirement and regulation of the "money market." Both are "economic" instruments inasmuch as they determine a certain framework within which banks may make their own decisions on the volume of credit.

1. Minimum Reserve Requirement

The minimum reserve requirement on deposits (*cunkuan zhunbeijin*) was introduced in 1985.[1] All special banks plus CITIC have to maintain a minimum reserve at the PBC. The PBC reviews the minimum reserve every 10 days[2] and necessary adjustments are made within 5 days.[3] Banks maintain their minimum reserve at the local PBC branch. If on the level

---

[1]   PBC 8 Oct. 1984 (a).

[2]   If the tenth day is a holiday, then on the day following the holiday.

[3]   On county level and below the minimum reserve is reviewed once a month with adjustments to be made during the first eight days of the following month.

The adjustment is made on the basis of the volume of deposits on the tenth day. If the volume of deposits varies from the volume at the time of last adjustment by more than 100,000 yuan, an adjustment is required.

77

concerned no PBC branch exists, the minimum reserve has to be maintained at a higher level PBC branch through the higher level branch of the same special bank. Interest payable on arrears is 0.3% per day on the amount outstanding. Minimum and excess reserves yield 5.04% and 6.48% per annum, respectively.[4]

The minimum reserve requirement differentiates between institutions. For the special banks and CITIC it amounted to 10% in 1985, 12% in October 1987,[5] and 13% after September 1988.[6] The requirement can be varied by the PBC as the monetary objectives might require. All special banks are treated uniformly whereas for other financial institutions it is not absolutely clear on which deposits a minimum reserve is required (or whether the item "reserves" in balance sheets can be regarded as minimum reserves).

Due to the proliferation of financial institutions, a number of special regulations became necessary.

— All insurance companies have to deposit 20% of their "cash capital" (*xianjin ziben*) at the PBC.[7] The PBC also determines how a number of different reserves of insurance companies are used.

— The minimum reserve requirement for trust and investment companies applies only to certain deposits which are not tied to particular projects and is determined by the PBC.[8]

— The rural credit co-operatives maintain their minimum reserves at the Agricultural Bank of China, which treats these reserves as normal deposits. The minimum reserve requirement can vary between 15% and 30% and is determined by the Agricultural Bank of China at the provincial level. Thus in 1988 the indirect minimum reserve

---

[4]   As of 1 September 1988. (Almanac 1989, 154.)

[5]   C.a. 1/88, 22.

[6]   The Wall Street Journal 1 Sept. 1988.

[7]   State Council 3 March 1985, Art. 9,17.
This deposit might not be regarded as a minimum reserve.

[8]   PBC 26 April 1986, Art. 16,26.
The minimum reserve on foreign exchange of trust and investment companies is to be maintained at the State Administration of Exchange Control. There is no information on where the minimum reserve on foreign exchange of other financial institutions is to be kept (the constitution of the Bank of China was passed in the same year the minimum reserve requirement was introduced).

requirement of the rural credit co-operatives at the PBC amounted to a final 1.95 to 3.9% of the volume of deposits at rural credit co-operatives.[9]

— The minimum reserve requirement for urban credit co-operatives is determined by the PBC at the provincial level. The minimum reserve is deposited at a special bank where the credit co-operative maintains an account (generally the Industrial and Commercial Bank of China), which passes the minimum reserves on to the PBC. Urban credit co-operatives can also directly deposit the minimum reserve at the PBC.[10]

If the minimum reserve requirement is increased, individual bank branches can (i) try to obtain more money from within their own bank hierarchy; (ii) increase utilization of the money market; (iii) reduce excess reserves; or (iv) increase loans from the PBC. If the reserve requirements for all financial institutions are increased simultaneously, the first two solutions are not viable and excess reserves may already have been run down. Yet loans from the PBC are determined politically. Hence if, as was the case in the past, the volume of refinancing of special banks by the PBC is to a large extent outside the control of the PBC, a minimum reserve does not make sense.[11]

That the minimum reserve requirement does not differentiate between the various types of deposits might be due to the separation into credit plan for enterprises and cash plan for consumers. There is no need for a minimum reserve to secure the liquidity of a bank if the use of enterprise deposits is severely restricted. Enterprise deposits may not be withdrawn in cash and are furthermore subject to administrative intervention. The behavior of individuals is supposed to be accounted for in the cash plan. Since the beginning of the reforms, however, credit plan and cash plan can no longer control the monetary system. The minimum reserve requirement could replace some of the restrictive influence formerly exercised through plans by keeping the multiplier effect of outside money under control.

---

[9] Agricultural Bank of China 12/84, 34.

The minimum reserve depends on the volume of deposits at the rural credit co-operative on the last day of the month. The adjustment is to be made within three days of the next month.

[10] State Council 17 July 1986.

[11] The minimum reserve requirement might simply have been copied from Western central banks at a time when enthusiasm for reform was running high. (Yuli 3/87.)

2. Money Market Instruments

After years of credit and cash plans, the "capitalist" money market, when rediscovered, first had to be legitimized. Chinese economists stress that plan and market both distribute money among different sectors, regulate economic efficiency, and determine the total amount of accumulation. Plans, however, are inferior to the market since they cannot take into consideration all details; since the distribution of loans among different sectors should depend on microeconomic efficiency, which, as years of planning have proven, is difficult to assess; and since the exact economic development would have to be known in order to determine the total volume of credit needed. The money market is said to solve all these problems via the interest rate. The money market allows for enterprise independence and for numerous different enterprise forms ranging from state-ownership to joint ventures and individual enterprises. The market renders credit planning futile and facilitates "horizontal" money flows whereas in the old system money, once handed down the hierarchy, is "never to be seen again." Finally, with a money market the central bank could gain a new instrument, open market policy.[12]

To avoid the "capitalist" expression "capital market" (*ziben shichang*), Chinese economists use the following expressions:

(i) short-term money market (*duanqi zijin shichang*)

   — interbank money market (*jinrong tongye chaijie shichang*)
   — (re)discounting of bills (*piaoju tiexian*)
   — short-term negotiable securities (*duanqi zhengquan*)

(ii) long-term money market (*changqi zijin shichang*) or "investment market" (*touzi shichang*)

   — stocks (*gupiao*)
   — bonds (*zhaiquan*)
   — long-term bank credit (*yinhangde changqi fangkuan*).[13]

---

[12]   Liu Hongru 1987, 93-99; Huang Min 1988, 169-172; Wu Jiesi 1987, 41-46.

[13]   Huang Min 1988, 167-169.
According to the author, the PRC does not yet have a market for short-term negotiable securities.

In the short run the PBC directly influences the availability of money in the banking system by controlling the interbank money market, while rediscounting of bills plays only a minor role. The administration of stocks and bonds with long-run effects of a possibly large magnitude is also under the direct control of the PBC (and other institutions).

Interbank Money Market Administration

The interbank money market, introduced in the first half of 1985,[14] is characterized by regional centers. One example is Shanghai, connected to 14 other cities, of which 7 are banking trial cities.[15] A supraregional trading net is only developing.[16] Central cities are to become the pillars of the interbank money market.

PBC branches do not participate in the lending, but the PBC "leads, organizes and administers" (*lingdao, zuzhi he guanli*) the trade in excess reserves at the PBC through "funds control groups" (*zijin diaodu xiaozu*) subordinate to either the director or one of the vice-directors at every PBC branch.[17] The conditions attached to interbank money market loans are negotiated by the participating banks, with the duration of loans generally being 3 months. The funds received may not be used for capital construction.[18] The strong involvement of the PBC in the interbank money market arises from the notion that "chaos" and "anarchy" have to be averted.[19] If the PBC can hardly monitor the implementation of the credit plan, however, how can it ever hope to monitor all movements in the money markets?

Shifting funds within a special bank hierarchy is considered by Chinese sources part of the interbank money market, accounting for more than 70%

---

[14] PBC 11/85, 28.

[15] Zhou Zhishi 1/88.

[16] C.a. 12/86, 764f.

[17] PBC 11/85, 28; ICBC 8 Oct. 1984, Art.8.

[18] PBC 1/87 (a).

[19] The PBC's involvement includes occasionally pressuring a special bank into lending its excess reserves in order to attenuate other special banks' money demand otherwise directed at the PBC.

In some cities the PBC branch is very actively pushing for an interbank money market, e.g., in Chongqing, a banking trial city. (Ren Junyin 9/87, 20f.)

of all lending. At the same time more than 70% of all lending is done locally,[20] possibly on very low administrative levels where a PBC branch does not exist.[21]

The funds lent by the Industrial and Commercial Bank of China (including funds shifted within its own hierarchy) amounted to about 20 b yuan in 1986. The figure for the Agricultural Bank of China was 15 b yuan. Nationwide in 1987 200 b yuan were traded.[22] The total amount for 1988 was 520 b yuan, and for 1989 290 b yuan.[23] For comparison: The year-end amount of loans from the PBC to special banks was approximately 324 b yuan (see Table 3 above). However, a direct comparison is not possible, as interbank money market figures are cumulative (the exact maturity of loans is not known).

Although the money market seems to be very improvised and unplanned, its potential in liberating financial institutions from plans and administrative regulations should not be underestimated. The only possibility for the PBC to clamp down on activities is by reducing the liquidity of the banking sector in total, as it did at the end of 1988 and all through 1989 and 1990.

Rediscounting

The reintroduction of bills[24] — that is, of commercial paper (*shangye chengdui huipiao*) and financial paper (*yinhang chengdui huipiao*) with a period of validity ranging from 3 to 9 months — can be seen as a further attempt to use market forces. The former clearing system in which a bank was asked by the creditor presenting a certificate of delivery to collect the

---

[20]   Cai Zhongzhi 3/88, 51.

[21]   According to a survey participants in the money market have very clear preferences as to the party they want to lend money to: First, to other local banks; second, to branches of the own special bank system within and outside the province; third, to other banks within or outside the province. (Zhang Shaojie 11/87, 17.)

[22]   Liu Hongru 1987, 100; Zhan Wu 3/88.
In Shanghai 19.8 b yuan were lent between July and September 1987 and 20.5 b yuan borrowed (Zhou Zhishi 1/88, 59), the difference is not accounted for.

[23]   Wu Qincheng 9/90, 24.

[24]   Discounting commercial paper was the backbone of the Shansi Banks in the last century (Yang Lien-sheng 1952, 81f), but has been used in the PRC since 1949 only for special purposes (Liu Hongru 1987, 67).

amount outstanding *(tuoshou chengfu jiesuan)*[25] has led to a large number of enterprise defaults with the financial institutions having to provide new loans.[26] If no new loans were given, the much-dreaded "chain reaction" occurred with enterprises successively being unable to meet their obligations and even suffering interruptions in production.[27] As a remedial action, the PBC and the Industrial and Commercial Bank of China passed the "Temporary Measures for Acceptance and Discounting of Bills" and the "Trial Regulations for Rediscounting through the PBC" in April 1985.[28] The objective of these measures was to facilitate clearing and to relieve banks of some of their responsibility by shifting the burden of checking the credit-worthiness of the buyer to the creditor. Banks are no longer responsible for bailing out enterprises which have not received their payments on time. Due to growing conservative influences in early 1990, however, the reform of the clearing system was stopped and all banks were asked to return to the former clearing system.[29]

Bills are discounted by banks at a rate slightly lower than the interest rate for working capital. All banks which maintain an account at the PBC may rediscount bills. The interest will be deducted from the amount paid to the bank. At maturity the PBC charges the account of that bank at the PBC which originally rediscounted the bill. Rediscounting is explicitly intended to provide short-term funds to banks for supporting trade.[30] In 1985 commercial and financial paper was rediscounted by the PBC in ten cities[31] at a rate of 3.75‰ per month. The rediscount rate is to be within 5 to 10% of the interest rate on a loan of comparable duration.[32]

---

[25]   This is the overall expression for several clearing methods used according to the local situation.

[26]   Liang Yingwu 5/86, 11.
An example: Such loans made by the Industrial and Commercial Bank of China amounted to 2.63 b yuan in July 1985, 5.63 b yuan in September 1985 and 9.38 b yuan at the end of 1985.

[27]   FEER 11 Dec. 1986, 85-88; ICBC 10 Oct. 1988.

[28]   PBC 4/85 (published in ZGJR more than one year later).

[29]   ZGJR 4/90, 1.

[30]   PBC 4/85, part 2.

[31]   The ten cities are: Beijing, Shanghai, Tianjin, Guangzhou, Chongqing, Wuhan, Shenyang, Harbin, Nanjing, Changzhou.

[32]   China Financial Statistics (1952-1987), 148; Almanac 1989, 154.

84

Although the first discounting of bills had already started in Shanghai in 1980,[33] as of 1991 discounting of bills was of small magnitude. Repeated exhortations[34] seem to have been without effect. In 1988 rediscounting by the PBC nationwide amounted to only 5% of all bridging loans, which in turn amounted to 14% of all loans by the PBC to special banks.[35] Thus rediscounting covered less than 1% of all money flowing from the PBC to special banks. One qualification, however, is necessary: rediscounting, in early 1989, was practiced only in the ten cities.

Commercial paper remains unpopular with enterprises, which prefer to rely on banks for collecting their money from the debtor and to obtain bank loans if a debtor cannot meet his obligations. Special banks, on the other hand, welcome rediscounting since it strengthens their independence from plans. Banks can use bills as a clearing instrument among themselves. Banks are allowed to endorse bills, non-banks are not.[36] Rediscounting allows banks to avoid bargaining with the PBC over new loans — the regulations do not specify whether examination of the bills presented to the PBC is only a "technical" examination or whether the PBC may reject bills on any grounds. With the volume of rediscounting, however, being as small as it presently is, rediscounting is hardly more than a partial replacement of bridging loans.

Administration of Stocks and Bonds

The legitimization for stocks and bonds is their ability to attract funds which are not deposited at banks either because of the low interest rates or in order to avoid state control. Enterprises can raise funds they might not be able to obtain through the credit plan and the use of these funds is expected to be efficient since high dividends have to be paid. The PBC might one day even start open market operations.[37] The "socialist" capital market, however, is said to differ from the "capitalist" capital market in that

---

[33]   Huang Min 1988, 172.

[34]   The vice-president of the Industrial and Commercial Bank of China, Shaanxi Province branch, even gave a speech to enterprise managers attempting to talk them into using commercial paper. (ICBC 10 Oct. 1988.)

[35]   Xu Jian 12 Dec. 1988.

[36]   State Council 22 Aug. 1988; PBC Taiyuan 1/86.

[37]   Wang Xiangpin 2/88, 38f; Wu Jiesi 1987, 164f.

the special banks play a dominant role, funds are provided chiefly by peasants, workers, and enterprises (not "capitalists"), and there is no connection with the international capital market.[38]

Since the beginning of the economic reforms a variety of stocks and bonds have emerged.

(i) stocks (*gupiao*)

(ii) bonds (*zhaiquan*)

(local) enterprise bonds (*(difang) qiye zhaiquan*)

financial bonds (*jinrong zhaiquan*) with a maturity of, as of 1988, 2 years

state bonds (*gongzhai*)

— treasury bonds (*guokuquan*) with a maturity of, as of 1988, 3 years
— state key construction bonds (*guojia zhongdian jianshe zhaiquan*)
— key enterprise bonds (*zhongdian qiye zhaiquan*) with a maturity of, as of 1988, 5 years
— capital construction bonds (*jiben jianshe zhaiquan*) with a maturity of, as of 1988, 5 years
— state construction bonds (*guojia jianshe zhaiquan*) with a maturity of, as of 1988, 2 years
— public bonds (*caizheng zhaiquan*) with a maturity of, as of 1988, 2 or 5 years
— value-guaranteed bonds (*baozhi gongzhai*) with a maturity of, as of 1989, 3 years
— special bonds (*tezhong guozhai*) with a maturity of, as of 1990, 5 years.[39]

---

[38] Yang Peixin 7 April 1986.

[39] Among others, Almanac 1989, 44,83,168.
The issuing procedure differs in most cases, e.g., the state key construction bonds are issued by the People's Construction Bank of China representing the Finance Ministry.

Figure 10. Shanghai's Stock and Bond Market

Stocks

8/84	The city government passes the "Provisional Administrative Measures for the Issuing of Stocks."
9/84	The first enterprise issues stocks to its staff and workers with official approval.
1/85	The first enterprise issues stocks to the public with official approval.
9/86	For the first time since 1949 stock trading is resumed.
12/86	The first state-owned enterprise is changed into a joint-stock company; stocks are sold to the public.
9/84 - 6/88	A total of 1,255 enterprises in Shanghai issue stocks valued at 1 b yuan (with official approval). The stocks of 8 enterprises are sold to the public.
9/86 - 6/88	Six stocks are traded. Total trading volume in this period is 2.6 m yuan. There are 9 security counters and 3 security companies.
12/90	Official opening of the Shanghai Securities Exchange (19 Dec. 1990).

Trading

The stock report in a Shanghai newspaper on 23 October 1988 listed the prices of 4 stocks, 3 treasury bonds, 5 financial bonds (3 issued by the Bank of Communications, 2 by the Industrial and Commercial Bank of China), 1 national key construction bond and 4 enterprise bonds at each of seven security counters (none of the stocks was listed at all seven security counters simultaneously).

Further information

Both PBC and city government are engaged in regulating the stock market.

The total volume of trading in stocks is low. By late 1990 the value of all daily trading on the Shanghai stock exchange was on average 1 m yuan, of which 95% in bonds.

The government controls up to 75% of the stocks listed on the Shanghai Securities Exchange; most stocks are issued to the staff and workers of the enterprise concerned.

Sources: Zhang Ning 28 Oct. 1988; Xinwenbao (Shanghai) 22 Oct. 1988; FEER 31 Jan. 1991, 34.

Stocks and Enterprise Bonds. The PBC together with the State Council passed a set of regulations in 1987[40] to reduce the many variations of "stocks" and "bonds." First of all, "stocks" and "bonds" had to be defined. Stocks earn dividends and are not returned to the issuing body; bonds are returned at maturity, pay interest (but not dividends or bonuses), and do not entitle to participation in an enterprise's decision-making. Neither stocks nor bonds bear any risk, being guaranteed by state organs. Bonds can be mortgaged, though not at the PBC,[41] and are inheritable but not transferable. Special banks and other financial institutions (both with approval of the PBC) are allowed to carry out trading.

State-owned enterprises are not permitted to issue stocks.[42] A small number of collective enterprises are allowed to issue stocks upon approval of the PBC. State-owned enterprises can issue bonds, whereas collective enterprises are not allowed to. The PBC, in co-operation with the State Planning Commission and the Finance Ministry, determines the annual total volume of bonds to be issued and divides the volume among the provinces. The PBC approves the issuing of bonds[43] and administers, supervises and examines the use of the funds raised. If the funds are to be used for investment in fixed assets the relevant authorities must give approval and the investment must be included in the plan. The interest rate on bonds may not exceed the interest rate on time deposits by more than 40%. Bonds can be issued by the enterprise itself or via a bank or other financial institution.

Although bonds are supposed to finance mainly state key projects within the state plan, the issuers of bonds seem to disagree. Time and again it is deplored that funds are "blindly" used for projects outside the plan and without giving any thought to whether similar investment is already being carried out elsewhere. Other problems are widely noted. When dividend and

---

[40] (1) "Provisional Regulations on the Administration of Enterprise Bonds" (State Council 27 March 1987);
(2) "State Council Circular Requesting the Strengthening of the Administration of Stocks and Bonds Nationwide" (State Council 7 April 1987);
(3) "Circular on Relevant Questions of the Administration of Enterprise Stocks, Bonds, and Other Financial Market Activities" (PBC 28 Sept. 1987).

[41] For different regulations in Shanghai see PBC Shanghai 3/88.

[42] Apart from two exceptions where approval from the State Commission for the Reform of the Economic System is necessary: participation in other enterprises, but these stocks may not be sold to a wider public except with special permission from the PBC; and a few trial enterprises.

[43] If the amount exceeds 30 m yuan, approval from the PBC Head Office is needed, otherwise approval can come from provincial PBC branches.

interest payments on stocks and bonds cannot be met, loans from banks become necessary. When stocks/bonds cannot be sold, staff and workers of the enterprise may be forced to help out. If funds raised through stocks and bonds are used for investment in fixed assets, as most of them are, special banks later on have to provide the working capital.[44]

The amount of funds raised up to August 1988 by issuing stocks and bonds has been estimated at 20 b yuan, of which 17 b yuan had been raised through the issuing of bonds.[45] While approximately 6,000 enterprises have issued stocks, the stocks of only 14 enterprises were traded in the 3 cities Shanghai, Wuhan and Chongqing in 1988.[46] In December 1990 the first stock exchange in the PRC since 1949 was formally opened in Shanghai. (See Figure 10.)

Financial and state bonds. Financial bonds, that is, bonds issued by financial institutions, are a convenient means to escape the PBC-mandated interest rate on deposits at special banks. In Shanghai in 1988, three issues by the Bank of Communications and the Industrial and Commercial Bank of China were traded. Nationwide the issuing of financial bonds began in 1985 and reached 6 b yuan in 1987 and 6.5 b yuan in 1988.[47] In 1990 the PBC and special banks sold financial bonds worth 7 b yuan and 6 b yuan respectively.[48]

After issuing "Victory Bonds" (*zhongguo renmin shengli zheshi gongzhai*) in 1950 and "Construction Bonds" (*guojia jingji jianshe gongzhai*) in 1954 and 1958, it was not until the high budget deficits in 1979 and 1980 that the PRC again issued state bonds. Maturity periods of these bonds were first 10

---

[44]   Wu Jiesi 1987, 66-70.

[45]   Hong Yuncheng 3/88, 39.
In comparison: The total amount of loans by all state banks (Consolidated Balance Sheet) was 1,000 b yuan in September 1988. (ZGJR 1/89.)
Almanac 1989, 83, gives the total amount of enterprise stocks issued in 1988 as 2.5 b yuan (with no issues before 1988) and of enterprise bonds issued in 1987 and 1988 as 3 b yuan (with no issues before 1987), yet the total figure "until 1988" for enterprise stocks and bonds is 3.5 b yuan and 16 b yuan respectively. In a footnote the excessive amount is said to stem from the years before 1986.

[46]   FEER 16 Feb. 1989, 48; FEER 9 March 1989.
No exact date is given, figures are probably for the end of 1988.

[47]   Hong Yuncheng 3/88, 39; Almanac 1989, 83.
No exact date is given.

[48]   Jinrong shibao 23 July 1990.

years, then 5 years, and since 1988 3 years. The PBC carries out issuing and repayment either itself or through a special bank.[49] Since 1985 units may use state bonds as security for bank loans (*diya daikuan*) and individuals may sell their state bonds to banks,[50] though not until two years after the issue date.[51] (See Table 8.)

In 1987 5.5 b yuan worth of state key construction bonds and 3 b yuan worth of key enterprise bonds were issued,[52] but were sold only with great difficulty.[53] The objective of the two issues was to guarantee certain large infrastructure projects on a national level. Such projects suffer most from a reduction in planned activities, because local governments and special bank branches prefer to support projects guaranteeing the development of the local economy.[54] In 1988 no state key construction bonds were issued, but key enterprise bonds worth 1 b yuan were. These bonds had to be purchased by other enterprises using 15% of their own funds "intended for capital construction." Three new types of bonds were created: public bonds (6.607 b yuan), possibly to finance the budget deficit, all sold to financial institutions; state construction bonds (3.065 b yuan); and capital construction bonds (8 b yuan), all sold to special banks. In 1989 and 1990 the central government invented further bond variants. In 1989 it issued value-guaranteed bonds worth 12 b yuan (with the interest rate linked to the inflation rate) and in 1990 special bonds worth 45 b yuan.[55]

---

[49]   State Council 23 Sept. 1983.

Repayment includes interest and is spread over 5 years at an annual repayment rate of 20%, allocated among individuals by drawing lots, whereas all enterprises are paid back 20% of the total annually.

[50]   Lu Peijian 2/85, 3.

[51]   C.a. 7/88, 516.

At the end of 1988 treasury bonds issued in 1985 and 1986 were traded in Shanghai.

[52]   Hong Yuncheng 3/88, 39.

[53]   In August 1987 the governor of the PBC, Chen Muhua, was still appealing for a complete subscription to the state key construction bonds of 1987. (Chen Muhua 8/87, 8.)

[54]   Zhang Shaojie 11/87.

Another reason why special banks might be reluctant to provide credit to such national infrastructure projects is the low interest rate on such loans.

[55]   State Council 31 July 1989; Jinrong shibao 9 June 1990; State Council 26 June 1990.

Most of the new types of bonds were issued besides those types already used in previous years.

Table 8. Issues of Treasury Bonds

Year	Par value (in RMB m)	of which sold to		Interest rate for	
		units	individuals	units	individuals
1981	4,866	4,855	11	4	4
1982	3.383	2,412	1,971	4	8
1983	4,158	2,071	2.087	4	8
1984	4,219	2,012	2,207	4	8
1985	6,060	2,182	3,878	5	9
1986	6,251	2,247	4,004	6	10
1987	6,307	2,258	4,409	6	10
1988	9,000	3,500	5,500	6	10

Note: In the Statistical Yearbook (e.g., in Statistical Yearbook 1988, 762) there are no entries for 1981. The reason stated is that although bonds have been issued to alleviate a budget deficit they have not been included in the state budget.
Sources: 1981-1987: Beijing Rundschau 16 Aug. 1988 (No.33).
1988: Herrmann-Pillath 2-89, 71f.

The State Council announcements list as prospective purchasers individuals, individually-owned enterprises, and all units. They mention that individuals should purchase bonds according to their income. Yet the request intensifies for the actual policy of forcing special banks, enterprises and individuals to purchase state bonds to be ended.[56] The government seems to have taken a liking to these new methods of raising and redistributing funds. From the point of view of the state and the PBC, the advantages of issuing state bonds are obvious: a reduction in purchasing power and the simultaneous financing of the government budget deficit. With, at the end of 1989, about 92 b yuan worth of state bonds in

---

[56] Li Xingbin 2/90.

circulation, the foundations are laid for later PBC open market operations.[57] Treasury bonds of the years 1982 to 1984, 1987, and 1988 were already freely traded by the public in most provinces.[58]

Problems. Despite the high demand for stocks and bonds and the eagerness of enterprises to tap this source of financing, the present economic system in China is inimical to large-scale issuing of stocks and bonds. (i) The irrational price structure impedes a "correct" assessment of enterprises and the interest paid on bonds is subject to state regulations and controls and thus not market-determined. (ii) Chinese enterprises, apart from some experiments, do not have any independence and responsibility when issuing stocks or bonds. They are jointly controlled by the PBC and other state organs and decisions on permitting an enterprise to issue stocks or bonds are more often than not political decisions. (iii) With larger numbers of stocks and bonds not always fully under the control of the PBC, the importance of the credit plan is reduced and the former system of credit administration as macroeconomic control mechanism loses its effectiveness.

As of 1991, the minimum reserve requirement has not been much used as a monetary policy instrument. The interbank money market still depends on both the general liquidity of the banking system and direct PBC control. Discounting of bills and rediscounting by the PBC never became widely accepted. Issuing of stocks and bonds suffered severe setbacks from braking manoeuvres since 1988. Altogether modern liquidity policy, although much publicized in the earlier years, never achieved a major impact on the monetary system.

---

[57] Almanac 1990, 71.
(Sum of relevant state receipts minus sum of disbursements.)

[58] Jingji cankao 7 June 1990.
The total amount officially traded in the first four months of 1990 was 1.5 b yuan nationwide, of which 0.8 b yuan in Shanghai; the black market offers treasury bonds at an average discount of 20 to 30%.

Chapter 4

Monetary Policy Instruments:
Interest Rates

Very pragmatic reasons are given for the existence of interest rates in the PRC: (i) interest rates stimulate savings, necessary to siphon off excessive cash in circulation; (ii) they offer some compensation for price adjustments (or inflation); (iii) enterprises are forced to work efficiently since interest payments increase their costs; (iv) the state can use interest rates to exercise macroeconomic control (e.g., channel funds by means of the interest rate structure); (v) banks can cover their costs with the difference in interest rates for loans and deposits.[1]

The most important function of interest rates is that of regulatory instrument. State monetary policy has at its disposal a multitude of different interest rates: Preferential interest rates (*youhui lilu*); subsidized interest rates (*tiexi lilu*); penalty and arrears interest rates (*jiashou lilu*); differential interest rates (*chabie lilu*) according to sectors, ownership and duration, possibly with slight variations decided upon by bank branches (*fudong lilu*); and special PBC interest rates (*zhuanxiang lilu*). The State Council approves interest rates and their structure as proposed by the PBC.[2]

---

[1] Huang Min 1988, 88-92.

[2] The interest rate adjustment of 1 Feb. 1989 (see Table 9) is the only interest rate adjustment not explicitly stating the participation of the State Council. (C.a. 1/89, 22.)

93

1. Interest Rate Structure

This first section introduces the various interest rates and analyzes their structure. The second section then looks at the implementation of this monetary policy instrument.

General Interest Rates

Until 1 September 1988 the interest rates on deposits by units were always below those on deposits by individuals.[3] (See Tables 9 and 10.) With enterprises not being allowed to choose their bank or to maintain accounts at different banks, and with cash usage by enterprises severely restricted, banks did not need to attract enterprise deposits. Only with the increasing lack of enforcement of these regulations in the course of reform did the need arise for banks to attract enterprise deposits, though still only on a very limited scale. On 1 September 1988 the interest rates on deposits by units were raised to the level of those on deposits by individuals. Yet on 10 September 1988 the interest rates for enterprises have not been linked to the retail price index as have been the interest rates on 3-, 5- and 8-year time deposits by individuals. The link was instituted because the inflation rate came to exceed interest rates on deposits by individuals. (Only for the case of an inflation rate exceeding the interest rate does the link go into effect.)

The considerable difference between interest rates on demand and time deposits seems to be an attempt to reduce latent purchasing power. The interest rate difference serves as an incentive to avoid immediately withdrawable demand deposits. (More will be said on the concept and implications of purchasing power in Part II.)

The development of differing lending rates clearly shows the change from state budget allocations to bank loans, a key component of industrial reform. "Medium- and short-term loans for the purchase of equipment and for large-scale repairs," covering the sub-group "equipment" of the fixed assets classification, first became "loans for technical updating and transformation" (in contrast to capital construction) and then "loans for investment in fixed assets" of all kinds. At the same time loans were made available for longer periods of time.

---

[3] Two differentiations are made in deposits: On the one hand between demand deposits and time deposits and, on the other hand, between deposits made by units and those made by individuals, the latter being called "savings" deposits (of the urban and rural population).

Table 9. Selected Interest Rates at Special Banks
(annual rates in %)

(1) Deposits at special banks	before 1982	1 Apr. 1982	1 Apr. 1985	1 Aug. 1985	June 1987	1 Sep. 1988	10 Sep. 1988	1 Feb. 1989
Units (enterprises, etc.)								
Demand deposits	1.80	1.80	1.80	.	.	2.88	X	.
Time deposits								
1 year	X	3.60	4.32	.	5.04	8.64	X	.
2 years	X	4.32	5.04	.	5.76	9.18	X	.
3 years	X	5.04	5.76	.	6.48	9.72	X	.
5 years	X	X	X	X	X	10.80	X	.
8 years	X	X	X	X	X	12.42	X	.
Savings deposits (of urban and rural individuals)								
Demand deposits	2.88	2.88	2.88	2.88	2.88	2.88	X	.
Time deposits								
6 months	4.32	4.32	5.40	6.12	6.12	6.84	X	9.00
1 year	5.40	5.76	6.84	7.20	7.20	8.64	X	11.34
2 years	X	X	X	X	X	9.18	X	12.24
3 years	6.20	6.84	7.92	8.28	8.28	9.72	•	13.14
5 years	6.84	7.92	8.28	9.36	9.36	10.80	•	14.94
8 years	X	9.00	9.00	10.44	10.44	12.42		17.64
Overseas Chinese: Time deposits								
1 year	5.76	6.48	7.20	8.28	8.28	9.72	X	.
3 years	6.48	7.20	8.28	9.36	9.36	10.80	X	.
5 years	7.20	8.28	9.00	10.44	10.44	11.88	X	.
Individually-owned enterprises in industry and commerce, and specialized households in agriculture	.	.	2.88	.	.	.	.	.

(2) Loans from special banks	before 1982	1 Jan. 1982	before 1 April 1985	1 Apr. 1985	1 Aug. 1985	1 Sep. 1988	1 Feb. 1989	21 March 1990
Working capital loans	5.04	7.20	7.20	7.92	.	.	9.00	10.08
Medium- and short-term loans for the purchase of equipment and for large-scale repairs[b]								
below 1 year	5.04	5.04	[c]					
above 1 year and below 3 years	5.04	5.76	[c]					
above 3 years and below 5 years	5.04	6.48	[c]					
Loans for technical updating and transformation								
below 1 year	X	X	5.04	5.04	.	[d]		
above 1 year and below 3 years	X	X	5.76	5.76	.	[d]		
above 3 years and below 5 years	X	X	6.48	6.48	.	[d]		
Capital construction loans	.	.	.	•				
Loans for investment in fixed assets								
below 1 year	X	X	X	X	5.04	7.92	9.00	.
above 1 year and below 3 years	X	X	X	X	5.76	8.64	9.90	.
above 3 years and below 5 years	X	X	X	X	6.48	9.36	10.80	.
above 5 years and below 10 years	X	X	X	X	7.20	10.08	13.32	.
above 10 years	X	X	X	X	7.92	10.80	16.20	.
Interest rate on arrears	+ 20%	+ 20%	.	.	.	+ 20%	+ 20%	.
Penalty rate[g]	+ 50%	+ 50%	.	.	.	+ 50%	+ 50%	.
Loans for advance payments	.	.	5.76	5.76	.	.	.	.
Preferential loans						3-7.2	3-8.28	.
Loans to urban and rural individually-owned enterprises in industry, trade, transport and services[h]	.	.	8.64	9.36-11.52	.	.	11.7	.
Agricultural loans (various types)	2.16-4.32	4.32-7.20	5.76-7.92	5.76-9.36	5.76-9.36	7.20-10.80	7.92-10.8	.

Notes: The above compilation is far from complete, China Financial Statistics (1952-1987) contains 12 pages and Almanac 1989 18 pages of various interest rates, the latter subdivided to the level of individual banks. Depending on the economic sector further differentiations have to be made.

a. Linked to retail price index.

b. "Equipment" is a subgroup of "fixed assets" which includes: (i) construction and installation, (ii) purchase of equipment, tools and instruments and (iii) other investment (Statistical Yearbook 1986, 750f).

c. See loans for technical updating and transformation.

d. See loans for investment in fixed assets.

e. Change from state allocations to loans.

f. See loans for investment in fixed assets.

g. A penalty rate has to be paid by the borrower if he pressured the bank into giving him a loan or if funds are not used as earmarked.

h. Interest rates on loans which do not mention the individually-owned enterprises seem to be valid only for state-owned and collective enterprises.

Sources: State Council, 23 Dec. 1981; State Council, 14 March 1985; State Council, 8 July 1985; State Council 3 Sept. 1988; Almanac 1989, 149-168; C.a. 8/88, 619; C.a. 1/89, 22; China Financial Statistics (1979-1985), 10,11; China Financial Statistics (1952-1987), 144,147; Zhou Zhengqing 4/90, 7f; Jingji cankao 15 April 1990; Yu Naidong 6/90, 29.

Table 10. People's Bank of China and Other Interest Rates (annual rates in %)	
(1) PBC (1 Sept. 1989, unless otherwise indicated)	
Deposits by:	
Special banks	
Minimum reserves	5.04
Excess reserves	6.48
Rural Credit Co-operatives (special deposits at PBC, 1987)	
6 months	7.56
1 year	7.92
Trust and Investment Companies, urban credit co-operatives (1987)	
Minimum reserves	4.32
Excess reserves (deposits)	5.76
Insurance companies (various types of deposits, e.g., "minimum reserves")	2.88-6.48
Loans to financial institutions	
Basic loans	8.28
Annual loans	8.28
Bridging loans	7.56
Daily money	6.48
Rediscount rate	within 5-10% of corresponding rates
Special loans: Differentiated between old revolutionary-base areas, development of local economy, RMB loans for the purchase of foreign exchange, 14 coastal cities and special economic zones as well as according to duration	4.68-16.20
(2) Interbank money market	determined by parties concerned
(3) Bonds (1988, unless otherwise indicated)	
Capital construction bonds (5 years)	7.50
Financial bonds	
1 to 3 years	9.00-11.00
3 to 5 years	9.00-13.00
Public bonds	
2 years	8.00
5 years	7.50
Key enterprise bonds (5 years)	6.00
State construction bonds (2 years)	9.50

Treasury bonds (3 years)	
Individuals	10.00
Units	6.00
Enterprise bonds	<40% above corresponding deposit rates
Value-guaranteed bonds (1989, 1 to 3 years)	1% above corresponding rates linked to Retail Price Index
Special bonds (1990, 5 years)	15.00
(4) Other financial institutions	
Deposits (1987) at:	
Trust and Investment Companies	5.76
Insurance Companies	1.80–6.48
Urban Credit Co-operatives	5.76
Agricultural Bank of China by Rural Credit Co-operatives (nationwide average)	
Minimum reserves	6.18
Other deposits	6.61
Rural Credit Co-operatives	within 20% of rates at special banks
Loans from:	
Urban Credit Co-operatives (examination and confirmation of rates by local PBC and approval by provincial PBC)	variable
Rural Credit Co-operatives	within 20% of 9.00 - 12.60
Other financial institutions	

Sources: (1) For 1989: Almanac 1989, 154f. For 1987: China Financial Statistics (1952 -1987), 140f. (2) PBC 1/87 (a) or Bank Regulations of 1986, Art.45. (3) China Financial Statistics (1952-1987), 152; State Council 31 July 1989; State Council 26 June 1990. (4) China Financial Statistics (1952-1987), 143; State Council 17 July 1986; Agricultural Bank of China 28 Feb. 1986, 51f.

Interest rates on loans are greatly differentiated, according to ownership, sector, and purpose. Interest rates on loans to individually-owned enterprises are the highest, whereas for certain sectors such as energy, communications and raw materials, reduced interest rates are in effect. Interest rate subsidies are permitted on loans to state key construction and to some technical updating and transformation projects; whichever state organ orders subsidies has to pay for them.[4] Minority regions, which make up more than half of China, enjoy special regulations. Banking trial cities experiment in various ways.[5] There is no indication of interest rate differentiation according to the risk associated with a loan.

The interest rates on working capital loans, generally for one year, have for years been slightly higher than the interest rates on long-term loans for investment in fixed assets (or their predecessors). With funds for investment in fixed assets being severely restricted by the credit plan, working capital comparatively easily provided by banks was channelled into investment in fixed assets. Hence liquidity policy annulled interest rate policy. The discrepancy in interest rates was redressed in August 1985. Since then interest rates on most working capital loans have equalled those on one-year loans for investment in fixed assets. This, however, did nothing to stop the illegal use of working capital loans for investment in fixed assets.

In agriculture the Agricultural Bank of China has been responsible for determining interest rates since 1 April 1985. However, approval is needed from the PBC. Since the abolition of the people's communes, a major change has occurred in that a large amount of credit is made available to individual households.[6] Interest rates charged by rural credit co-operatives are close to market rates, even if that means disregarding regulations, since loans made outside financial institutions — e.g., through "People's Banks" — are always a viable alternative.

A comparison between the interest rates on working capital loans and loans for investment in fixed assets vs. those on time deposits reveals an astonishing fact. The PBC (or State Council) allows for only a very narrow

---

[4] There also exists a host of penalty interest rates, interest rates on arrears and special interest rates on items such as loans for advance payments.

[5] In Chongqing, for example, working capital loans in 1987 were further structured, with different interest rates according to maturity. (Ren Junyin 9/87, 21.)

[6] At the end of 1989 38% of all loans (by volume) by rural credit co-operatives had gone to individual households, 52% to rural enterprises, and 10% to agricultural collectives. (For comparison, the volume of all loans by rural credit co-operatives was 1.2 times the volume of "agricultural loans" in the Consolidated Balance Sheet of all state banks, including the Agricultural Bank of China, but excluding rural credit co-operatives.) (ZGJR 5/90, 61.)

interest rate margin (Table 11). If preferential loans are not completely subsidized, banks will more likely than not incur losses. The objective of state monetary policy is clearly not one of maximizing special bank profits.

Table 11. Selected Interest Rates on 1 September 1988 (annual interest rate in %)			
	Time deposits	Loans for	
		investment in fixed assets	working capital
1 year	8.64	9.00	9.00
2 years	9.18	.	X
3 years	9.72	9.90	X
5 years	10.80	10.80	X
8 years	12.42	.	X
10 years	.	16.20	X
Source: See Table 9.			

People's Bank of China and Other Interest Rates

Interest rates on excess and minimum reserves maintained at the PBC are below the interest rates on time deposits of individuals at special banks and in general below interest rates on loans from banks to enterprises. (See Tables 9 and 10.) But by paying some interest on special bank excess reserves, the PBC can reduce the pressure on special banks to increase the volume of loans even more. With the interest rates on loans from the PBC to special banks being independent of the volume of refinancing, any amount of refinancing, if the money was given to enterprises, promised higher profits to special banks.

The PBC acquires the seemingly permanent surplus of deposits over loans at rural credit co-operatives through compulsory deposits by rural co-operatives at the PBC (apart from the minimum reserve requirement). The surplus might otherwise remain unexploited, given the decentralized organization of the approximately 61,000 rural credit co-operatives. In 1987 interest rates on these compulsory deposits were in the range of 2- to 3-year time deposits by individuals at special banks.

Interest rates on the various bonds sold to individuals in 1988 were all above those on comparable savings deposits at special banks. Since the interest rates on bonds held by individuals usually exceed those on bonds held by units, units try to pass their bonds on to individuals.

While the interest rates on deposits at trust and investment companies and insurance companies in 1987 in general approximated those for deposits of units at special banks, interest rates at some of the more recently established financial institutions may well differ due to the lack of control through the PBC.[7]

2. Limits of Interest Rate Policy

The Demand for Loans from Special Banks

Interest payments constitute only a small part of an enterprise's costs.[8] As long as enterprises are not completely independent and their managers not responsible for profit and losses, the interest rate will remain a minor factor in enterprise decision-making. It is generally not the interest rate that constitutes a restraint on borrowing, for a high interest rate can be offset — for example, by higher prices or lower tax payments. Rather, the restraint on borrowing is simply the availability of credit.[9]

Assuming that enterprises were to regard the interest rate as a cost factor, the problem of determining the "correct" interest rate remains, since a market rate would lead to a large number of bankruptcies. The interest rate would have to differ from industry to industry in order to take into account

---

[7]   According to the Bank Regulations of 1986, every special bank has the right to vary its interest rates within a certain range (Art. 42). It is questionable whether this right exists in practice. Chinese economists often discuss whether the PBC's power to determine interest rates should not be reduced by limiting its authority to determining a maximum interest rate on deposits and a minimum interest rate on loans. (Wu Jiesi 1987, 142f.)

[8]   Wu Jiesi 1987, 125, offers a few figures.
   The share of interest costs in total costs for the energy sector is 0.7%; for most important raw materials 0.1 to 0.8%; for light industry 0.4 to 0.9%; for agriculture 0.2%. Since these figures are for 1981, however, loans for investment in fixed assets have not been included. (In 1981 investment in fixed assets was not supposed to be financed through bank loans.)

[9]   In a few cases enterprise managers have been given interest costs as one of the reference numbers for which they are responsible.

the different profit margins as established through state priorities and the corresponding price system.[10] With state-decreed prices, however, it cannot be determined which enterprises are efficient and which are not. Inefficient enterprises might be offered large amounts of credit at low costs, thus further straining the economy.

Local governments tend to plead for low interest rates in order to keep interest costs low and investment cheap. With PBC branches (as well as special bank branches) subject to local government interference, active interest rate policy making on the part of the PBC is improbable.[11]

The Volume of Deposits

Long-term savings, such as savings to provide for the education of children, prepare for emergencies, or secure an income for old-age, are rather stable and independent of short-term changes in the interest rate. The same is true of medium-term savings, such as savings for the purchase of an expensive commodity. Savings due to an inadequate supply of those commodities which are demanded now, however, can become highly instable. Since individuals cannot purchase investment goods, the smaller the supply of consumer goods and the lower the interest rate the more excessive purchasing power will be held in cash (or as demand deposits rather than time deposits, for unexpected purchases if desired goods suddenly become available).[12]

If, however, the interest rate drops significantly below the inflation rate and is expected to stay there, almost any available consumer goods will be purchased in order to avoid a loss of purchasing power. In August 1988 a panicking urban population purchased not only those goods for which administrative price rises were anticipated, but any goods available. The larger the discrepancy between interest rate and inflation rate, the more savings will be withdrawn. If the state is not willing to reduce purchasing power by lowering income, only a readjustment (increase) of the interest

---

[10] With sectorally differentiated interest rates or even individual interest rates for different enterprises as sometimes proposed, all incentives to work efficiently would again be lost. "To take away from the rich and to give to the poor" leads back to central planning.

[11] Li Yining 4/86; Wu Jiesi 1987, 136-139; Zhou Zhishi 12/87.

The market interest rate far surpasses the interest rates charged by special banks. (See Wenzhou below.)

[12] Li Yining 4/86, 58-60.

rate can stop the run on banks. On 1 September 1988 the interest rates on savings deposits were increased and on 10 September 1988 the rates on 3-, 5-, and 8-year savings deposits were linked to the Retail Price Index.

Units face a similar problem once the interest rate is lower than, or approximately equal to, the inflation rate. They will attempt to disburse funds allocated through the credit plan as well as their own funds as fast as possible or ask their staff and workers to "store" enterprise funds in their savings accounts. Before September 1988 interest rates on individual savings exceeded those on deposits by units; when some savings deposits were linked to the Retail Price Index on 10 September 1988, deposits by units were not. For units one alternative to deposits is purchase of state bonds traded with a steep discount on the black market.[13]

The Inflation Rate as a Determinant of Interest Rates

The inflation rate thus determines interest rates on savings deposits, which in turn influence savings and deposits by units. (See Table 12.) If special banks are to cover their costs through income earned via interest rate margins, then interest rates on loans must follow interest rates on savings deposits, or a lower interest rate on loans must be subsidized.

In determining monetary policy the PBC and the State Council are forced to react to changes in the inflation rate by adjusting interest rates. Interest rates may be used only to a limited degree as an independent variable of monetary policy. If there is some link between credit volume and inflation rates — such as loans being used to make bonus payments to staff, who then increase their demand for goods — then the PBC's only important monetary policy variable is the volume of credit. Interest rates will simply have to be adjusted accordingly.

From 1980 until 1984 the inflation rate as measured by the Retail Price Index and the Living Cost Index was almost always above the interest rate on demand deposits of units and approximately equal to the interest rate on demand deposits of individuals. Since 1985, both indices have far exceeded interest rates. Only in 1988 did the PBC link interest rates to the Retail Price Index; inflation rates were then double or triple the interest rates and the population had started to withdraw savings from banks on a large scale. It is possible, however, that with special banks and other financial institutions competing for funds and trying to attract deposits in order to

---

[13]   Zhao Baowei 1/90, 31f.

Table 12. Comparison Between Various Interest Rates and Official Inflation Rates
(annual rates in %)

	1980	1981	1982	1983	1984	1985	1986	1987	1988
Annual interest rate on deposits by									
Units									
Demand deposits	1.80	1.80	1.80	1.80	1.80	1.80	1.80	1.80	2.88
Time deposits (1 year)	X	X	3.60	3.60	3.60	4.32	4.32	5.04	8.64
Individuals									
Demand deposits	2.88	2.88	2.88	2.88	2.88	2.88	2.88	2.88	2.88
Time deposits (1 year)	5.40	5.40	5.76	5.76	5.76	7.20	7.20	7.20	8.64
Inflation rates									
Retail Price Index	6.0	2.4	1.9	1.5	2.8	8.8	6.0	7.3	18.5
Cost of Living Index (staff and workers)	7.5	2.5	2.0	2.0	2.7	11.9	10.7	8.8	20.7

Sources: Table 9; China Financial Statistics (1952-1987), 142,201; C.a. 1/89, 22; State Statistical Bureau, 19 Jan. 1989; Almanac 1989, 149,153.

escape the credit plan, actual interest rates offered on savings (including premiums paid in kind) were higher than those decreed by the PBC.

Despite the high inflation rates in 1988 and the linkage of interest rates on some savings deposits to the inflation rate, interest rates on loans have not been adjusted accordingly. In 1988 and 1989 — and in some cases even since 1985 — interest rates on loans were lower than some interest rates on deposits. This implies that the linkage from interest rates on savings deposits to the inflation rate had to be subsidized by either the PBC or by the government and that enterprises had even more reason to ask for new loans.

Chapter 5

Influence of State Budget Deficits and of Financial Institutions on Monetary Policy

When determining monetary policy or regulating the monetary system the PBC has to take into consideration state organs and other financial institutions.

The close relationship between the PBC and the state has already become obvious above. The PBC is by no means the one and only institution responsible for determining monetary policy and for regulating the monetary system. Yet how serious is the direct effect of the state via budget deficits on monetary policy?

Financial institutions (partly due to their proliferation and the lack of control over them) strongly influence the implementation of monetary policy. What are the major trends in the past few years and, if they are not intended, how does the PBC respond to them?

1. State Budget Deficits

A summary of the involvement of state organs in the monetary sphere is given in Figure 11. The authority of the state is all-pervading and the PBC is not expected to take independent action.

The one quantifiable influence of state organs on monetary policy is the financing of state budget deficits by the PBC. While budget surpluses approximately balanced budget deficits in the years before 1979, only one

---

Figure 11. Summary of State Involvement in the Monetary System

General relationship between the state and the PBC

   PBC — State Council/monetary policy. "The PBC is the ... organ of the State Council ..." (PBC Constitution of 1983) and there is a state monetary policy which, implicitly, is not determined by the PBC.

   Local governments. "Local governments at all levels shall facilitate and supervise the implementation by the PBC of the guiding principles and policies of the State, but they shall not interfere with the routine operations of the Bank." (PBC Constitution of 1983).

   PBC — Board of Directors. The Board of Directors of the PBC must ask the State Council for a decision on all important questions; the Board of Directors includes representatives of at least 3 ministries; one of the duties of the PBC is the development of the economy; the "Board of Directors" of a PBC branch includes representatives of local government.

   Appointments. The State Council appoints the head of the PBC for an unlimited tenure and seems to be able to recall him any time.

   PBC services to state. Services provided by the PBC to the state include: Management of state foreign exchange reserves; issuing of state bonds; loans to the state.

   Stocks and bonds. Regulations on stocks and bonds are passed by the PBC and/or the state.

   Interest rates. The State Council approves changes in interest rates.

Relationship between the state and special banks

   Special banks - State Council. Special banks are "economic entities at the bureau level" subordinate to the State Council (PBC Constitution of 1983).

   Budget allocations for investment. Budget allocations for investment in fixed assets are made via the People's Construction Bank of China.

   Establishment of commercial banks. The State Council approves the establishment of special banks and national trust and investment companies; local governments may not establish local banks (Bank Regulations of 1986).

   Renunciation of loan repayment. The State Council may waive the repayment of loans by units (Bank Regulations of 1986).

Relationship between the state and monetary plans

   Monetary plans and State Council. The State Council approves credit, cash, and foreign exchange plans.

   Credit plan. The credit plan and its implementation depend on the real plan as well as on extra-budgetary funds and quasi-mandatory loans.

   Cash plan. The cash plan depends on state measures in the real economy.

   Foreign Exchange Plan. The Ministry of Finance and the Ministry of Foreign Economic Relations and Trade participate in drawing up the foreign exchange plan.

year since 1979 has seen an "official" budget surplus — 1985.[1] The
"creeping" budget deficits from 1981 to 1985 corresponded to rising price
subsidies, which increased from 8% of all state expenditures in 1978 to
16% in 1985. (See Table 13.) Price subsidies and subsidies to loss-making
enterprises amounted to approximately 25% of total government
expenditures in 1988, if the subsidies to loss-making enterprises are
included in expenditures. Since 1979 the share of revenues from issuing
state bonds has increased continuously. This was necessary to finance an
increasing actual budget deficit (calculated by not counting the receipts from
the sale of state bonds as revenue).[2] The issues of state bonds already being
included in the state budget, the official budget deficit remained to be
financed by other means. From the end of 1978 until the end of 1989, the
state received loans worth 68.46 b yuan from the PBC, whereas total state
deposits in the same period increased by only 20.87 b yuan (taking into
consideration changes in the statistics due to the inclusion of the People's
Construction Bank of China in 1985).[3]

Is deficit financing through the PBC macroeconomically important? In the
period examined above, loans by the PBC to the state accounted for 3.5%
of all state expenditures, while the amount of all new state loans minus all
new state deposits accounted for 2.4%. The increase in loans and the
issuing of state bonds accounted for 9.3% of all state expenditures. In 1989
the share of loans to the state in all loans was 4.5%, and the share of
deposits by the central government in all deposits was 4.9%; if the deposits
by state organs ("authorities and state organizations"), which are not
allowed to take out loans, are considered, the state share in all deposits
reached 10.2%.[4] With the amount of deposits by state organs exceeding the
amount of loans to all state organs there is hardly any reason for anxiety.

---

[1]   Official PRC budgeting practice includes all (planned) issues of state bonds as
revenues.

[2]   As the purchase of state bonds by the population reduces purchasing power, this
measure helps reduce (excessive) demand for commodities. Revenue obtained from state bonds
issued abroad was used to pay for the import of goods which were then partly sold to the
population, thus also reducing purchasing power.

[3]   The surplus in loans of 47.591 b yuan falls short of the accumulated budget deficit
from 1978 to 1989 of 74.633 b yuan. What has happened to the balance of 27.042 b yuan? If
the difference is not due to time differences in accounting procedures, then manipulations such
as transfers between enterprises receiving new loans and the state budget are conceivable, with
these transfers not being recorded as state revenues. Another possibility could be that the
PBC's profits are transferred to the state, for which, however, there is no evidence.

[4]   ZGJR 5/90, 61.

Table 13. State Revenues and Expenditures
(in RMB b)

	1970	1975	1978	1979	1980	1981	1982	1983	1984	1985	1986	1987	1988	1989
Total state revenues of which:	66.29	81.56	112.11	110.33	108.52	108.95	112.40	124.90	150.19	186.64	222.03	234.66	258.78	291.92
Tax revenue	28.12	40.28	51.93	53.78	57.17	62.99	70.00	77.56	94.76	204.08	209.08	213.48	237.58	274.06
Subsidies to loss-making enterprises (-)	.	.	.	.	.	.	.	.	.	.	-27.62	-37.55	-44.58	-59.98
Issue of state bonds domestically	-	-				(4.86)	4.38	4.16	4.22	6.06	6.25	6.31	13.10	14.01
abroad	-	-	-	3.53	4.30	7.31	4.00	3.78	3.48	2.92	7.57	10.30	13.00	13.42
Total state expenditures of which:	64.94	82.09	111.10	127.39	121.27	111.50	115.33	129.25	154.64	184.48	229.11	242.69	266.83	301.46
Capital construction	29.84	32.70	45.19	51.47	41.94	33.06	30.92	38.28	48.89	58.38	65.57	61.20	61.95	61.26
Interest on and repayment of state bonds	-	-	-	-	2.86	6.29	5.55	4.25	2.89	3.96	4.40	7.52	7.68	7.26
Price subsidies	.	.	9.39	18.07	24.21	32.77	31.84	34.17	37.00	29.95	25.75	29.41	31.70	37.03
Budget surplus (+)	+1.35	-0.53	+1.02	-17.07	-12.75	-2.55	-2.93	-4.35	-4.45	+2.16	-7.08	-8.03	-8.05	-9.54
Loans from PBC	-	-	-	9.02	17.02	17.02	17.02	19.96	26.08	27.51	37.01	51.50	57.65	68.46
Deposits at PBC	17.68	14.02	18.74	14.87	16.45	19.74	17.99	19.79	16.59	32.64 / 36.84[a]	31.15	30.70	27.09	43.80
Change in loans from PBC	-	-	-	+9.02	+8.00	-	-	+2.93	+6.12	+1.43	+9.50	+14.5	+6.15	+10.81
Change in deposits at PBC	X	-3.66	+4.72	-3.87	+1.58	+3.29	-1.74	+1.79	-3.20	+16.1	-5.70	-0.45	-3.61	+16.72

Note:

a. Because of the inclusion of the People's Construction Bank of China in the Consolidated Balance Sheet the base of the deposits changes in 1985. Loans are not affected.

Sources: In general: 1970-1985: Caizhengjuan 1987, 720-725. 1986-1987: C.a. 4/87, 279; C.a. 3/88, 196. 1988: Statistical Yearbook 1989, 566; Almanac 1989, 51; State Council 27 April 1989. 1989: State Council 27 April 1990; ZGJR 5/90.

State bonds: Domestic: Beijing Rundschau 16 Aug. 1988, No.33. Abroad: Statistical Yearbook 1988, 762.

Capital construction: 1970-1985: Statistical Yearbook 1988, 755. 1986-1987: C.a. 4/87, 279; C.a. 3/88, 196.

Interest on and repayment of state bonds: 1970-1985: Statistical Yearbook 1988, 762. 1986-1987: C.a. 4/87, 279; C.a. 3/88, 196.

Price subsidies: Statistical Yearbook 1988, 763.

Loans from and deposits at PBC: China Financial Statistics (1952-1987), 7,24; Financial Statistics of China (1979-1985), 2f; ZGJR 4/87 4/88 4/89.

But how can the PBC implement a consistent monetary policy if the state can violate all plans by incurring unplanned budget deficits which then have to be financed by the PBC?

2. Financial Institutions

The latest developments in banking trial cities pose a big challenge to the traditional administrative management by the PBC and the strong involvement of the state in the monetary sphere. The PBC, furthermore, experiences difficulties in exerting its control over an increasing number of financial institutions, and is affected by the changing role of special banks in the course of economic reforms.

Financial Institutions in the Banking Trial Cities

A survey of the business objectives of the heads of special bank branches in banking trial cities[5] (see Figure 12) reveals that first, the objectives of managers in all banks surveyed is to maximize their profits (more deposits mean more loans and more authority as well as higher profits through interest receipts). Second, the objectives of the PBC or special bank head offices enjoy only low priority. Such objectives are maintenance of the credit structure prescribed by the credit plan, acceleration of the circulation of funds, implementation of the central macroeconomic policy, implementation of assignments and requirements of superior bank branches, and exhortation of enterprises to improve their management. Third, to supply enterprises with money is not an objective of the special banks surveyed — although the financing of bankrupt enterprises might well be forced upon them by local governments.

---

[5]   This survey, of which other results have already been cited above, was conducted in the second half of 1986 in branches of the Industrial and Commercial Bank of China and the Agricultural Bank of China in 9 banking trial cities. This survey is not representative of the situation in the whole country (apart from the doubtful quality of a survey the number of participants in which seems to have been very small as judged by the three ties). Nevertheless it is one of very few surveys available in this field. The priorities described in this survey are confirmed by statements in other sources.

Figure 12. Business Objectives of Special Banks in Banking Trial Cities	
Question: What is the most important objective of your bank management under current circumstances within the present monetary system?	
Answers	assess- ment
1. To attract as much deposits as possible	3.779
2. To increase the bank's profit	1.998
3. To secure economic development	1.887
3. To increase the scope of business and business volume	1.887
5. To set priorities when making loans for investment	1.554
6. To accelerate the circulation of funds	1.111
6. To implement the macroeconomic policy of the center	1.111
8. To preserve the bank's business reputation	0.777
9. To fulfill the assignments and requirements of the superior branch	0.444
9. To induce enterprises to improve their management	0.444
11. To ensure the supply of funds to enterprises	0
Source: Zhang Shaojie 11/87, 13.	

This movement towards professional management is reflected by the "six rights" which were introduced to branches of the Industrial and Commercial Bank of China in 27 banking trial cities and in all of Guangdong Province in 1987 after prior trial in Guangzhou and 4 other cities. They include the right of the bank branch to direct business activities on its own; to autonomously choose between different projects when giving loans; to vary interest rates; to employ, dismiss, reward and punish staff; to autonomously determine its organization and bonus payments; and to autonomously distribute its retained profits. At the same time banks experimented with different types of responsibility systems such as the "bank-director-responsibility system" (hangzhang zerenzhi).[6] In 1988 the six rights were supposed to be given to banks in all cities.[7] If the six rights were to be

---

[6]   Guanche 2/88, 11; PBC 12/87.

[7]   Xu Jian 12 Dec. 1988.

realized, this would constitute a break-through for the banking system and the collapse of administrative management of the monetary system by the PBC, yet there is every reason to believe that these reforms are not being fully implemented.

The most well-known example for the developments in banking trial cities is Wenzhou,[8] Zhejiang province, a city with 500,000 inhabitants and with 6 m more people living in the surrounding areas. Wenzhou's financial system is characterized by traditional credit associations[9] which operate completely outside any state control. These associations have been facilitated by the predominance of collective and individually-owned enterprises. Instead of passing through the elaborate and sometimes humiliating procedures at state banks, small enterprises and individuals participate in credit associations, depositing a small amount of money at certain times and receiving a large loan once.[10] A different form of financing is the personal loan between two persons (*minjian daikuan* or *ziyou daikuan*), which is illegally but uncontrollably organized by professional agents.[11] A second variation is the raising of funds by collective enterprises from their own staff and workers, a method used not only in Wenzhou but also elsewhere.

Due to these private credit arrangements, the share of special banks and credit co-operatives in all financial transactions in Wenzhou hardly amounted to one-third. Wenzhou's fame travelled as far as Beijing, and in March 1986 the leadership of the PBC and the special banks[12] arrived in Wenzhou to gain some first-hand experience of a situation so foreign to state planning and state control.

In August 1986 Wenzhou was named a banking trial city, and a state counter-attack was launched. The special banks and particularly the credit

---

[8] Sources are, if not otherwise stated: Han Yuting 2/88; Zhan Wu 23 Sept. 1987; FEER 27 Oct. 1988, 42; International Herald Tribune 8 Aug. 1988.

[9] At the end of the nineteenth century 3 types of credit associations existed: The *lunhui* in which, according to a certain agreed-upon order, a loan was given to each person in turn; the *yaohui* in which the person to receive a loan was chosen by throwing dice; the *piaohui* in which loans were auctioned off. (Yang Lien-Sheng 1952, 75-78.)

[10] A report warning of the "chaos" in Wenzhou mentioned one man who headed 80 credit associations (with more than 2,000 people), of which 3 eventually went "bankrupt."

[11] Individuals are not allowed to establish banks or other financial institutions or to carry out financial transactions. (Bank Regulations of 1986, Art. 28.)

[12] The governor of the PBC, Chen Muhua; the vice-governor of the PBC, Qiu Qing; the president of the Industrial and Commercial Bank, Zhang Xiao; the president of the Agricultural Bank of China, Ma Yongwei; and the president of the Bank of China, Wang Deyan.

co-operatives were to use a double-track interest rate system: PBC-determined interest rates for certain projects or types of credit, with banks otherwise at complete liberty to set rates themselves.[13] The interbank money market was strengthened and new types of credit were introduced; the independence of the lower level bank branches was guaranteed; the egalitarianism in remuneration was replaced by autonomy in personnel decisions and a "responsibility system by objectives" (with remuneration according to achievement of different objectives); the division of labor between different special banks was abolished; and the minimum reserve requirement of credit co-operatives was lowered from 24% to 15%. As a result the market share of credit co-operatives increased, while the special banks were still fighting for the repayment of loans given to state-owned enterprises.

The episode Wenzhou shows that once the real economy no longer consists mainly of state-owned enterprises but of collective and individually-owned enterprises, the PBC's concept of credit administration and interest rate determination is untenable. The only solution possible is transition toward liberation of special banks and credit co-operatives and toward indirect control through the PBC. Special banks and credit co-operatives can then offer one advantage at otherwise equal conditions which credit associations cannot: security.

Proliferation of Other Financial Institutions

Although the Bank Regulations of 1986 clearly state procedures for establishing special banks and other financial institutions, the PBC repeatedly seems to have lost control.[14] Already in 1985 an announcement by the PBC was necessary to prohibit the establishment of financial institutions without prior approval.[15] In September 1988 the PBC enacted a general ban on the establishment of new non-state financial institutions.

The reason for the increase in financial institutions approved of could well be that for financial institutions to be established below the provincial level only the approval of the provincial PBC branch (or a corresponding lower level branch) is needed. Every provincial (or lower level) PBC branch also

---

[13]   Market interest rates were reaching 50% annually.

[14]   For the establishment of new special banks or national trust and investment companies the State Council is the approving authority; otherwise, the PBC is.

[15]   PBC 16 Feb. 1985. For a province, see Heilongjiang Government 4/85.

represents the interests of the locality and is subject to pressure exerted by the local government.

Some of the more recently established financial institutions are the following.

The Bank of Communications, a bank whose capital was raised by issuing shares with the state as the major shareholder, has been expanding to all large cities nationwide. It has also opened branches within enterprises, as in a pharmaceutical combine in Shenyang where the branch serves as a clearing house between individual factories.[16] No mention is made of a credit plan. Since its scope of business includes all kinds of financial transactions, it constitutes a competitor to all other banks.

"Internal" banks within enterprises (*neibu yinhang*) are among the latest developments, being in charge of all monetary relationships between the enterprise and outside suppliers or customers. At times even a branch of the Industrial and Commercial Bank of China has been involved in setting up such banks, once sufficient pressure had been applied.[17]

The number of trust and investment companies, including leasing and bond trading companies, increased to more than 600 by mid-1988.[18] Although very concise regulations exist for trust and investment companies,[19] they seem to constantly evade state control.[20] Time and again local governments are admonished not to establish their own banks in the guise of trust and investment companies, and special banks are reminded to make their trust and investment companies independent or to include them in the credit plan. An investigation of several hundred trust and investment companies in 1985 revealed that more than one third of the companies under examination did not possess sufficient capital, did not maintain adequate minimum reserves, ignored reference numbers, dealt in

---

[16] Zhang Xuezhi 2/88, 24.

[17] C.a. 8/86, 493f; Tang Yongyi 2/88.

[18] Liu Hongru in: China Daily 17 June 1988.
According to China Financial Statistics (1952-1987), 137,165, at the end of 1987 there were 561 trust and investment companies with a total credit volume of 44 b yuan. This equalled 0.5% of all credit in the PRC (Consolidated Balance Sheet without rural credit co-operatives). (ZGJR 4/88.)

[19] PBC 26 April 1988; Bank Regulations of 1986.

[20] The discussion on trust and investment companies has never stopped since their first appearance in the mid-1980s (Byrd 1983, 81f). ZGJR in the late 1980s offers some insight into the ongoing discussion.

money markets instead of trust business, offered loans in cases in which they were not allowed to do so, and violated interest rate regulations.[21]

Urban credit co-operatives, although still on a very small scale, effectively compete with state banks for customers among collective and individually-owned enterprises. Although they maintain a minimum reserve at the PBC, generally through the Industrial and Commercial Bank of China, they are not under the direct control of the PBC. Their number amounted to approximately 1,600 in 1988.[22]

A large number of other financial institutions ranging from bank combines and co-operative banks (consisting of several credit co-operatives), through companies for the assessment of a customer's credit-worthiness, to building and loan associations now exist.[23] These institutions more often than not operate outside the law or, if they are subject to some legal restrictions, are less controlled than, for example, special banks.

These free-wheeling financial institutions are not (or only to a limited degree) part of the old system of administrative management as far as the planning system is concerned. With a Western-type monetary system not yet in place the PBC has great difficulty in controlling these institutions, especially if they enjoy the protection of local state organs.

Fundamental Problems of Special Banks

Enterprises, not being fully autonomous, are not responsible for profits and losses and cannot be held responsible for damage done to special banks. There are no self-restraint mechanisms limiting the demand for loans. The interest rate mechanism is ineffective, and credit limits can, with the help of state organs, be ignored.

Local governments are responsible for the fate of "their" enterprises and are willing to influence banks regarded as subordinate,[24] in some cases

---

[21]   PBC 14 Nov. 1988.

[22]   Liu Hongru 17 June 1988 in China Daily.

According to China Financial Statistics (1952-1987), 165, there were 1615 urban credit co-operatives at the end of 1987. No entry exists for 1986 (0?).

[23]   C.a. 2/88, 106f; FEER 10 Sept. 1987, 59; Ye Yixin 2/88.

[24]   The municipal administration of Shanghai has promised the foreign buyers of 26 municipal enterprises preferential treatment in the supply of water, electricity, gas and raw materials as well as *loans*. (C.a. 9/88, 685.)

exerting influence through personnel appointments.[25] If need be, local financial institutions are established to circumvent state regulations.

Special banks are state departments when entrusted by the local government with special tasks or when participating in the collection of taxes. At the same time, they are also independent units striving for profitability, liquidity and stability. Is it still their duty to provide all state-owned enterprises with working capital, or should loans be given to enterprises only in accordance with their efficiency?

These problems encountered by special banks in turn also affect the PBC. In the absence of any restraint mechanism on the demand for loans, the PBC has to rely on its administrative management of the monetary sphere to restrict the supply of credit. With state organs and special banks increasingly able to undermine the PBC's administrative management of the monetary sphere, the PBC can no longer control the supply of credit.

While the state budget deficit seems to have no major impact on the monetary sphere, the changes in the banking system pose a severe threat to the PBC's control over the monetary system. As poorly equipped with monetary policy instruments as the PBC is at this stage in the economic reforms, one would expect the disturbances in the monetary part of the economy to spill over into the real economy. This is the subject of Part II.

---

[25] A counterproposal suggests having the directors of the special bank branches appointed by the PBC (Ni Liangtao 6/85). Yet the PBC is also subject to state influence.

Part II

MONETARY POLICY AND
THE ECONOMY

Chapter 6

Monetary Policy

In Part I the PBC's monetary policy instruments and their limitations were introduced. (For a summary of the instruments see Figure 13.) In the case of administrative management within liquidity policy, the PBC has lost its full control over credit, cash in circulation and foreign exchange. The system of monetary plans is inadequate to indirectly control the economy through special banks and other financial institutions. The PBC furthermore does not formulate an independent monetary policy but is subject to state interference on all levels. In the case of economic control within liquidity policy, the new instruments are not yet well-established. Their use parallel to administrative management in the monetary sphere at a time when central planning and state-owned enterprises still prevail in the real economy does not make sense. The PBC, finally, due to the nature of the economic system, and to state interference, is incapable of conducting an active interest policy. Interest rates are determined by the inflation rate.

The PBC is prevented from achieving its objectives by (i) the increasing number of independent decisions by individuals and other economic units (mainly enterprises) in the real and monetary economies, endangering control over the monetary system; and (ii) its lack of independence from the state together with a general lack of authority, preventing an adequate response to changes in the real and monetary economies. The old system of administrative management can no longer, and the new system of economic control can not yet, perform the necessary control functions.

The second part of this book analyses the interaction between the monetary and real economies. Chapter 6 looks at the intermediate objectives linking monetary policy and real economy and describes the behavior of the

Figure 13. Monetary Policy Instruments				
Objectives	Instruments			
(1) Economic development (2) Currency stability	Liquidity policy	Administrative management	PBC — non-banking sector	Deposit policy
				Special loans
				Administration of gold, silver and forex
				Regulations on use of cash and forex
			PBC — special banks and other financial institutions	Administration of credit: Credit, cash and forex plan Refinancing at PBC Special deposits at PBC Sale of state bonds Credit limit Administration of treasury accounts
				Control: Internal auditing Reports Moral suasion
				Establishment/dissolution of fin. institutions
				Other regulations
			PBC — state	State-determined monetary policy
				Financing of government budget deficits
				Other regulations
		Economic control		Minimum reserve requirement
				Interbank money market administration
				(Re-)discount policy
				Stocks and bonds administration
				Open market transactions
	Interest rate policy	Determination of rates between	PBC — special banks	Rates: Deposit interest rates Credit interest rates
				Interest rate structure
			Special banks — non-banking sector	Rates: Deposit interest rates Credit interest rates
				Interest rate structure

variables chosen as intermediate objectives (together with other monetary variables) since the transformation of the PBC into a solely central bank. Chapter 7 then establishes the mechanisms through which monetary and real economic variables interact.

1. Intermediate Objectives of Monetary Policy

Volume of Credit and Cash in Circulation

In the centrally planned economy, the volume and structure of credit as well as the amount of cash in circulation are the most effective measure for implementing state economic policy via the monetary system. The volumes of credit and cash in circulation are variables easily and quickly ascertained. As long as loans are given in strict accordance with the real bills principle, that is, as a mirror-image of flows in the real economy, credit is non-inflationary (apart from the fact that in the centrally planned economy most prices in the production sphere are set by planners). Money in the inter-enterprise circuit does not matter except as a unit of account and a medium of exchange. The intermediate objective "volume and structure of credit" can be achieved simply by adhering to the plans. Inherent to the cash circuit, however, is the danger of inflation. If the demand by consumers for commodities the prices of which are determined by the market exceeds the supply of these commodities at a certain point of time, prices are likely to rise. Therefore the amount of cash in circulation has always been one of the main concerns of the PBC and the State Council.

As of 1991, the volume and, to a lesser degree, the structure of credit as well as the amount of cash in circulation are still the main intermediate monetary objectives. These objectives are achieved via "administrative management," i.e., credit plan, cash plan and foreign exchange plan, as well as through a host of unorthodox measures like appeals to the population to save a larger percentage of income.

Money Supply

Within the concept of economic control the PBC has been aiming for indirect control of the monetary system as practiced in Western countries. The increase in the supply of money (not only cash) serves as an intermediate objective. On how this intermediate objective is to be attained, no explanation has been offered. Occasionally Chinese economists have proposed to use the monetary base to regulate the money supply,[1] with the monetary base in turn being fine-tuned with the help of the minimum reserve requirement, rediscount policy and eventually open market operations. So far the PBC has only used the first two instruments and on a scale too small to have any significant impact.

But even if they had a significant impact, the partial (intended and unintended) break-down in plan enforcement would still render the relationship between the monetary base and the money supply highly instable.[2] For instance, the ratio of cash in circulation to savings deposits dropped from 1.00 in 1978 to 0.46 in 1989 (with two reversals, in 1984/85 and 1988).[3] Furthermore, the enforced contraction of currency in circulation in the first half of every year leads to large seasonal changes in the ratios. Seasonal changes could be predicted if the contraction were a sufficiently stable phenomenon. However, the contraction depends much on the enforcement of monetary policy. With different degrees of enforcement depending on the political situation, the seasonal ratios of cash to savings deposits can only be very roughly predicted.

The monetary base itself is a factor outside the sole control of the PBC. The monetary base is politically determined through State Council decisions concerning both the amount of cash in circulation and PBC refinancing of special banks. In practice, therefore, the PBC still attempts to control the amount of cash in circulation directly through the cash plan, and to control credit (and indirectly deposits) through administrative credit management for enterprises and state institutions.

---

[1] Zhou Jun 4/86; Lin Jiken 6/87.

The money supply (*huobi gongyingliang*) is defined synonymously to Western concepts as a function of the monetary base (*jichu huobi*) with, as the multiplier, e.g., [1 plus (cash/deposits)] divided by [(cash/deposits) + (minimum reserves/deposits) + (excess reserves/deposits)].

[2] The distortion in the relationship between money supply and monetary base due to the limited use of cash in the economy does not necessarily hamper the use of the money supply as an intermediate objective, as long as the limitations are strictly enforced (or as long as the degree of enforcement is exactly known).

[3] The ratio cash in circulation divided by urban and rural savings deposits is derived from figures given in Appendix A below. The multiplier itself has not been calculated due to the lack of figures on minimum and excess reserves (apart from the dubious quality of those few figures published).

Despite all the talk about the money supply no official definition of "money supply" exists. All unofficial definitions[4] have in common differentiation of deposits according to their duration and special consideration given to deposits by the state. In accordance with the available statistical material (Consolidated Balance Sheet without rural credit cooperatives) the definition used below is as follows:

M_o = cash in circulation (*liutongzhong huobi*)

M_1 = M_o + deposits by enterprises (*qiye cunkuan*)
+ deposits by organizations (*jiguan tuanti cunkuan*)
+ deposits for investment in capital construction (*jiben jianshe cunkuan*) — until 1981 or 1985, depending on the statistics used

M_2 = M_1 + savings deposits by urban individuals (*chengzhen chuxu cunkuan*)
+ rural deposits (*nongcun cunkuan*)

M_3 = M_2 + deposits by the state (*caizheng cunkuan*)
+ other deposits (*qita cunkuan*) — beginning 1980 or 1988, depending on the statistics used.[5]

---

[4] Sheng Mujie 1989, 280-284, distinguishes between four different concepts according to: (1) IMF, (2) Liu Hongru (former vice-governor of the PBC), (3) Department of Investigation and Statistics at the PBC, and (4) a definition based on the Consolidated Balance Sheet (two versions, with or without rural credit cooperatives). (Zhou Jun 4/86; Huang Min 1988, 43; Liu Zhiqiang 11/88, 35.)

[5] Because of changing statistical conventions, the following inconsistencies occur:
— The deposits for investment in capital construction (in M1) after 1981/1985 are found in both deposits by enterprises (in M1) and deposits by the state (in M3).
— Other deposits since 1980/1988 are not explained further and at the time of their introduction reduced M1 and M2 considerably. (At the end of 1989 other deposits amounted to 6.2% of all deposits (ZGJR 4/90, 61).)
The overall tendency due to statistical changes is therefore an increase in M3 and a reduction in M2.

2. Monetary Policy from 1984 to 1990[6]

While Chapters 3 to 5 in Part I examined the various monetary policy instruments individually, this section looks at the simultaneous application of all monetary policy instruments over time to achieve the — not always published — intermediate monetary objectives. It becomes obvious that the PBC faces the same problems year after year without any solution in sight.

1984 to 1986

The transformation of the PBC into a solely central bank in September 1983 had no effect on monetary policy in 1983.

When it was announced at the end of 1984 that the credit plan in 1985 would be based on the amount of loans given at the end of 1984, the discipline imposed by the concept of "control of the balance" between deposits and loans broke down. More than half of the high increase in the amount of loans in 1984 (+ 32.8% as compared to the previous year) occurred in December 1984.[7] Cash in circulation increased by 49.6% compared to the previous year, an increase which might have at least partly been due to lenient cash administration during the PBC's transformation period, when cash at lower levels was administered by the Industrial and Commercial Bank of China.

As a consequence of the increases in 1984, the PBC decided on a policy of scarce money in 1985, with withdrawal of some of the cash in circulation during the first half of 1985. However, the PBC did not succeed in reducing the amount of cash in circulation in 1985 but only in lowering the rate of increase as compared to the previous year. Due to the new regulations on credit administration in 1985, which included more autonomy for provincial branches of special banks, the beginning of the interbank money market, and more freedom for special banks in determining loans, the amount of new loans was difficult to rein in.[8] The sudden increase in retail prices and living costs required increases in interest rates, which took place on 1 April

---

[6] See Appendix A below for figures underlying the following explanations.

[7] C.a. 4/85, 232.

[8] The excess reserves of the special banks at the PBC at the end of 1985 — 46 b yuan — would have allowed new loans on the scale of 138 b yuan as compared to existing loans of 591 b yuan, assuming a minimum reserve requirement of 10% and a uniform cash rate (cash/deposits) of 20%. (Derived from China Financial Statistics (1952-1987), 28f.)

and 1 August 1985. The record deficit in the current account, which helped increase the supply of goods on the domestic market and thus reduce the danger of inflation, had to be financed through borrowing abroad.

In 1986 the policy of scarce money was to be continued. Yet when it became obvious that economic growth would suffer, the contractionary monetary policy was scaled down under a new policy of "easing with stability" (*wenzhong qiusong*), leading to a renewed increase in credit and cash in circulation.

The years from 1984 to 1986 were characterized by two trends, which persisted in subsequent years: (i) of all loans, the loans to industrial and construction enterprises as well as for investment in fixed assets increased overproportionally when compared to the amount of credit for working capital investment; (ii) savings deposits[9] increased by more than deposits by enterprises, at a higher rate than in the years before 1984 and at a higher rate than loans. Savings deposits for the first time exceeded deposits by enterprises in 1986.

1987 and 1988

The years 1987 and 1988 saw a full circle of monetary policy. While the expansion of credit and cash in circulation could be kept under control in 1987, the year 1988 saw the worst — as yet — loss of control.

The year 1987 started with new regulations for credit administration. The new regulations no longer guaranteed the refinancing of special banks by the PBC, differentiated between different types of refinancing, and made the money supply an intermediate objective. The slogan for 1987 was "tightening with enlivening" (*jinzhong youhuo*) — i.e., a general tightening of credit and cash but enlivening of selected enterprises. In July 1987 figures for the planned increase in cash in circulation and in credit for 1987 were given as 25 b yuan and 140 b yuan respectively.[10] The actual increases did not exceed these amounts.

The measures taken by the PBC to limit the expansion of credit and cash, mainly in the fourth quarter, were:

---

[9]   "Savings deposits" here mean urban and rural savings deposits (of individuals) at special banks and rural credit co-operatives.

[10]   Zhang Yongyu 4/88, 26.
These figures were determined by the "center" (State Council?).

— an increase in minimum reserve requirements by 2 percentage points and strict control over the amount of short-term refinancing;

— an increase in interest rates for the refinancing of special banks by the PBC (e.g., on annual loans, from 4.68% to 7.2%);

— special deposits of 5 b yuan by rural credit co-operatives at the PBC;

— limitation of loans to enterprises by both the Agricultural Bank of China and rural credit co-operatives (to the amount lent at the end of June and August respectively);

— increased pressure on special banks to sell state key construction bonds by threatening reluctant or tardy special banks with a reduction in credit plan reference numbers for investment in fixed assets and for the use of extra-budgetary revenue deposits in providing new loans;

— selection of "best" enterprises when giving new loans (*zeyou xianlie*); reduction of loans for ordinary projects and guaranteed loans for key projects; accelerated readjustment of the sectoral structure and the commodity structure.[11]

Of these measures, the supply of funds to certain state key projects was the most questionable one, comparable to abandoning all efficiency criteria in lending to the state. Professional management of banks (i.e., orientation towards profitability) was not mentioned at all.[12]

While the strict implementation of the measures in 1987 resulted in the lowest growth rates of credit and cash in circulation in several years, the demand for credit and cash could no longer be restrained in 1988. The volume of credit increased even in the first quarter, instead of shrinking as in previous years. The amount of cash in circulation, normally decreasing during the first half of the year, decreased only slightly during the first quarter to increase in the second quarter. One reason for the developments in 1987/88 may be that in 1987, for the first time ever, loans included in the credit plan for 1987 but not given in 1987 could be transferred to the

---

[11]   Zhou Zhengqing 3/88, 6; Zhang Yongyu 4/88, 25-27.

The last measure was decided on jointly by the PBC and the Economic Commission in May 1987.

[12]   Wang Zhi 27 Feb. 1989.

next year. This transfer could help account for the achievement of the objectives in 1987 and the increases already in early 1988.[13]

Refinancing with the PBC likewise could not be reduced by as much as planned during the first half of 1988. Of the planned reduction in the amount of loans by 30.06 b yuan (25 b yuan in short-term loans and 5.06 b yuan in annual loans), less than one third was achieved.[14] Cash in circulation was to be increased by 20 b yuan in 1988, but later this figure was adjusted by the State Council to 40 b yuan, only to be surpassed by the end of the year by another 28 b yuan, resulting in a total increase of 68 b yuan. The projected volume of credit for 1988 had to be readjusted to 180 b yuan.[15]

The reasons for the large increase in cash in circulation include extensive purchase of agricultural and sideline products at increased prices,[16] redemption of IOUs,[17] increased salary and wage payments,[18] an unusually high reduction in existing savings deposits[19] and increased cash disbursements by (administrative) enterprises.[20] Except for the higher rate of liquidization of savings deposits, all other events were of recurring nature (although in 1988 larger than ever before). The extraordinary liquidization of savings deposits was due to the inflation rate of about 20% in 1988, exceeding all interest rates — a discrepancy only redressed with the linking of some interest rates to the Retail Price Index in September 1988. Competition from financial institutions evading state control and "People's Banks" also reduced the amount of savings deposits held at special banks, especially prior to September 1988. At the same time 60% to 70% of the large amount of new state bonds issued were bought by liquidating savings

---

[13] Chen Muhua was replaced by Li Guixian as governor of the PBC in April 1988. The lack of control in early 1988, especially of those reference numbers dear to the leadership, might well have contributed to Chen Muhua's removal.

[14] Song Feng'e 3/88, 10; Song Feng'e 6/88; C.a. 10/88, 768.

[15] PBC 19 Aug. 1988.

[16] Zhichi 9/88, 11.

[17] FEER 2 March 1989, 83.

[18] Ibid.; Li Guixian 7/88, 4.

[19] See Table 5 above.

[20] PBC 10/88, 19.

deposits.[21] The reduction in savings deposits at special banks increased the pressure on the PBC for refinancing, and the PBC, already charged with financing an increasing budget deficit, gave in.

The PBC had started the year 1988 with the slogan "control the volume, readjust the structure [of credit]" (*kongzhi zongliang, tiaozheng jiegou*) but soon had to decree another host of individual measures. The minimum reserve requirement was raised by 1%, interest rates were first increased and then interest rates on time deposits of individuals (3 to 8 years) were linked to the Retail Price Index. The PBC required special deposits by trust and investment companies[22] and withdrew all loans to nonbank financial institutions.[23] The cash administration was rigorously enforced[24] and credit ceilings for all financial institutions were to be strictly heeded.[25] Enterprises were asked to use funds more efficiently,[26] to reduce their commodity inventories and to sell their unused equipment, constituting about 4% to 5% of their fixed assets; overdue loans (approximately 10% of all loans) were to be repaid.[27] The State Council guaranteed loans for the production of everyday necessities, for salary and wage payments, for bonuses and subsidies determined by the state, for the purchase of agricultural and sideline products, for certain energy and communication projects, for the purchase of export products, for the production of certain, highly demanded goods and for key projects.[28] Internally, "work standards" for directors (*hangzhang gangwei guifan*) of PBC branches on the second level and on the county level were adopted; the decisions of the superior PBC branch and various laws and regulations were to be

---

[21]   Wang Lijuan 8/88, 58f.

Dai Genyou 9/88 shows how savings were shifted from time deposits to demand deposits in the first half of 1988 just before the largest reductions in savings deposits at special banks occurred.

[22]   Song Feng'e 11/88, 13.

[23]   Ibid.

[24]   State Council 8 Sept. 1988; State Council 12 Sept. 1988.

[25]   Neue Zuercher Zeitung 26 Oct. 1988; Neue Zuercher Zeitung 24 Dec. 1988.

[26]   PBC 19 Aug. 1988.

[27]   Zhou Zhengqing 8/88, 8.

[28]   State Council 18 Aug. 1988; Jianding 12/88.

obeyed.[29] Finally, the State Council together with the PBC launched a "large-scale investigation" of the credit, cash and foreign exchange situation nationwide (starting October 1988).[30]

All these measures had in common that they again far exceeded any "economic control." They resembled a desperate attempt to maintain control of the monetary system by administrative means.

1989 and 1990

With control over the monetary system and therefore over the whole economy in such disarray, more "conservative" measures were introduced in 1989 and 1990. The Third Plenum of the Thirteenth Central Committee (16 to 30 September 1988) ordained a two-year break in the reforms to restore order to the economic system. During a meeting with the directors of provincial PBC branches in early 1989, Li Guixian (governor of the PBC) announced monetary measures "in the spirit" of this Plenum. Li's measures covered two areas: contractionary overall monetary policy and "structural adjustments." The slogan for 1989 was "control the volume, readjust the structure, guarantee key projects, reduce ordinary [loans], adjust in good time, and increase efficiency" (*kongzhi zongliang, tiaozheng jiegou, baozheng zhongdian, yasuo yiban, shishi tiaojie, tigao xiaoyi*). Strict credit ceilings for special banks were imposed; PBC control over amount, interest rate, maturity and use of funds raised through enterprise bonds was tightened; and a "social credit outline" (*shehui xinyong guihua*) for all financial institutions was drawn up. Ten types of enterprises (including rural

---

[29]   PBC 11/88.

Branch directors also have to conscientiously study the basic principles of Marxism-Leninism ...

[30]   Jiaqiang jilu 11/88.

Ma Delun, an auditor of the PBC reports in his "diary entry" of 7 October 1988 (Ma Delun 12/88, 29) some of the violations of regulations he encountered in several northern provinces:

— In some cities all special banks ignored the credit ceiling.
— Enterprises could no longer regularly withdraw deposits.
— All special banks operated urban credit co-operatives without approval.
— Trust and investment companies openly violated PBC regulations.
— As no funds were available, urgent appeals were lodged with municipal governments asking them to intervene with the State Council to obtain higher credit ceilings.
— Some banks refused an investigation by the PBC.
— The minimum reserve requirement was disregarded, and deposits that had to be passed on to the PBC were not passed on.

industries) were denied new loans, while the State Planning Commission determined preferential loans for particular industrial sectors. Loans for foreign trade business and the purchase of cereals were subsidized, and the PBC increased its loans via special banks to enterprises.[31] The monetary system returned to a higher degree of central planning.

Li Guixian thus reverted to pure administrative management. Control of the money supply was not even mentioned. The stricter control of loans for working capital (approximately 86% of all loans in 1989) became necessary, with the realization that a large part of these loans would never be repaid.[32] Structural adjustment therefore would only be possible by properly placing new loans. The total volume of loans, although it was not supposed to increase as in previous years, still attained a 17.6% increase over 1988. Almost all of this increase took place in the second half of 1989, when it became obvious that state-owned enterprises would otherwise not survive the credit crunch.

The situation was well characterized by the observation that "deposits cannot be attracted and withdrawals are not possible; there are no funds for new loans and old loans are not repaid; transfer payments from outside [one's city or county] are not practicable, and transfer payments which arrive cannot be disbursed in cash."[33]

In 1990 the PBC, as in the year before, was struggling to keep the supply of credit under control and to adjust the credit structure. In addition to the 1989 slogan a new slogan was formulated for the administration of credit: "annual planning, quarterly inspections, monthly examinations, and adjustment on time" (*quannian liangdi, anji jiankong, anyue kaohe, shishi tiaojie*).[34]

With a few variations, past monetary policy measures were continued. A proportion of new deposits at special banks was to be used for loans to key projects and enterprises — with full support for all 234 "two guarantees" large- and medium-sized key enterprises[35] designated by the state. Financial institutions were required to deposit compulsory "excess" reserves

---

[31]   Li Guixian 2/89, 6f; Li Guixian 1/90; Xie Ping 1/90.
The last point hints at return of the PBC to commercial banking.

[32]   Xie Ping 1/90, 24, speaks of 10% of all working capital loans being definitely lost, with the rest not likely ever to be repaid.

[33]   Dai Yuanchen 20 Feb. 1989.

[34]   Li Guixian 2/90, 6.

[35]   The state guarantees the supply of all material inputs and the purchase of all output.

amounting to 5 to 7% of their deposit-liabilities (besides minimum reserves) in the first six months. The PBC gave new annual loans to special banks for "policy loans" as determined by the state while converting some past short-term loans to the special banks into annual loans.[36] The credit volume became an imperatively planned figure to be strictly obeyed, the volume of loans to rural enterprises could only be reduced, and loans for purchase of agricultural and sideline products were to be increased. Interest rates were lowered, but linkage to the inflation rate was retained, for those types of deposits where practiced before. (If the inflation rate dropped below the official interest rate, interest was to be calculated according to the official interest rate.) The banking system was to return to the former clearing system (*tuoshou chengfu*).[37]

Central planning seemed once more to be in full control of the monetary system. But enterprises were neither able nor willing to repay loans. The special banks and other financial institutions, in turn, could not repay loans obtained from the PBC. Central planning was in control of constants (loans which could not be repaid) with new loans still being provided to the state-owned enterprises as directed by the state, although these loans could most probably never be recovered. Instead of central macroeconomic control by economic means, in 1990 the monetary system had drifted further towards loss of control.

Has the monetary system thus completely returned to central planning? The answer is a clear "No" for two reasons. First, there is still some room at the edges of the monetary system that state control cannot reach (for example, some of the operations of "other" financial institutions). Second, monetary decisions are now made not only at the center but increasingly at the local level. Local bank branches are supposed to work closely together with the local Planing Commission, Economic Commission and Party.[38] The most important decision, to whom loans will be available, is mainly made locally.

---

[36] It seems that most short-term loans by the PBC to special banks are de facto annual loans.

[37] Li Guixian 2/90, 6; Li Guixian 4/90; Zhou Zhengqing 2/90; Zhou Zhengqing 4/90; Jinrong shibao 24 Feb. 1990.

[38] Li Guixian 4/90.

Chapter 7

Monetary Overinvestment

Monetary policy during the economic reform years performed poorly in achieving its intermediate objectives. Could the PBC nevertheless accomplish its tasks of stabilizing the currency and promoting economic growth?

This chapter is an adaption of the business cycle theory of monetary overinvestment to the special case of China.[1] A comparison of the behavior of certain key macroeconomic variables together with the insights into the functioning of central banking gained in Part I allow conclusions on how the monetary and real economies interact to result in the phenomena experienced since the beginning of economic reform.

All statistical material used in this chapter, except where otherwise noted, has been included in Appendix A.

---

[1]   Hayek 1933; Haberler 1955, 41-76; Paraskewopoulos 1985, especially 67-70.

Chen Caihong 2/88 states in his article "Investment and Economic Cycles" that the basic reason for economic fluctuations in the PRC is the contradiction between supply and demand structures. He does not, however, go beyond multiplier models, and ignores monetary aspects. Jia Geng 5/88 in "To Reduce Money Supply and Investment" is of the opinion that excessive investment in fixed assets is in general due to the government and banks, yet that in the PRC, in contrast to Western countries, the problem lies solely with the government.

135

1. The Market for Consumer Goods

At the heart of the theory of monetary overinvestment lies the concept of a discrepancy between the supply and demand for consumer goods, with the supply of consumer goods being determined by the volume of resources destined for investment in fixed assets.

This first section discusses the market for consumer goods. The second section introduces investment in fixed assets. The third section combines the two aspects into a circular flow model.

Demand for and Supply of Consumer Goods

As demand for consumer goods is a quantity difficult to measure, a decision has to be made as to how to approximate it. Due to the lack of figures, the supply of consumer goods must likewise be approximated. In a third step, the comparison of demand and supply leads to results employed further below.

To determine the demand for commodities, the concept of "Purchasing Power (of Society)" (*shehui shangpin goumaili*) will be used as it comes closest to "disposable income."[2] "Disposable income," in turn, is assumed to be the main determinant of the demand for consumer good. Since the beginning of the economic reforms, nominal (and, in most years, real) purchasing power has increased by more than Total Output Value of Society, National Income and in most years, Gross National Product. The increase in purchasing power has exceeded the increase in labor productivity and living costs together.

On the other hand, retail sales, as a substitute for the production of consumer goods, increased at approximately the same rate as the various national income measures. Retail sales (*shehui shangpin lingshou*) consist of sales of consumer goods (*xiaofeipin*) — in 1989, 87% of all retail sales — and sales of agricultural investment goods (*nongye shengchan ziliao*) — in 1989, 13% of all retail sales.[3] Using the concept of retail sales as an approximation of the production of consumer goods ignores inventory

---

[2] In 1989 7.3% of all Purchasing Power of Society was not exercised by Chinese individuals but, among others, by "social institutions." (Statistical Yearbook 1990, 614.)

[3] Individuals are not supposed to be able to purchase other investment goods besides agricultural ones. For figures on the share of consumer goods and agricultural investment goods in retail sales see Statistical Yearbook 1990, 622.

investment, for which no figures are available. Qualitative statements in official reports note excessive inventory investment by state enterprises only in 1990 and 1991.

Combining demand and supply leads to the conclusion that — at least during the reform period — the increases in income (as approximated by Purchasing Power of Society) exceeded the increases in the supply of consumer goods (as approximated by retail sales).[4] If the approximations are correct, markets clear either through price rises or rationing. Rationing of some consumer goods was a common feature of the Chinese economy in the past but is more and more replaced by the price mechanism.

The Price Level of Consumer Goods

The growing inflation rate can no longer be dismissed as "planned increases in some prices" to create a "rational price structure," since a "rational price structure" could also be achieved by lowering some prices.

What are the causes of the increases in the inflation rate (for consumer goods) as measured by the Living Cost Index? While the living expenses per head of the urban population more than doubled between 1981 and 1989 to 1,210.95 yuan and similar expenses of the rural population almost quintupled between 1978 and 1989 to 535.37 yuan, the share of expenditures for goods with state-determined prices continuously decreased.[5] Almost constant retail prices and increasing procurement prices for these commodities led to higher price subsidies.[6] The expenditures of the population for food, clothing and basic consumer goods together made

---

[4]   The approximations are justified by the fact that excluding and including the remaining items in the various concepts yields the same results, their percentage share having remained almost stable throughout the years of reform.

   Other items in Purchasing Power, besides expenditure for retail sales, are expenditure for services, tax payments and "others." The figures for 1989 were 86.8% (for retail sales), 5.6%, 0.9%, and 6.7% respectively. (Statistical Yearbook 1990, 614.)

[5]   Rent in cities: in 1981, 1.39% of all living expenses of the urban population; in 1989, 0.72%. Cereals in cities: in 1981, 12.95%; in 1989, 6.76%. All figures on living expenses here and below are from Statistical Yearbook 1988, 807,823, and Statistical Yearbook 1990, 300,316.

[6]   State price subsidies continuously increased to more than 37 b yuan in 1989.

up three quarters of all living expenses.[7] The prices of these goods, with the exception of some food items, are less and less subject to state control.[8] The increases in the inflation rate, as measured by the Living Cost Index, can thus be traced back mainly to price increases of goods not controlled by the state. That the market has allowed these prices to rise could be attributed to excessive demand which, in turn, is due to income increases exceeding increases in the supply of retail goods.

The inflation rate is low as long as prices of commodities controlled by the state are stable and, if necessary, subsidized and the excess purchasing power is siphoned off into savings deposits. Once the real interest rate on savings deposits drops below zero — as it did in late 1988 — the only efficient way of saving money consists of purchasing commodities. The panic purchases in August 1988 were not restricted to those goods for which price increases were expected (tobacco products and spirits).[9] Consequently, the inflation rate could no longer be controlled and interest rates on savings deposits had to be linked to the Retail Price Index (in September 1988).

Repressed Inflation

The official inflation rate, however, need not be the "true" inflation rate, if commodities are scarce and some commodity prices state-determined. The scale of "repressed" inflation can only be estimated. Repressed inflation corresponds to the amount of money that is saved or held as cash because the commodities demanded at the given price are not in sufficient supply. In one study the "true" inflation rate was estimated at 2.5 times the official inflation rate.[10] Rationing, queuing, black markets and rampant corruption

---

[7] Expenditures for food amounted to 54.45% of all living expenses of the urban population in 1989, and to 54.09% of all living expenses of the rural population. The corresponding figures for clothing were 12.32% and 8.29%; for basic consumer goods 11.06% and, including other expenses, 8.29%.

[8] According to FEER 30 June 1988, 50, the prices of more than one third of all "agricultural products and retail goods" are determined solely by the market.

[9] C.a. 9/88, 687.
There have also been panic purchases before (see C.a. 8/88, 618f).

[10] Feltenstein 5/87 asks which "true" inflation rate with no restraint on prices and the same supply of retail goods would induce the population to hold the same amount of money (cash and savings deposits) as it did. The "true" inflation rate thus derived was approximately
(continued...)

in commercial transactions support the hypothesis that repressed inflation exists.

It is true that savings and cash in circulation increased tremendously since the beginning of the reforms, more so than retail sales or Gross National Product, thus leading to a decrease in the velocity of money. Yet decreases in the velocity of money need not be the result of an insufficient supply of commodities (at — at least partly — state-determined prices). In the PRC a decrease in the velocity of money as measured by the volume of retail sales divided by cash in circulation[11] might also be due to, first, an ever larger amount of goods being traded by non-state trading institutions (for example, direct trade between peasants and urban consumers or between peasants themselves). Transactions not recorded by official statistics signify a de facto increase in "retail sales" rather than a decrease in velocity of cash in circulation. A second reason could be larger cash holdings by individuals and individually-owned enterprises in order to carry out non-retail purchases — that is, purchases of products not supposed to be bought by individuals. Third, enterprises have built up their cash holdings due to the increased decision-making power of enterprise management and the need to evade state cash regulations in order to ensure steady supply of material inputs.

Decreases in the velocity of money as measured by GNP divided by M_2 might likewise be due to statistics on the real economy not reflecting the "true" state of the economy. Production and distribution outside the state-controlled realm of state-owned and collective enterprises remains difficult to measure.[12]

2. Investment in Fixed Assets

In contrast to the production of consumer goods, the growth rates of investment in fixed assets clearly exceeded the growth rates of Total Output

---

[10](...continued)
2.5 times the official inflation rate.

For a critique of the model see Herrmann-Pillath 2-89, 30-38.

[11] Such a definition of velocity of money (in terms of cash) is justified and necessitated by the intended separation into cash and credit circuits.

[12] On the other hand, depending on the scope of financial transactions by financial institutions not under control of the PBC, M2 might be larger than officially stated.

Value of Society, National Income[13] and Gross National Product. The largest increase occurred in 1985, the first year the PBC moved away from strict implementation of the credit plan and the first year with a distinctly higher inflation rate than before.

The share of state budget allocations in funding investment in fixed assets decreased continuously (from 28.1% in 1981 to 1.3% in 1989). The share of domestic loans, on the other hand, increased (from 12.7% in 1981 to more than 20% in the years 1985 to 1988 and 17.3% in 1989).[14] The large scale of "self-raised funds and others"[15] — over 50% even before the tax reform, and 67.8% in 1989 — is due largely to extra-budgetary funds. Extra-budgetary funds were comparable to 89% of the regular state budget in 1988; they originate mainly in "state-owned enterprises and responsible departments"[16] and are used by the same institutions. This large volume of "self-raised funds and others" is dangerous in that it is difficult for the state to control the use of these funds. The state, having given up its large share in the financing of investment in fixed assets and working capital as well as much of imperative planning, now lacks control mechanisms.

In 1985, according to the plan, investment in fixed assets was not to exceed the amount of 1984. The result, however, was an increase of 38.8%. In 1986 and 1987 the plans called for maintaining, but not exceeding, the 1985 level of investment in fixed assets; in both years the limit was exceeded. In 1986 the increase over 1985 was 18.7%; in 1987

---

[13]   Although the share of consumption (1 - accumulation) in National Income is almost constant (Appendix A), the share of Purchasing Power of Society in National Income increased from 59% in 1978 to 82% in 1987. The shares of consumption and accumulation in National Income remaining constant corresponds to an ever-increasing part of the Purchasing Power of Society going into savings deposits.

The amount of investment in fixed assets within accumulation (as part of National Income) is lower than "investment in fixed assets" in investment statistics, as National Income does not include depreciation.

[14]   The increase in loans for investment in fixed assets as shown in the Consolidated Balance Sheet is lower than the loans given as source for investment in fixed assets in investment statistics. Some of the reasons are that (i) the Consolidated Balance Sheet accounts only for the special banks and not for other financial institutions; (ii) old loans for investment in fixed assets are repaid and lent anew during the period concerned, thus increasing the actual amount of new loans; and (iii) working capital loans are used for investment in fixed assets.

[15]   Only since 1986 are "other funds" listed separately: 1986, 11%; 1987, 11%; 1988, 10%; and 1989, 11% of all funds. (Statistical Yearbook 1989, 404; Statistical Yearbook 1990, 154.)

[16]   In 1988 80% of all extra-budgetary funds accrued in "state-owned enterprises and responsible departments." (Statistical Yearbook 1990, 243.)

investment in fixed assets was up 43.2% over 1985. In 1988 the overall limit of 330 b yuan was exceeded by 30.7%, and the limit for state-owned enterprises alone, 206 b yuan, was exceeded by 30.8%.[17]

One result of high investment in fixed assets was an increase in the demand for working capital, at a time when the state almost completely cut off its working capital allocations and asked the banks to provide the planned amount of working capital.[18] A result of "blind" investment in fixed assets (i.e., in assets duplicating similar projects elsewhere, possibly outside the plan, with no consideration given to the supply of material inputs or to market demand for final products) was an increase in bottlenecks in the supply of raw materials and energy; some completed projects were operating only a few days a week due to such shortages.[19]

3. Production of Consumer Goods, Investment in Fixed Assets, and Purchasing Power of Society

The interaction between the various macroeconomic variables is described in Figure 14. The desire for a higher level of investment in fixed assets (shown at the top of the figure), accommodated by monetary policy, triggers a discrepancy on the market for consumer goods (shown near the center of the figure). This discrepancy has feedback effects on monetary policy. Given the absence of endogenous restrictive mechanisms, the discrepancy on the market for consumer goods can only be mended through administrative countermeasures.

---

[17] The planned figures are given in Wang Lan 11/88, 18. According to Li Guixian 7/88, 5, the discrepancy between plan and reality is even larger.

[18] There were many miscalculations for funding for investment in fixed assets and underestimations of the need for working capital. Between 1984 and 1986, in 88 % of all 235 large and medium projects completed, 21.3% more funds were needed than planned. (WEH 27 Feb. 1989, 6.)

[19] FEER 9 March 1989, 81f, speaks of a scarcity of energy impairing one third of industrial capacity. The (annual?) losses due to the scarcity of energy are estimated at 200 b yuan, a figure almost as high as all state budget revenue (FAZ 12 April 1989; according to Guangming Ribao).

Figure 14. Course of Monetary Overinvestment

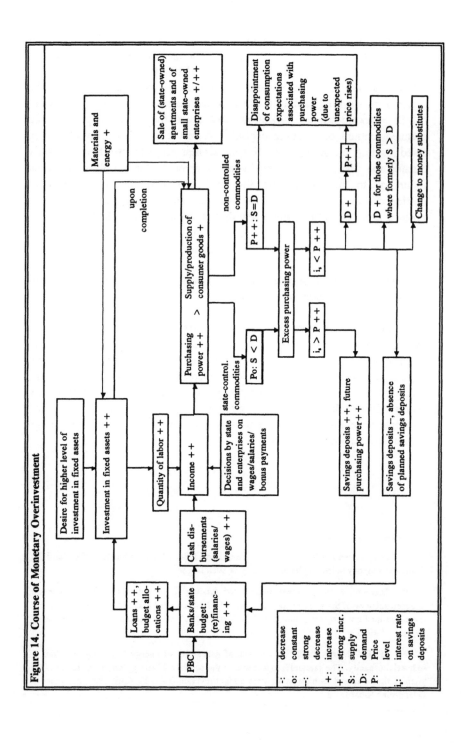

Consequences of the Different Growth Rates

During the years of economic reform in the PRC, any gains in labor productivity were immediately offset by increases in labor remuneration. The price of labor (translating into corresponding purchasing power) is determined politically. The "success" of the economic reforms must increase the income of the population. First, salary and wage disbursements increased with higher wages and salaries per head, as well as an increasing number of persons employed. Second, state purchase of agricultural and sideline products took place at increasing prices, with retail prices of these goods being kept constant or with wages and salaries being adjusted correspondingly. Third, bonus payments increased partly because of a lack of restrictions, or disregard of existing restrictions. High increases in labor remuneration, exceeding gains in labor productivity, led to high increases in purchasing power. On the other hand, investment in fixed assets increased unperturbed, with enterprises and all levels of government trying to increase their power bases and to lay the foundations for a future golden age of consumption. Both trends were supported by new loans, made possible through sufficient refinancing of special banks by the PBC, and by state budget allocations.

In accordance with the theory of monetary overinvestment, the resulting excess demand for consumer goods, the prices of which are market-determined, leads to price rises. Excess demand for commodities for which price limits exist leads to bottlenecks, black markets, and corruption. The excess demand for consumer goods explodes whenever the inflation rate exceeds the interest rate on savings by a margin wide enough to be noticed by the population. The authorities then have a choice between (i) hyperinflation caused by even higher excess demand due to decreased savings deposits and a further increase in the credit supply to finance the investment planned; and (ii) an increase in the interest rate on savings deposits. In the PRC the decision has always been in favor of an increase in the interest rate on savings deposits (or even linkage to the Retail Price Index, in 1988). Increasing savings deposits continue to alleviate the demand for consumer goods. Depending on how successfully the amount of savings can be increased, the excess demand on the market for consumer goods can be reduced and inflation reined in.[20]

---

[20] Investment in fixed assets can also, after completion, contribute to the production of consumer goods. Yet by that time both demand for consumer goods and investment in fixed assets will have increased further, and more likely than not, by more than the supply of

(continued...)

An increase in the interest rate on savings deposits, however, requires an increase in the interest rate on loans to enterprises in order to maintain the special banks' profit margin. An increase in the interest rate on loans increases the costs of investment for enterprises to whom, however, the decisive factor is not the cost of a loan but rather its availability. Interest costs in the PRC were passed on to the state via reductions in tax payments or increases in state subsidies. With enterprise bankruptcy not yet a serious option, the state had to bear the higher interest costs through a larger budget deficit — i.e., the issuing of an increasing volume of bonds and further loans abroad and from the PBC. The state can, as it did, also counter the increase in the interest rate on savings deposits by directly subsidizing the interest rate for loans. The overall effect is similar.

A reduction of accumulated savings deposits to a "voluntary" level is possible through (i) an inflationary decrease in the real value of savings deposits; (ii) a drastic currency reform; (iii) a reduction in real income; (iv) a shift from investment to the production of consumer goods, lowering economic growth by possibly as much as it has before exceeded the level desired by the population; and (v) an increase in the range of commodities available to consumers (to include, for example, investment goods).

High inflation or a currency reform are politically not feasible. Up to 1989, the population of the PRC has never given up, but only delayed, consumption — mainly through (probably involuntary) savings. Hence future economic growth at a stable price level depends on whether the PRC succeeds in limiting income and increasing the production of consumer goods fast enough. An easy way out would be to increase the supply of consumer goods by, for instance, selling state property. Premier Li Peng in 1988/89 promoted the sale of apartments and small state-owned enterprises.[21] Such sales, however, were never implemented on a large scale.

Any of the countermeasures would reduce savings and at the same time possibly solve the problem of the budget deficit. The options open to the government in 1989 were few in number, but a choice among these options

---

[20](...continued)
consumer goods. Completed investment in fixed assets, apart from assets being inefficient or standing idle for lack of energy and material inputs, will at least partly be devoted to serving further investment instead of contributing to an increase in the production of consumer goods.

[21]   Li Peng 1/89, 6.

had to be made because there exists no endogenous restrictive mechanism which would impede major discrepancies.[22]

Countermeasures

To reduce the discrepancy between purchasing power and the supply of retail goods within the present economic and political framework, on the one hand the production of consumer goods would have to be increased — i.e., investment in fixed assets would have to be reduced. This means starting fewer new projects or stopping some of the projects already under construction, in order to provide scarce material inputs and loans for the production of consumer goods. On the other hand, salary and wage payments, plus the amounts spent on the purchase of agricultural and sideline products, would have to be reduced or at least be allowed to stagnate in order to reduce purchasing power.

The Third Plenum of the Thirteenth Central Committee (26-30 September 1988) initiated a two-year period of consolidation in order to "improve the economic environment." The most important countermeasures implemented after the Plenum were to stop or delay 14,400 investment projects in fixed assets and thus save 44.2 b yuan,[23] to levy a 30% tax on projects financed through units' own funds and bank loans,[24] and to reduce target growth for agriculture in 1989 to 4% and for industry to 7.5%.[25] These measures, taking into consideration the various ways of circumventing them, were hardly more than a start in the right direction. A reduction of income, apart from the regular implementation of regulations on salaries, wages and bonus payments, was not even mentioned.

It was not until 1989 that the state finally succeeded in reducing investment in fixed assets significantly by reducing the number of capital construction projects of state-owned enterprises by 43,000 to 123,000;

---

[22] Foreign trade as a balancing factor is eliminated through state planning and administrative management of the monetary aspects of foreign trade.

[23] State Statistical Bureau 7 March 1989, 3f.

But compared to the total amount of investment in fixed assets in 1988 of 449.7 b yuan, the amount saved was almost negligible. Furthermore, most of the projects suspended had either not yet been under construction or were then completed ahead of time. (C.a. 11/88, 843f.)

[24] FEER 2 March 1989, 59.

[25] In 1988 growth rates in Gross Industrial and Agricultural Output Value were 20.8% and 4.0% respectively. (Handelsblatt 22 March 1989; C.a. 3/89, 164; Appendix A.)

37,000 new construction projects were started in 1989, down 41,000 from 1988. At the same time, the total amount of investment in fixed assets was reduced by almost 50 b yuan below the level in 1988, to about 400 b yuan in 1989. For 1990 the total amount of investment in fixed assets was set to rise to 410 b yuan, up only 2.5% in nominal terms, with 251 b yuan in state-owned enterprises and 159 b yuan in collective and individually-owned enterprises.[26] At the same time the average annual income of the urban population available for covering living costs in 1989 was 1,260 yuan, down 5.2% in real terms. The respective figure for the rural population was 602 yuan, down 7.3% in real terms.[27]

The Fifth Plenum of the Thirteenth Central Committee on 9 November 1989 passed the "Decision on Further Improving the Economic Environment, Straightening Out the Economic Order, and Deepening the Reforms," which extended the period of consolidation three more years, calling for a reduction in the inflation rate to below 10% and for an end to budget deficits. Total investment in fixed assets in 1990 and 1991 was to be limited to the 1989 level and cash in circulation and credit volume in 1990 to the 1989 levels, while individual incomes were to be strictly controlled.[28]

The results of the 1989 reductions in investment and income were almost immediate: the situation in the PRC in 1990 was characterized by an excess supply of consumer goods. The main factors were the reductions in investment and real income made politically feasible in the aftermath of 4 June 1989, and the linkage of the interest rate on some savings deposits to the Retail Price Index (thus leading to an increase in savings). Although the reduction in excess demand for consumer goods was exactly the result necessary to stop the economic situation from developing completely out of control, it was achieved not by economic means but through administrative directives and the political climate after 4 June. Yet by trying to regain control over the economy with one huge administrative effort the PRC government only shifted the problem to another arena: the state budget.

The "market slump" (*shichang piruan*) of 1989 and 1990, as the situation came to be called, caused an increase in unplanned inventory investment by

---

[26]   State Statistical Bureau 27 Feb. 1990, III; State Council 27 April 1990.

[27]   State Council 27 April 1990. Statistical Yearbook 1990, 301,316, gives slightly different figures.

[28]   Decision 1989, IV,V.

enterprises.[29] Enterprises, forced to accumulate unplanned inventory, were unable to repay their debts to other enterprises, if they did not receive new loans. The ensuing situation, called "triangular debt" (*sanjiaozhai*), resulted in almost all enterprises not being able to pay back their bank loans or loans from other enterprises[30] and not being able to purchase material inputs because of the state-ordered credit crunch. Price reductions for goods stocked excessively were not possible, since contractual reference numbers including profits and losses could not be violated. (A devalued stock or sales at lower prices would decrease profits.)[31] In addition, the state did not subsidize prices by as much as originally planned; neither did it cover as many losses of enterprises as originally planned.[32] With the share of their own funds in working capital having dropped in past years,[33] enterprises had to rely more and more on loans — which, in 1989, were not available.

Subsequently the whole country was asked to help "clean up" the debt situation. Banks and local governments intervened, tried to swap debts between enterprises and to obtain the largest possible effect with the few new loans allowed.[34] Yet these efforts met only with partial success. By the end of 1989 the State Council had to raise the overall credit ceiling and allow new loans to state-owned enterprises. Without new loans these enterprises would not have been able to pay their taxes to the government. The 17.6% increase in loans in 1989 thus remained as high as in the years

---

[29] The stocks of 24,036 state-owned industrial enterprises doubled in 1989 (from 33.5 b yuan in 1988 to 61.7 b yuan in 1989) (Liu Yiqun 8/90, 35). For comparison: In 1989 there existed 100,230 state-owned industrial enterprises (Statistical Yearbook 1990, 15).

[30] According to a survey of 300 enterprises, more than 90% of those investigated had not paid back their loans from other enterprises on time. (Shi Xiaofeng 4/90, 43.)

[31] Liu Yiqun 8/90, 35.

[32] Wu Xingdong 7/90, 5; Jin Weihong 9/90.

[33] The proportion of state-owned enterprises' own funds in all working capital dropped from 40% in 1983 to 20% in 1989 (Jin Weihong 9/90, 34). Enterprises preferred to spend their own funds on increasing capital construction and individual incomes.

[34] According to one source by early 1990 120 b yuan had been "cleaned up;" another source speaks of 40 to 50 b yuan in irregular supplier credit. (ZGJR 9/90, 22; Wu Xingdong 7/90, 4.)

before. But the consequence of new loans, namely the danger of renewed inflation, was not the only problem the government faced.[35]

Despite the pledges in the Central Committee decision of 9 November 1989, the actual budget deficit, consisting of the issuing of domestic bonds, the increase in state foreign debts, and the official deficit, again increased in 1990.[36] The number of loss-making state-owned enterprises was estimated to have reached one third of all state-owned enterprises. The tightening of credit beginning in 1989 resulted in 7% of all rural industries being shut down or merged,[37] with a consequent fall in employment and in the output growth rate. Urban unemployment in 1989 was officially given as 2.6%,[38] but according to unpublished statistics of the Labor Ministry stood at 5%.[39] Disguised rural unemployment was estimated by Chinese economists to have reached 40%.[40]

It seems that repeated administrative interference in the economy, necessitated by lack of any endogenous restraint mechanism in the monetary system, is at the heart of the wide swings in economic growth and inflation during the reform period. The leadership is incapable of finding the right measures in the changing economic environment, yet is unwilling to surrender discretionary powers to market mechanisms.

---

[35] The linkage of the interest rate on some savings deposits to the Retail Price Index remained in place, despite the (temporary) drop in the inflation rate to 2.1% in 1991 (Retail Price Index) or 3.1% (Living Cost Index). (State Statistical Bureau 3-91, V.)

[36] The budget deficits so calculated were 36.97 b yuan in 1989 and 50.90 b yuan in 1990. See, for instance, FEER 25 April 1991, 46.

[37] Rural enterprises consist of collective industrial enterprises run by townships, villages or rural co-operatives. State-owned enterprises under the administration of townships and villages do not exist. (Statistical Yearbook 1990, 409.)

[38] Statistical Yearbook 1990, 130.

[39] FEER 19 July 1990, 49.

[40] Ibid.

The "Proposals for the Formulation of the Ten-Year and Eigth Five-Year Plan for Economic and Social Development" issued by the Seventh Plenum of the Thirteenth CCP Central Committee on 30 December 1990, did not signify any about-turn in economic reform policies, yet neither did it take any of the bold steps necessary to solve the problems of budget deficit, loss-making state-owned enterprises and inflation.

Conclusions

The lack of an endogenous mechanism restraining the volume of credit and cash in circulation turned out to be a major factor in the cycle of monetary overinvestment characteristic of the PRC. Yet lack of an endogenous restraint mechanism simply means lack of a market-clearing mechanism. One way to allow markets to clear would be to make the central bank independent and to give it the authority to implement economically sound monetary policy. This would mean the end of "socialism." In fact, continuation of present economic policies might not lead to a very different outcome.

1. Lack of a Market-clearing Mechanism

From the point of view of some Chinese economists, the causes of all economic problems can be traced back to the high investment in fixed assets, caused by a corresponding state policy: "the strategic mistake of the center in pressing for success too impatiently." The dynamic behavior of investment in fixed assets, however, is due not only to the center but also to local governments interested in development of their local economies. That region which does not press for excessive investment in fixed assets would not only lag behind in economic growth but would also suffer bottlenecks in the centralized supply of material inputs caused by other regions.[1]

---

[1]   Jia Geng 5/88.

Yet excessive investment (together with excessive wages and salaries) is only the trigger of the process outlined in the last chapter. The process can evolve because no operational mechanism exists to limit the supply of money.

Why does the interest rate mechanism not operate in the PRC? The obvious answer is simply that the PBC administratively determines the interest rate. But more importantly, the interest rate, however determined, is without much effect on lending to state-owned enterprises. The interest rate lacks the function of a price for scarce funds for two reasons: (i) the general price structure is distorted; and (ii) funds are not scarce. Investment in fixed assets is based not so much on profitability calculations — which are meaningless, anyway, given the arbitrary price structure — but on state plans and the requests of local governments. Funds are in general not scarce since loans (and cash supply) can be expanded to an almost unlimited degree through banks, due to a relaxation of the credit plan and a soft refinancing quota with the PBC. The market for loanable funds thus is not between banks and enterprises but within the PBC, which cannot point to any objective mechanism for restricting loans. If all prices in the real economy were state-determined, the lack of a market-clearing mechanism would not be a problem. The population could be relieved of as large a part of its income via savings deposits as desired. But the reforms in the real economy no longer allow for this solution; administrative management of the monetary system has been made at least partly obsolete. Western-style monetary instruments, which would include the interest rate as an endogenous restraint mechanism, are not yet fully employed. A Western-style monetary policy would require further changes in the real economy that seem politically infeasible. The only possible way to prevent the economy from overheating is through political decisions of the center and successful implementation.[2]

---

[2]   Chinese sources characterize economic development in the PRC with the slogan "liberate, chaos, take back, death" (*fang, luan, shou, si*), i.e., decentralization of decision-making power, chaos, recentralization of decision-making power and finally the abrogation of local autonomy and no economic growth. (Jia Geng 5/88, 14.)

2. Independence of the Central Bank and Establishment of a Legal Framework in the Monetary System

Again, what could be changed to let monetary policy work? One possible answer is: The PBC could be made independent of any outside authority and thus be allowed to maintain a monetary policy with currency stability as its main objective. At the same time, a strong legal framework is necessary for the implementation of monetary policy and for the regulation of financial institutions.

Historically, dependence of banks on the state has been the iron rule in China. Prior to the PRC the size of the country and changing centers of power were responsible for several currencies being used simultaneously at flexible exchange rates. Regional rulers regarded monetary policy as a regional privilege:

> The financial commissioner [local official responsible for the local mint] was directly responsible only to the governor and the latter communicated directly with the Emperor. Censors or the Board of Revenue might denounce deviations from the established rules, but the governor could usually support the deviation as locally necessary, and the Emperor had little practical alternative but to approve if the evidence available — and it usually came from provincial sources — gave prima-facie support to the provincial position.[3]

It was not until 1928, 16 years after the foundation of the Republic in 1911/1912, that the first central bank of the Guomindang government was established in Shanghai. It was not a solely central bank, not responsible for all of China, and not independent.

A uniform currency for all of China was created only with the foundation of the PBC on 1 December 1948. During the next 35 years the PBC was to serve mainly as a clearing and accounting organ for the Ministry of Finance before changes in the real economy required transformation of the PBC into a solely central bank on 17 September 1983.

One of the main tasks since the transformation has been to bring about a "change in consciousness" (yishi de gaibian) about the role of the PBC. Judged by the importance attached, in the annual government reports to the National People's Congress, to monetary reforms — as compared to

---

[3] King 1965, 128 (on the situation at the end of the 19th century).

For the monetary system before the foundation of the PRC also see Yang Lien-Sheng 1952; King 1965; and Weber 1920, 276-290.

enterprise or price reforms — the level of success has been low. Nevertheless, there is a growing number of voices calling for subordination of the PBC to the National People's Congress, the parliament of the PRC. The intention is to reduce the influence of the State Council, the highest organ of government. The question of independence has not even been raised. The advantage of making the PBC subordinate to the National People's Congress would be that objectives for monetary policy could only be formulated once a year, since the National People's Congress meets annually. In the meantime, the PBC would be free to pursue these objectives. Yet the National People's Congress is a rather weak institution with its representatives not directly elected and subject to the State Council's influence. At most, the threshold against government intervention would be raised somewhat, but intervention would certainly not be eliminated.

Apart from the dubious separation of power in monetary policy decision-making, there remains the equally fundamental problem of disobedience to the few existing laws and regulations.

Neither for the monetary system nor for the PBC does there exist a formal law passed by the National People's Congress. The "PBC Constitution of 1983" is a State Council "decision" (*jueding*), and the "Bank Regulations of 1986" a State Council "regulation" (*tiaoli*), yet both are elemental rules on which most of the later regulations are based. The PBC Board of Directors, according to the Bank Regulations of 1986, shall "discuss and draw up drafts of laws and regulations" for the monetary system and "determine basic rules and regulations for the monetary system." Thus the PBC not only implements monetary policy, controls the special banks, issues bonds as an agent of the state, and regulates the money market, but also seems to possess, apart from the State Council, the Ministry of Finance and the individual special banks, some legislative sovereignty over the monetary system.

No matter how sophisticated the division of legislative powers may be in practice, the resulting laws and regulations are widely disregarded. PBC regulations are repeatedly published in the *State Council Bulletin* together with short State Council messages admonishing obedience to the regulations published. The State Council itself draws up and publishes regulations on the monetary system and even old State Council decisions are reprinted to encourage compliance to the law.

Besides obeying regulations, bank cadres and the population are asked to act "in the spirit of ..." Party or State Council decisions, in the spirit of the reform of the economy, in the spirit of opening to the outside world, etc.[4] But what is "in the spirit of ... "?

When talking of "ideological work" in early 1990, Li Guixian, governor of the PBC, stated that "effort shall be put into the study of policies, laws and regulations. Political work shall be studied. The speeches of central leaders and the documents of the Fourth and Fifth Plenum shall be conscientiously studied. Marxism, especially Marxist economic theory shall also be conscientiously studied; this is very important for properly carrying out financial work. Furthermore, attention shall be paid to the study of relevant economic laws, regulations, and policies."[5]

Importing a Western-type central bank and Western-type monetary policy into such an environment may be doomed to fail. Replacing strict subordination to monetary decision-makers with political campaigns and bargaining is a contradiction to Western-type banking itself. Li Guixian's words reveal how removed he, and probably other bank cadres with him, are from Western-type central banking.

3. Outlook

Scenario I: Independence of the People's Bank of China

If the PBC were to receive approval from the National People's Congress for a certain increase in the supply of money or a maximum expansion of loans to special banks each year, it would be free to pursue the objectives of currency stability and development of the economy. According to Liu Hongru, until 1989 a vice-governor of the PBC, in practice this would lead

---

[4]   Li Guixian, governor of the PBC, in his first speech to the meeting of directors of the provincial PBC branches in January 1989: "The biggest challenge in the monetary system in 1989 is the implementation of the spirit of the Third Plenum of the Thirteenth Central Committee of the Party ..." (Li Guixian 2/89, 6.)

[5]   Li Guixian 3/90, 5.
Liu Hongru is well aware of the problem of implementing laws. In the last chapter of one of his books (Liu Hongru 1987) he lists four fields which still have to be covered systematically by laws (PBC, banks in general, money market and foreign exchange sector) and stakes out their contents. On the obedience to laws he does not elaborate.

to the priority of currency stability.[6] Liu Hongru has stated explicitly that "the emphasis of China's monetary policy is on currency stability."[7]

A more independent PBC could, in order to safeguard currency stability, abandon the administrative management of the monetary system which has, with the reforms in the real economy, proven more and more inefficient. The new monetary instruments would be rediscount policy, a minimum reserve requirement, and open market operations. Interest rates would be determined on the market, and special banks would be independent of the PBC. All state preferential policies would have to be accompanied by state subsidies. The PBC would refuse to refinance the special banks on a scale exceeding the limits set by the National People's Congress. Interest rates on loans by special banks to enterprises would then rise because of the scarcity of loanable funds. The effects on the private economy and most collective enterprises would be minor, since these enterprises already now obtain most of their funds at market interest rates from sources not controlled by the state.

Most hurt by higher interest rates would be state-owned enterprises whose costs would rise correspondingly and who would no longer be able to rely on new bank loans to pay their taxes or salaries and wages. If higher costs were not to lead to less tax revenue and possibly higher enterprise subsidies, salaries and wages would have to be cut or the prices of material inputs lowered. Both measures are improbable, if not impossible. Less tax revenue and higher enterprise subsidies would result in a larger budget deficit, which in turn would have to be financed exclusively by issuing state bonds once the PBC refuses to extend further loans to the state. In order to compete with market interest rates on savings deposits, these bonds would have to carry a high return. The state would have to issue new bonds every year and bear an increasing debt burden, transferring the problem into the future. The state could also try to reduce investment in fixed assets and thus

---

[6]   Liu Hongru, as of early 1991, retained his post as vice-minister of the Commission for the Reform of the Economic System; for his demise at the PBC in 1989 no reason could be found. His economic views and the date suggest a possible relationship to 4 June 1989, especially with Liu Hongru having been in charge of the educational work at the PBC.

[7]   Liu Hongru 1987, 243.

Liu Hongru, in books, articles, and speeches also tried to accelerate the reform of the monetary system on the basis of experience gained by Western central banks. It was often he who, together with the governor or vice-governors of the PBC, headed the meetings of the directors of provincial PBC branches and promoted the implementation of reforms there. Liu Hongru together with Qiu Qing, another vice-governor since the transformation of the PBC in 1983, seem to have been the driving forces behind most of the reforms in the monetary system implemented so far.

reduce the demand for loans, especially by state-owned enterprises. But the momentum gathered by local governments could foil this attempt as long as the central government did not resort to strict central planning of the whole economy.

In such a scenario, independence of the central bank could lead directly to the abandonment of the concept of state-owned enterprises as the backbone of the Chinese economy. Their inefficiency could no longer be supported, and the resulting state budget deficits would become unbearable. Both for a decision on whether to let an enterprise go bankrupt and for the privatization of a state-owned enterprise, a valuation of the enterprise is necessary. With a politically determined price structure that is arbitrarily readjusted every so often, there is no possibility for an accurate enterprise assessment. On the other hand, with the state abandoning the concept of "state-owned enterprises," hardly any need for state-determined prices remains. Thus, independence of the central bank with currency stability as the main objective is very likely to translate, through the abandonment of state-owned enterprises and state-determined prices, into a market economy.

Scenario II: No Further Reforms in the Monetary System

What would happen if excessive investment in fixed assets and high income were to continue unchanged and the PBC were to continue its "administrative management" of the monetary system?[8]

As of the early 1990s state-owned enterprises will continue to incur losses due to inefficiency and state interference. (Almost constant state-determined sales prices lead to losses if the prices of inputs — such as labor or materials purchased on the market — increase.) The state so far has not allowed state-owned enterprises to go bankrupt but has subsidized their increasing losses. The state likewise finances increasing price subsidies. With increasing budget deficits, either lending from the PBC or the issuing of state bonds (or, most probably, both) will continue to increase. The possibility exists that a real decrease in salaries and wages combined with a sufficiently high real interest rate on savings deposits reduces the pressure on retail prices, as it did in 1990; yet real decreases in salaries and wages

---

[8]   Decision 1989, XIII, states: "The need for banks to be managed in the manner of enterprises should not be over-emphasized."

Li Guixian's speeches resound with the old campaign rhetoric yet show no understanding at all of control of the monetary system by economic means. The time of professional management of banks seems bygone.

cannot be expected to be long-lived. The state budget deficit (as well as the state domestic and foreign debt) increased even in 1990, when inflation stood at approximately 3%.

Individuals presently try to dispense of their increasing cash holdings by investing in rural industrial enterprises[9] or by supporting credit associations and "People's Banks," all of which are institutions not covered by any plans in the monetary or real economy. Urban credit co-operatives and the trust and investment companies operate under the auspices of local special bank branches that want to increase their profits, and under local governments that want to accelerate the development of the local economy; control by the PBC or the center is minimal. With rural industries mainly run by lower-level administrations (or even under truly collective ownership), a large part of the PRC's industry is also outside the range of the center's authority.

Meanwhile, the resentment of the population against the central government is likely to increase for several reasons. Wide-spread discontent with the compulsory purchase of state bonds continues. In the future the government might have to abandon this source of deficit financing to some extent and increase its borrowing from the PBC, which is likely to fuel inflation. The corruption of cadres, especially at a time when real salaries and wages of the population on average decrease, is seen as the biggest "social problem" and the machinations of Party members as the biggest "political problem." Anti-corruption campaigns have met with little success.[10] The Chinese leadership has long been well aware of the problems. Premier Li Peng described the inflation rate, "some" corruption in government and Party, and the unjust income distribution as the biggest concerns of the people.[11] Nevertheless, the central government since 1988 has lost the initiative.

The PBC cannot be blamed for the increasing state budget deficit, for the loss of control over the economy, or for popular resentment against the government. The PBC with its monetary instruments, however, would be

---

[9]   The Gross Output Value of rural industries (township enterprises, village enterprises, and rural co-operatives, all in industry) tripled during the four years from 1986 to 1989 and reached 22 % of GIOV in 1989. (Statistical Yearbook 1989, 224.)

[10]   FEER 2 March 1989, 62f.

Liu Hongru in his speech to the directors of the provincial PBC branches in August 1988 emphasized that bank cadres in the future would not be allowed to accept presents... (Jin zuida 10/88, 7.)

[11]   Li Peng 2/89.

well-positioned to solve these problems were it not that the main decisions on monetary policy are not its own; they are political decisions.

Before 4 June 1989, a discussion was raging through the weekly Shanghai newspaper *Word Economic Herald* on the "New Authoritarianism" (*xin quanwei zhuyi*)[12] — i.e., on whether the PRC needs a strong authoritative leader or group of leaders. In view of the emphasis on increasing the material well-being of the population,[13] and of the strong centrifugal forces (especially in the peripheral provinces of China), New Authoritarianism seems no longer a viable option. Due to changing ownership structures with the rapid development of private and truly collective enterprises as well as joint ventures, decision-making in the real economy has become strongly decentralized.[14]

The CCP Central Committee decision on consolidation in September 1988 was the first in a number of attempts by the Chinese leadership to regain some control over the economy. Whereas from 1978 to 1988 the choice of reform rested with the Chinese leadership, since 1988 it can only react. With its traditional economic measures meeting no more than partial success, the leadership must choose: Recentralize decision-making authority or permit far-reaching reforms. The first option is hardly feasible any more; the latter will limit and possibly end the dictatorial powers enjoyed by the leadership. By choosing the path followed since 1988 — namely, not to move resolutely in any direction — the leadership in fact paves the way toward a segmented and disorderly market economy.

The political system of the PRC is characterized by the intentional superiority of the CCP to the law. An efficient economy, however, requires self-regulatory mechanisms not subject to discretionary political decisions opportune at one point in time. The CCP (i) even if it desired to implement sound monetary policy, simply cannot obtain and process on time the information necessary to guarantee currency stability, to develop the economy steadily, and to increase economic efficiency; and (ii) is not willing to give up its control over the economy, since the political fortunes

---

[12] See, for example, Fan Di 20 March 1989; Huang Youguang 6 Feb. 1989; Li Yining 6 March 1989; Li Yunqi 27 Feb. 1989; Wu Jiaxiang 6 Feb. 1989; Yu Haocheng 6 Feb. 1989; Yuan Zhiming 6 Feb. 1989; Zhang Xiaojun 30 Jan. 1989; Zhang Xiaojun 13 March 1989; Zhang Xin 20 March 1988.

[13] Central "leaders" of all shades have confirmed that raising the material well-being is the main task of the CCP: Zhao Ziyang in Report 1987, 6; Li Peng in Report 1988, 11; and Deng Xiaoping in Deng Xiaoping 1990, 101f.

[14] As of the first half of 1992, state-owned industrial enterprises produced little more than one third of GIOV.

of the CCP are likely to decrease as its economic power diminishes. Past experiments and experiences in the monetary sphere have prepared the ground for a quick transition to Western-type monetary instruments, if only the PBC were given the authority to strictly impose sound monetary policy. In the real economy, however, factors such as the lack of a social security net, the absence of an efficient tax system, the 'iron rice bowl', and 'eating from the same pot' are difficult to change[15] — always assuming that the CCP would allow a change.

As of 1992 all major reforms in the monetary sphere are still on hold with Li Guixian as governor of the PBC and Chen Yuan, son of Chen Yun, as one of the vice-governors. With a reformist tide rising in the PRC in 1992 it would not be astonishing if before long a more reform-oriented team were to take over the leadership of the PBC and, parallel to the changes in the real economy, once more set out to modernize central banking.

---

[15] The economic policy measures introduced at the end of 1988 led to the closure of some industrial enterprises. With a total of more than 500 m workers, staff, and peasants, a few hundred thousand more unemployed (C.a. 2/89, 86, talks of "hundred thousands") might seem a small figure. However, in a society without unemployment insurance and a large number of unemployed not supported by any units, wide-spread unemployment is a political risk.

APPENDIX A:

ECONOMIC DATA

All data in RMB b, if not otherwise stated

(1) Monetary statistics

	1978	1979	1980	1981	1982	1983	1984	1985	1986	1987	1988	1989
Cash in circulation (M_0)	21.2	26.8	34.6	39.6	43.9	53.0	79.2	98.8	121.8	145.4	213.4	234.4
Change against previous year in %	X	26.3	29.3	14.5	10.8	20.7	49.6	24.7	23.3	19.4	46.8	9.8
Loans (by state banks)	185.0	204.0	241.4	276.5	318.1	359.0	476.6	590.6	759.1	903.3	1,055	1,241
Change against previous year in %	X	10.2	18.4	14.5	15.0	12.9	32.8	23.9	28.5	19.0	16.8	17.6
of which to:												
Industrial Enterprises	35.2	36.3	42.8	47.8	51.3	57.0	78.9	98.5	141.7	170.7	208.5	272.5
Change against previous year in %	X	3.3	17.7	11.7	7.3	11.3	38.3	24.9	43.9	20.4	22.1	30.7
Commercial enterprises	111.8	123.2	143.7	164.2	178.8	197.9	227.3	264.9	308.9	350.6	410.1	477.5
Change against previous year in %	X	10.3	16.6	14.2	8.9	10.7	14.9	16.6	16.6	13.5	17.0	16.4
Investment in fixed assets	-	0.8	5.6	13.3	23.8	30.7	45.2	70.5	100.6	128.7	155.9	177.6
Change against previous year in %	X	X	702.5	239.5	79.2	29.0	47.1	56.1	42.6	27.9	21.1	13.9
Construction enterprises	-	-	-	4.6	4.2	4.8	18.5	26.7	36.9	46.7	49.5	60.1
Change against previous year in %	X	X	X	X	-8.6	13.1	387.6	44.8	38.3	26.3	6.0	21.4
Deposits (at state banks)	113.4	133.9	166.2	202.7	237.0	278.9	358.4	426.5	535.5	651.7	742.6	901.4
Change against previous year in %	X	18.0	24.1	22.0	16.9	17.7	28.5	19.0	25.6	21.7	13.9	21.4
of which (by):												
Enterprises	36.8	46.9	56.3	85.2	100.6	114.0	163.9	173.6	224.3	267.1	293.7	308.5
Change against previous year in %	X	27.3	20.1	51.3	18.0	13.3	43.8	5.9	29.2	19.1	10.0	5.0
of which by:												

Industrial enterprises	18.6	22.5	26.8	32.6	34.6	38.3	45.7	43.3	57.4	67.6	·	·
Change against pr. year in %	X	20.9	19.2	21.5	6.4	10.6	19.3	-5.2	32.5	17.8	·	·
Commercial enterprises	6.9	10.6	11.8	14.6	16.0	20.2	41.4	44.7	56.1	66.9	·	·
Change against pr. year in %	X	53.6	10.5	24.2	9.9	26.2	204.4	8.0	25.6	19.2	·	·
Construction enterprises	-	-	-	17.5	24.4	27.5	39.1	49.4	60.7	70.5	·	·
Change against pr. year in %	X	X	X	X	39.3	12.7	42.1	26.5	22.8	16.2	·	·
Urban savings deposits	15.5	20.3	28.3	35.4	44.7	57.3	77.7	105.8	147.2	206.8	265.9	373.5
Change against previous year in %	X	30.8	39.4	25.4	26.3	28.0	35.6	36.2	39.1	40.5	28.6	40.5
of which: Time deposits	12.9	16.6	22.9	28.9	36.5	46.4	61.5	84.1	118.9	164.8	204.5	·
Rural deposits (at state banks)	15.4	20.4	24.0	27.8	33.0	39.1	37.2	45.0	56.0	62.6	67.0	71.6
Change against previous year in %	X	31.9	17.7	16.1	18.5	18.6	-4.8	20.7	24.5	11.9	7.0	5.9
At all financial institutions in the PRC:												
Rural savings deposits	5.6	7.8	11.7	17.0	22.8	32.0	43.8	56.5	76.6	100.6	114.2	141.2
Change against previous year in %	X	40.8	49.2	45.0	34.5	40.2	36.9	28.9	35.6	31.3	13.5	23.6
of which: Time deposits	-	·	7.6	10.7	15.4	21.8	28.6	38.4	54.0	70.8	79.2	·
Refinancing of special banks at the PBC	X	X	X	X	X	X	·	224.9	272	279	324	428
Monetary aggregates:												
M1	85.0	105.2	131.1	157.7	177.6	204.8	275.4	305.0	385.7	457.5	546.4	591.3
Change against previous year in %	X	23.8	24.6	20.3	12.6	15.3	34.5	10.7	26.5	18.6	19.4	8.2
M2	115.9	145.8	183.3	221.0	255.3	301.2	390.3	455.7	588.8	726.9	879.3	1,036
Change against previous year in %	X	25.8	25.7	20.5	15.5	17.9	29.6	16.8	29.2	23.4	21.0	17.9
M3	134.6	160.7	200.7	243.2	280.9	331.8	437.6	525.3	657.3	797.2	956.1	1,136
Change against previous year in %	X	19.3	24.9	21.1	15.5	18.1	31.9	20.0	25.1	21.3	19.9	18.8

	1978	1979	1980	1981	1982	1983	1984	1985	1986	1987	1988	1989
Velocity of money:												
v_0 (retail sales/M_0)	7.4	6.7	6.2	5.9	5.9	5.4	4.3	4.4	4.1	4.0	3.5	3.5
v_2 (GNP/M_2)	3.0	2.7	2.4	2.1	2.0	1.9	1.7	1.8	1.6	1.5	1.6	1.5
(2) National Income Accounting												
National income (formation)	301.0	335.0	368.8	394.0	426.1	473.0	565.0	703.1	788.7	932.1	1,177	1,313
Change against previous year in %	X	11.3	10.1	6.8	8.1	11.0	19.5	24.4	12.2	18.2	26.3	11.5
National Income Index (deflated, 1952 = 100)	453.4	485.1	516.3	541.4	586.2	643.8	730.6	826.6	892.5	985.9	1,097	1,133
Change against previous year in %	X	7.0	6.4	4.9	8.3	9.8	13.5	13.1	8.0	10.5	11.3	3.3
National income (use)	297.5	335.6	369.6	390.5	429.0	477.9	570.1	748.0	840.6	968.4	1,227	1,358
Consumption (in %)	63.5	65.4	68.5	71.7	71.2	70.3	68.5	64.8	65.2	65.9	65.5	65.6
Accumulation (in %)	36.5	34.6	31.5	28.3	28.8	29.7	31.5	35.2	34.8	34.1	34.5	34.4
of which: Investment in fixed assets (absolute value)	78.3	83.8	89.3	77.8	96.9	112.5	145.3	195.4	222.8	269.3	336.0	295.3
in % of accumulation	72.0	72.0	76.7	70.3	78.4	79.2	80.9	74.3	76.2	81.5	79.4	63.2
Gross National Product (GNP)	348.2	387.9	433.6	462.9	503.8	562.7	676.1	833.0	945.7	1,105	1,402	1,568
Change against previous year in %	X	11.4	11.8	6.8	8.8	11.7	20.2	23.2	13.5	16.8	26.8	11.9
Total Output Value of Society	684.6	764.2	853.2	907.2	996.6	1,113	1,317	1,659	1,907	2,308	2,985	3,460
Change against pr. year in %, deflated	13.1	8.5	8.4	4.7	9.5	10.2	14.7	17.1	10.3	14.1	15.8	5.2
of which:												
Industry	423.7	468.1	515.5	540.0	581.1	646.1	761.7	971.7	1,119	1,381	1,822	2,188
Change ag. pr. year in %, deflated	13.6	8.8	9.3	4.5	7.8	11.2	16.3	21.4	11.7	17.7	20.8	8.3
Agriculture	139.7	169.8	192.3	218.1	248.3	275.0	321.4	362.0	401.3	467.6	586.5	655

Change ag. pr. year in %, deflated	8.1	7.5	1.4	6.4	11.3	7.8	12.3	3.4	3.4	5.8	4.0	3.3
(3) (Total) Purchasing Power of Society												
Formation	176.5	209.4	253.6	274.7	302.6	344.1	445.7	564.5	634.0	757.3	960.3	1,082
Change against previous year in %	X	18.6	21.1	8.3	10.2	13.7	29.5	26.7	12.3	19.4	26.8	12.7
minus relative change in the Retail Price Index	X	16.6	15.1	5.9	8.3	12.2	26.7	17.9	6.3	12.1	8.3	-5.1
of which:												
Rural income (in % of "formation")	55.7	57.4	58.9	58.9	59.8	61.5	63.9	64.8	63.1	64.5	65.5	65.9
Urban Income (in % …)	37.2	35.6	34.6	34.3	33.4	31.6	29.3	28.4	29.2	27.8	27.3	27.5
Value of consumer goods purchased by foreigners (in % …)		0.2	0.2	0.3	0.3	0.3	0.3	0.3	0.4	0.4	0.3	0.2
Value of consumer goods purchased by urban social institutions (in % …)	7.2	6.8	6.3	6.5	6.5	6.6	6.5	6.5	7.3	7.3	6.9	6.4
Use												
Expenditures	172.1	197.6	233.1	255.7	282.8	316.9	393.3	509.5	555.5	654.8	834.3	932.7
Change against previous year in %	X	14.8	17.9	9.7	10.6	12.1	24.1	29.5	9.0	17.9	27.4	11.8
minus relative change in the Retail Price Index	X	12.8	11.9	7.3	8.7	10.6	21.3	20.7	3.0	10.6	8.9	-6.0
of which for retail sales	155.9	180.0	214.0	235.0	257.0	284.9	337.6	430.5	495.0	582.0	744.0	810.1
Change against pr. year in %	X	15.5	18.9	9.8	9.4	10.9	18.5	27.4	15.1	17.6	27.8	8.9
of which:												
Consumer goods	126.5	147.6	179.4	200.3	218.2	242.6	289.9	380.1	437.4	511.5	654.2	708.4
Means of agric. production	29.4	32.4	34.6	34.8	38.9	42.3	47.7	50.4	57.6	70.5	89.9	101.7

	1978	1979	1980	1981	1982	1983	1984	1985	1986	1987	1988	1989
Excess (cumulative)	48.1	58.5	79.1	98.1	117.9	145.1	197.4	252.4	321.0	423.5	549.5	698.5
Change against previous year in %	X	21.7	35.1	24.0	20.2	23.0	36.1	27.9	27.1	31.9	29.8	27.1
of which:												
Savings deposits (cumulative)	30.9	36.9	50.9	64.8	80.6	99.3	131.5	170.4	223.8	307.3	380.2	513.5
Change against pr. year in %	X	19.4	37.9	27.2	24.4	23.3	32.5	29.6	31.3	37.4	23.7	35.1
Cash holdings by individuals	17.1	21.6	28.1	33.3	37.3	45.8	65.9	82.0	97.2	116.1	169.3	185.0
Change against pr. year in %	X	25.9	30.3	18.4	12.1	22.7	43.9	24.4	18.5	19.5	45.8	9.3
Share of (annual) change in excess (as %) in Purchasing Power of Society (Formation)	X	5.0	8.1	6.9	6.6	7.9	11.7	9.7	12.4	13.5	13.1	13.8
Share of (annual) change in (cumul.) savings deposits (as %) in Purchasing Power of Society (Formation)	X	2.9	5.5	5.0	5.2	5.4	7.2	6.9	8.4	11.0	7.6	12.3
(4) Price indices												
Change of Retail Price Index against previous year in %	0.7	2.0	6.0	2.4	1.9	1.5	2.8	8.8	6.0	7.3	18.5	17.8
Change in Staff and Workers Cost of Living Index against pr. year in %	0.7	1.9	7.5	2.5	2.0	2.0	2.7	11.9	7.0	8.8	20.7	16.3
Change in Purchasing Price Index for Agricultural and Sideline Products against previous year in %	3.9	22.1	7.1	5.9	2.2	4.4	4.0	8.6	6.4	12.0	23.0	15.0
Increase in labor productivity against previous year in %	10.5	4.8	3.6	1.6	4.7	6.6	10.0	9.2	4.7	7.4	7.9	1.3
plus increase in living costs	11.2	6.7	11.1	4.1	6.7	8.6	12.7	21.1	11.7	16.2	28.6	17.6

(5) State Budget												
Extrabudgetary funds	34.7	45.3	55.7	60.1	80.3	96.8	118.8	153.0	173.7	202.8	227	.
compared to state budget revenues (as % of state budget revenues)	31.0	41.0	51.4	55.2	71.4	77.5	79.1	82.0	78.2	89.7	88.9	.
Share of local revenues in total state revenues in %				79.4	77.0	70.2	65.1	63.0	59.4	61.8	60.2	.
Share of local expenditures in total state expenditures in %				46.0	50.1	50.3	52.2	56.7	58.7	57.9	60.8	.
(6) Energy production (change against previous year in %)	11.3	2.9	-1.3	-0.8	5.6	6.7	9.2	9.9	3.0	3.6	5.0	6.1
(7) Investment in fixed assets	X	X	X	96.1	123.0	143.0	183.3	254.3	302.0	364.1	449.7	413.8
Change against previous year in % of which by (in %):	X	X	X	X	28.0	16.2	28.2	38.8	18.7	20.6	18.5	-8.0
State-owned enterprises				66.8	84.5	95.2	118.5	168.1	197.9	229.8	276.3	253.5
Collective-owned enterprises				11.5	17.4	15.6	23.9	32.7	39.2	54.7	71.2	57.0
of which: rural (in %)				72.6	75.4	70.8	73.2	60.8	62.6	66.8	64.2	67.4
Individual-owned enterprises				17.8	21.1	32.2	40.9	53.5	64.9	79.6	102.2	103.2
of which: rural (in %)				93.3	94.2	94.8	92.7	89.4	88.5	87.4	84.7	86.4
Sources of funding (in %):												
State allocations				28.1	22.7	23.8	23.0	16.0	14.6	13.1	9.0	8.3
Domestic loans				12.7	14.3	12.3	14.1	20.1	21.1	23.0	20.3	17.3
Foreign funds				3.8	4.9	4.7	3.9	3.6	4.4	4.8	5.7	6.6
Self-raised funds and others				55.5	58.1	59.3	59.1	60.3	59.9	59.2	63.9	67.8

Definitions:

a. Total Purchasing Power of Society (*shehui shangpin goumaili*) consists of (i) wages and salaries to staff and workers in state-owned, urban collective-owned and various jointly-owned units, and net money income of urban individual laborers, (ii) income of peasants from the sale of agricultural and sideline products, labor remuneration, budget appropriations, agricultural loans and advance payments by banks and credit co-operatives as well as from other sources, (iii) the value of consumer goods purchased by foreigners, and (iv) the value of consumer goods purchased by urban social institutions. It is used for (i) the purchase of consumer goods, (ii) the purchase of means of agricultural production, and (iii) to a small part for expenditures on services and recreation, tax payments, net decreases of agricultural loans from banks and credit co-operatives and for other expenditures. The difference between "formation" and "expenditures" equals the increases in savings deposits and cash holdings. (Statistical Yearbook 1988, 680f,716; Statistical Yearbook 1989, 517.)

b. National Income (*guomin shouru*) is the net output value of total material production (in the 5 sectors agriculture, industry, transportation, construction and commerce), that is, the Total Output Value of Society minus material inputs (interenterprise purchases and depreciation). It is distributed via the remuneration of labor in the material production sectors, taxes, profit and interest "etc.". (Statistical Yearbook 1988, 91)

c. Gross National Product (*guomin shengchan zongzhi*) is the sum of value-added production in all sectors of the economy (value of final products and services; SNA, not MPS). It is distributed via the remuneration of labor, tax, profit, interest and depreciation "etc." and is used for consumption, investment in fixed assets, inventory investment and net export of goods and services. (Statistical Yearbook 1988, 92)

d. Total Output Value of Society (*shehui zongchanzhi*) is the total output value (list price x quantity produced) of all five material production sectors. (Statistical Yearbook 1988, 21)

— Total Output Value of Society = interenterprise purchases + depreciation + Net Output Value (National Income, MPS)

— Gross National Product = National Income (MPS) + depreciation + services

Sources and notes:

(1) Monetary statistics

— Cash in circulation, loans and deposits: China Financial Statistics (1952-1987), 5,24f,28f,54,63; ZGJR 4/89 5/90; Almanac 1987, II-9; Almanac 1989, 65; Li Yuping 6/90, 30.

— The People's Construction Bank of China is included starting 1981. All "other deposits" are listed separately starting 1980.

— The remaining loans are made to material supply and marketing enterprises, to urban collectives, to individual-owned industrial and commercial enterprises, to agriculture and to "others".

— Besides deposits by enterprises and savings deposits by urban and rural individuals there further exist deposits by the state, offices and organizations, deposits earmarked for capital construction (until 1980) and "other deposits". The remaining enterprise deposits are by state agriculture, collective-owned enterprises, individual-owned enterprises and "others".

— Urban deposits at state banks equal urban savings deposits at all financial institutions in the PRC.

— Of the figures for refinancing of state banks at the PBC only that for 1985 is absolutely reliable (Almanac 1987, II-9). Figures from 1986 to 1989 are based on Li Yuping 6/90, 30, who does not offer any total figures but only relative and absolute annual increases which, probably due to rounding, partly contradict each other. Here the total of 1985 has been taken from Almanac 1987, II-9, and figures for all following years are derived by using the relative changes given by Li Yuping 6/90, 30.

(2) National Income Accounting

— National Income: Statistical Yearbook 1989, 24f,28; Statistical Yearbook 1990, 34f,42,47; Economic Yearbook 1988, 11-27.

— Gross National Product: Statistical Yearbook 1988, 36; Statistical Yearbook 1989, 23; State Statistical Bureau 2/90, I,II.

— Total Output Value of Society: Statistical Yearbook 1988, 44,46; C.a. 3/89, 164; Statistical Yearbook 1989, 35f; Statistical Yearbook 1990, 49f.

(3) (Total) Purchasing Power of Society: Statistical Yearbook 1988, 680-684; Statistical Yearbook 1989, 517; Statistical Yearbook 1990, 614; State Statistical Bureau 2/90, I,II.

(4) Price Indices

— Retail Price Index and Cost of Living Index: Statistical Yearbook 1988, 777; C.a. 1/89, 22; State Statistical Bureau 2/90, I,II.

— Purchasing Price Index of Agricultural and Sideline Products: Statistical Yearbook 1990, 249.

— Increase in labor productivity: Statistical Yearbook 1988, 72; Statistical Yearbook 1989, 45; Statistical Yearbook 1990, 65.

(5) State Budget

— Extrabudgetary revenues: Statistical Yearbook 1988, 763f; Statistical Yearbook 1989, 579f; FEER, 6 April 1989, 77.

— Share of local revenues/expenditures: Statistical Yearbook 1988, 763; Statistical Yearbook 1990, 242.

(6) Energy production (without organic energy, solar or nuclear power): Statistical Yearbook 1990, 487.

(7) Investment in fixed assets (including, since 1988, the 3 special economic zones Shenzhen, Zhuhai and Shantou): Statistical Yearbook 1988, 72; Statistical Yearbook 1989, 404; State Statistical Bureau 7 March 1989; State Statistical Bureau 2/90, V.

APPENDIX B:

GLOSSARY OF CHINESE TERMS

baitiao	IOU
baoxian jijin zuzhi	Insurance Funds Organization
baozhi gongzhai	value-guaranteed bonds
caiwu gongsi	corporate finance companies
caizheng cunkuan	state deposits
caizheng tizhi	financial system
caizheng zhaiquan	public bonds
caizhengbu	Ministry of Finance
chabie lilu	differential interest rates
changqi zijin shichang	long-term money market
chengshi xinyong (hezuo) she	urban credit co-operatives
chengzhen chuxu cunkuan	savings deposits by urban individuals
cunkuan zhunbeijin	minimum reserve requirement
daimao	"wearing a hat," determination of bank loans by state departments
dangzu shuji	secretary of the leading Party group
duanqi zhengquan	short-term negotiable securities
duanqi zijin shichang	short-term money market
fangzhen zhengce	general and special policies (guidelines and policies)
faxingku	money-issuing deptartment/vault
fei yinhang jinrong jigou xindai jihua	Credit Plan for Non-bank Financial Institutions

fenxiang xindai zijin shouzhi jihua	Concise Credit Funds Income and Expenditure Plan
fudong lilu	variable interest rates
gongzhai	state bonds
guanli	to control, to administer
guoji shouzhi jihua	International Revenue and Expenditure Plan
guojia jianshe zhaiquan	state construction bonds
guojia jingji jianshe gongzhai	state economic construction bonds
guojia waihui guanli ju	State Administration of Exchange Control
guojia waihui kucun	state foreign exchange stock
guojia waihui shouzhi jihua	Foreign Exchange Plan
guojia zhongdian jianshe zhaiquan	state key construction bonds
guojia zonghe xindai jihua	State Comprehensive Credit Plan
guokuquan	treasury bonds
guomin shengchan zongzhi	Gross National Product (SNA)
guomin shouru	National Income (SNA)
gupiao	stocks
hangzhang zerenzhi	bank director responsibility system
heli gongei, guiding qixian, youjie youhuan, zhouzhuan bianyong	rational supply of loans, fixed duration, guaranteed repayment, and preference for circulation
hezuo yinhang	co-operative banks

hongguan kongzhi	macroeconomic control
hui (lunhui, yaohui, piaohui)	credit associations (various forms)
huidui	remittances
huobi gongyingliang	money supply
huobi liutong sudu bianhua	changes in the velocity of money
huobi shichang	money market
jiaotong yinhang	Bank of Communications
jiashou lilu	penalty and arrears interest rates
jiben jianshe cunkuan	deposits for investment in capital construction
jiben jianshe zhaiquan	capital construction bonds
jichu huobi	monetary base
jiguan tuanti cunkuan	deposits by (state) offices and organizations
jihe	auditing
jihua danlie chengshi zhuanye yinhang fenhang	special bank branches in cities with provincial status
jijiexing daikuan	seasonal loans
jingji heli zengzhanglu	"rational" economic growth rate
jinrong gaige shidian chengshi	banking trial cities
jinrong gongsi	factoring companies
jinrong jigou	financial institutions
jinrong shichang	financial market

jinrong tizhi	monetary system, banking system
jinrong tongye chaijie shichang	interbank money market
jinrong zhaiquan	financial bonds
jinzhong youhuo	"tightening with enlivening" (a monetary policy)
kongzhi shuzi	reference numbers
kongzhi zongliang, tiaozheng jiegou, baozheng zhongdian, yasuo yiban, shishi tiaojie, tigao xiaoyi	control the volume of loans, readjust the structure of loans, guarantee key projects, reduce ordinary loans, adjust loans in good time, and increase efficiency
lao shao bian qiong diqu	"liberated" areas (Chinese soviets before 1949), minority, border and poor areas;
lianxi huiyi	joint conference
liutong zhong huobi	cash in circulation
minjian daikuan (or: ziyou daikuan)	personal loans (no financial intermediaries)
neibu yinhang	internal banks (within enterprises)
niandu xindai zijin shouzhi jihua	Annual Credit Funds Income and Expenditure Plan
nianduxing daikuan	annual loans
nongcun cunkuan	rural deposits
nongcun xinyong (hezuo) she	rural credit co-operatives
nongfu chanpin caigou	purchase of agricultural and sideline products
nongye shengchan ziliao	agricultural means of production

piaoju tiexian	(re)discounting of bills
qiye cunkuan	enterprise deposits
qiye zhaiquan	enterprise bonds
qiyehua	professional management
qu, zhen banshichu	local offices
quannian liangdi, anji jiankong, anyue kaohe, shishi tiaojie	annual planning quarterly inspections, monthly examinations, and adjustment on time
renmin yinhang xindai jihua	PBC Credit Plan
richaixing daikuan	call money, bridging loan
sanjiaozhai	triangular debt
shangye chengdui huipiao	commercial paper
shao shang yinhang	Shao Trade Bank
shehui shangpin goumaili	(Total) Purchasing Power (of Society)
shehui shangpin lingshou	Retail Sales
shehui xinyong guihua	Social Credit Outline
shehui zongchanzhi	Total Output Value of Society (MPS)
shehui zonghe xinyong guihua	Social Comprehensive Credit Outline
shichang piruan	market slump
tezhong guozhai	special bonds
tiaotiao kuaikuai	central and regional
tiexi	subsidized interest rates

tongshou tongzhi, tongcun tongdai	unified state control over revenues and expenditures, savings and credit
tongyi jihua, fenji guanli, cundai guagou, cha'e kongzhi	unified planning, administration on different levels, linking of deposits and loans, and control of the balance
tongyi jihua, huafen zijin, shidai shicun, xianghu rongtong	unified planning, division of funds, deposit of credit funds, and mutual money flows
tuoshou chengfu jiesuan	(traditional clearing system between banks)
waihui chubei	state foreign exchange stock plus foreign exchange balance of the Bank of China
waihui zhankuan	(PBC) foreign exchange
waizi, hezi, qiaozi yinhang	banks at least partly foreign-owned (solely foreign owned, jointly owned, owned by overseas Chinese)
wenzhong qiusong	"easing with stability" (monetary policy)
wujia jihua shangshenglu	planned increases in the price level
xiang renmin yinhang jiekuan jihua	PBC Refinancing Plan
xiaofeipin	consumer goods
xingzheng qiye	(administrative) enterprises
xintuo touzi gongsi	trust and investment companies
yewuku	business vault
yinhang chengdui huipiao	financial paper

yinhang tizhi	banking system
yinhangde changqi fangkuan	long-term bank credit
youhui lilu	preferential interest rates
yusuanwai zijin	extra-budgetary funds
zai ... de jingshen xia	in the spirit of ...
zaitiexian	rediscounting
zhaiquan	bonds
zhongdian qiye zhaiquan	key enterprise bonds
zhongguo gongshang yinhang	Industrial and Commercial Bank of China
zhongguo nongye yinhang	Agricultural Bank of China
zhongguo renmin baoxian gongsi	People's Insurance Company of China
zhongguo renmin jianshe yinhang	People's Construction Bank of China
zhongguo renmin shengli zheshi gongzhai	Victory Bonds
zhongguo renmin yinhang	People's Bank of China
zhongguo renmin yinhang shengshiqu fenhang (yiji fenhang)	PBC branches on provincial level (including the 3 municipalities directly under the central government and the 5 autonomous regions)
zhongguo renmin yinhang erji fenhang (diqu suozaidi (shi) fenhang, zhongxin zhihang)	PBC branches on second level (in districts, cities on district level and central cities)
zhongguo renmin yinhang jihua danlie chengshi	PBC branches in cities with provincial status
zhongguo renmin yinhang xian zhihang (banshichu)	PBC branches on county level

zhongguo renmin yinhang zonghang	PBC Head Office
zhongguo touzi yinhang	China Investment Bank
zhongguo yinhang	Bank of China
zhongguo yinhang waihui jiecun	foreign exchange balance of the Bank of China at the end of the year from business transactions
zhongxin shiye yinhang	Zhongxin Industrial and Commercial Banks
zhuanxiang lilu	special interest rates
zhuanye yinhang	special bank (commercial bank)
zhuanye yinhang shengshiqu fenhang	special bank branches on provincial level
zhuanye yinhang shizhihang	special bank branches in cities on the second level
zhuanye yinhang xian zhihang	special bank branches on county level
zhuanye yinhang zonghang	special bank head office
zhunbeijin cunkuan	minimum reserves
ziben shichang	capital market
zijin shichang	funds market
zongheng lianxi huiyi	"horizontal and vertical" joint conference
zongxiang zhuanye lianxi huiyi	"vertical, special" joint conference
zulin gongsi	leasing companies

SELECTED REFERENCES

Agricultural Bank of China. "Guanche zhixing < xindai zijin guanli shixing banfa > ruogan wenti de zanxing guiding" (To Implement the Temporary Provisions on Some Problems of the < Trial Measures for Credit Administration >). ZGJR 12/84: 32-35.

Almanac 1987. *1987 Zhongguo jinrong nianjian* (1987 Almanac of China's Finance and Banking). Beijing 1987.

Almanac 1989. *1989 Zhongguo jinrong nianjian* (1989 Almanac of China's Finance and Banking). Beijing 1989.

Almanac 1990. *1990 Zhongguo jinrong nianjian* (1990 Almanac of China's Finance and Banking). Beijing 1990.

An Zhiwen. "Nuli tansuo jinrong tizhi gaige de luzi" (To Make All Efforts to Explore the Path for the Reform of the Financial System). ZGJR 2/87: 10ff.

Bank Regulations of 1986. See State Council 7 Jan. 1986.

Barnham, Oliver. "Banking and Financial Reform in China." *China News Analysis* 1356 (15 March 1988): 1-9.

Bartke, Wolfgang. *Who's Who in the People's Republic of China*. 2. ed. Muenchen 1987.

Who's Who in the People's Republic of China. 3. ed. Muenchen 1991.

Beijing Rundschau. Beijing. Weekly magazine (German version of Beijing Review).

Beijing Review. Beijing. Weekly magazine.

Bendig, Helmut. "Das Bankwesen der Volksrepublik China" (The Banking System of the People's Republic of China). *Die Bank* 10/81: 501-508.

Berger, Peter L. and Hsin-Huang, Michael Hsiao (Ed.). *In Search of an East Asian Development Model*. New Brunswick 1987.

Bo Fulin. *Zhonghua renmin gongheguo guoshi* (History of the PRC). Harbin, PRC, 1988.

Buduan. "Buduan kaituo chuangxin wanshan xindai zijin guanli tizhi" (Continuously Bring Forth New Ideas and Perfect the Administrative System of Credit Funds). ZGJR 3/88: 25-27.

Byrd, William. *China's Financial System*. Boulder 1983.

C.a. *China aktuell*. Hamburg. Monthly journal (published by Institut fuer Asienkunde in German).

Cai Zhongzhi. "Lun jinrong gaige" (Analysis of the Reform of Finance). JJYJ 3/88: 51-58.

Caizhengjuan (Chinese-Chinese dictionary on finance). Shanghai 1987.

Carver, Dean. "China's Experiment with Fiscal and Monetary Policy." In *China's Economy Looks Toward the Year 2000, Volume 1, The Four Modernizations*. Washington D.C. 5/86: 110-131.

Cash Regulations 1988. See State Council 8 Sept. 1988.

CCP Research Agency. *Zhonggong nianjian* (CCP Annual). Taipei 1990.

Chang Gong. "Gaijin zhuanxiang daikuan guanli, cujin shangpin jingji fazhan" (To Improve the Administration of Special Credit and to Accelerate the Development of the Commodity Economy). ZGJR 3/88: 31f.

Chen Caihong. "Touzi yu jingji zhouqi" (Investment and Economic Cycles). JJYJ 2/88: 50-54.

Chen Huan-Chang. *The Economic Principles of Confucius and His School*. New York 1911.

Chen Muhua. "Chen Muhua tongzhi zhuchi zhaokai renmin yinhang lishihui" (Comrade Chen Muhua Presides Over a Meeting of the People's Bank of China Board of Directors). ZGJR 10/85: 2f.

"Yao jiakuai jinrong tizhi gaige de bufa" (To Quicken the Pace of Reform of the Financial System). ZGJR 2/87: 4-7.

"Jianchi 'jinzhong youhuo' fangzhen, renzhen luoshi gexiang jinrong zhengce cuoshi" (To Maintain the General Principle 'Tightening with Contraction' and Conscientiously Implement All Special Monetary Policy Measures). ZGJR 8/87: 8f.

"Kongzhi zongliang, tiaozheng jiegou, shenhua gaige, zhichi jingji wending fazhan" (To Control the Volume, Adjust the Structure, Deepen Reform and Support the Steady Development of the Economy). ZGJR 2/88: 4-7.

Chen Xigu. "Qianyi sheng yiji renmin yinhang zhixing zhongyang yinhang zhineng wenti" (Short Analysis of Problems Occurring with the Central Functions of the People's Bank of China On the Provincial Level). ZGJR 5/84: 25f.

Cheng Chuyuan. *Monetary Affairs of Communist China*. Hong Kong 1959.

China Business Guide. Hong Kong 1986.

China Daily. Beijing. Daily newspaper (published in English).

China Financial Statistics (1979-1985). *Zhongguo jinrong tongji* (China Financial Statistics). Edited by People's Bank of China, Investigation and Statistics Department. Beijing 1987.

China Financial Statistics (1952-1987). *Zhongguo jinrong tongji* (China Financial Statistics). Edited by People's Bank of China, Investigation and Statistics Department. Beijing 1988.

Chu, Franklin D. "Banking and Finance in the China Trade." In *Foreign Trade, Investment and the Law in the People's Republic of China*, edited by Michael J. Moser. Hongkong 1987.

Communique 1978. "Kommunique der 3. Plenartagung des 11. Zentralkomitees der Kommunistischen Partei Chinas" (Communique of the 3rd Plenum of the 11th Central Committee of the Chinese Communist Party). *Beijing Rundschau* 15 (No. 52) 31 Dec. 1978.

Dai Genyou et. al. "Jiating chuxu: Qingkuang, wenti he duice" (Private Savings Deposits: Present Situation, Problems and Counterpolicies). ZGJR 9/88: 30-32.

Dai Yuanchen. "Guanyu zhili jingji huanjing yu bimian jingji weisuo de tongxin taolun" (Correspondence On Ordering the Economic Environment and Avoiding an Economic Contraction). WEH 20 Feb. 1989: 7.

Decision 1989. "Decision on Further Improving the Economic Environment, Straightening Out the Economic Order, and Deepening the Reforms (Excerpts)." *Beijing Review* 33 (No. 7) 12 Feb. 1990: I-XVI.

Dembinski, Pawel H. "Quantity Versus Allocation of Money: Monetary Problems of the Centrally Planned Economies Reconsidered." *Kyklos* 41 (1988): (Fasc. 2) 281-300.

Deng Xiaoping. *Deng Xiaoping tongzhi lun zhexue* (Comrade Deng Xiaoping on Philosophy). Beijing 1990.

Domes, Juergen. "China auf dem Wege zu einem 'marktwirtschaftlichen' Sozialismus? Entwicklungen, bisherige Ergebnisse und Zukunftsperspektiven der Politik der Wirtschaftsreformen in der VR China" (China on the Way to a 'Market' Socialism? Developments, Previous Results and Future Perspectives of the Policy of Economic Reforms in the PRC). *Zeitschrift fuer Politik* 33 (Neue Folge, Heft 4, 1986): 351-371.

"Signale fuer die Zukunft? Der 13. Parteitag der KPCh (25.10.-1.1.87)" (Signals For the Future? The 13th Party Congress of the CCP (Oct. 25 - Jan. 1, 1987)). In *VR China im Wandel*. Bonn: Bundeszentrale fuer politische Bildung, 1988: 156-165.

Economic Yearbook 1988. *Zhongguo jingji nianjian* (1988 Economic Yearbook of the PRC). Beijing 1988.

Euromoney. London: Euromoney Publications PLC. (Monthly magazine.)

Fan Di et. al. "Shenmo shi shichang shehui zhuyi gongyouzhi shengchan de mudi zhide sansi" (What Is the Target of Production under Market-Socialist Society Ownership, Is Worth Three Thoughts). WEH 20 March 1989: 6.

Faxue cidian (Chinese-Chinese dictionary on law). Shanghai 1984.

FAZ. *Frankfurter Allgemeine Zeitung*. Frankfurt. Daily newspaper (in German).

FEER. *Far Eastern Economic Review*. Hong Kong. Weekly magazine.

Feltenstein, Andrew and Fahadian, Ziba: "Fiscal Policy, Monetary Targets and the Price Level in a Centrally Planned Economy: An Application to the Case of China." *Journal of Money, Credit and Banking* 19 (No. 2, 5/87): 137-156.

Feng Chunlin. "Xue Lei Feng xue 'er Lan' gao hao jingshen wenming jianshe" (To Study Lei Feng and the 'Two Lans' and to Do Well in the Construction of a Spiritual Civilization). ZGJR 5/90: 11-13.

Gao Shangquan. *Jiunian laide zhongguo jingji tizhi gaige* (Nine Years of Reform of the Economic System in China). Beijing 1987.

Gongzuo yanjiu. "Gongzuo yanjiu: Zhongyang yinhang shishi hongguan kongzhi yao jiejue quanshao fashao de wenti" (Work Research: When Exercising Macroeconomic Control the Central Bank Must Solve the Problems of Lack of Power and Laws). ZGJR 7/85: 33f.

Guanche. "Guanche hongguan jinsuo fangzhen, shenhua gongshang yinhang qiyehua gaige" (To Implement the General Macroeconomic Policy of Contraction and to Deepen the Reform Towards Professional Management Within the Industrial and Commercial Bank). ZGJR 2/88: 10-12.

Haberler, Gottfried. *Prosperitaet und Depression* (Prosperity and Depression). 2nd ed. Tuebingen 1955.

Hagemann, Ernst. *Statistik in China* (Statistics in China). Ein Literaturbericht. Bericht des Bundesinstituts fuer ostwissenschaftliche und internationale Studien. Koeln 5-88.

184

Han Yuting et. al. "Dute jingji geju xia de jinrong shijie, Wenzhou jinrong diaocha shouji" (The Financial World in an Unique Environment, Notes from a Financial Investigation in Wenzhou). ZGJR 2/88: 25-28.

Handelsblatt. Daily newspaper on commerce (in German).

Hayek, Friedrich A. Monetary Theory and the Trade Cycle. New York 1966 (Reprint, first publ. in 1933).

Heilongjiang Government. "Guanyu chexiao wei jing pizhun de jinrong jigou de tongzhi" (Circular on the Dissolution of Unlicensed Financial Institutions). ZGJR 4/85: 12.

Herrmann-Pillath, Carsten. Inflationsprozesse in der VR China seit 1979 (Inflationary Processes in the PRC Since 1979). Berichte des Bundesinstituts fuer ostwissenschaftliche und internationale Studien. Koeln 44-87.

"Das Grundproblem der Geldverfassung in den juengsten wirtschaftspolitischen Erfahrungen der Volksrepublic China" (The Fundamental Problem of the Monetary Constitution in the Latest Economic Policy Experiences in the People's Republic of China). Zeitschrift fuer Wirtschaftspolitik 37 (Heft 2-3, 1988): 139-187.

Die chinesische Wirtschaftsreform in der Phase beschleunigter Inflation: Neue theoretische und empirische Anlaysen (The Reform of the Chinese Economy in the Phase of Accelerated Inflation: New Theoretical and Empirical Analysis). Berichte des Bundesinstituts fuer ostwissenschaftliche und internationale Studien. Koeln 2-89.

Herrmann-Pillath Carsten and Ute. "Kultur- und Wirtschaftsordnung in der VR China: Korporativismus und begrenzter Individualismus" (Cultural and Economic Order in the PRC: Corporativism and Limited Individualism). Asien 22 (1/87): 1-24.

Hong Yuncheng et. al. "Jiakuai fazhi jianshe, shenhua jinrong gaige" (To Quicken the Establishment of a Legal System and to Deepen the Financial Reform). ZGJR 3/88: 39f.

Hsue, Immanuel C.Y. China Without Mao: The Search for a New Order. 2. ed. New York 1990.

Hu Xiaolian and Tang Sining. "Dui woguo waizhai chengshou nengli he changhuan nengli de panduan yu fenxi" (Analysis and Assessment of China's Ability to Bear and to Repay Foreign Debts). ZGJR 7/90: 39f.

Huang Gangming. "Fahui erji fenhang de jiji zuoyong" (To Give Play to the Positive Functions of the Second-Level Bank Branches). ZGJR 2/86: 22f.

Huang Min. *Shehui zhuyi huobi yinhang xue* (Socialist Money and Banking). Wuhan 1988.

Huang Renzhen et. al. "Qiye jituan de jinrong zudai" (The Financial Organization and Links of Enterprise Groups). ZGJR 8/88: 39f.

Huang Youguang et. al. "Weihe zhongguo ying yitiao guohe de jinxing minyinghua" (Why China Should Cross the River in One Leap to Democratization of Management). WEH 6 and 20 Feb. 1989: 12f and 15.

ICBC. See Industrial and Commercial Bank of China.

Industrial and Commercial Bank of China. "Zhongguo gongshang yinhang xindai zijin jihua guanli shixing banfa" (Provisional Measures in the Planned Administration of Credit Funds of the Industrial and Commercial Bank of China). ZGJR 12/84 (passed on 8 Oct. 1984): 30-32.

"Zhongguo gongshang yinhang Shaanxi sheng fenhang fuhangzhang Shang Xiaomei huyu qiyejia yao liyong hao yinhang zhege 'lingqiao jiqi'" (Zhang Xiaomei, Vice-Director of the Industrial and Commercial Bank of China, Shaanxi Province, Appeals to Entrepreneurs to Well Use the Bank, This 'Ingenious Machine'). WEH 10 Oct. 1988: 5.

International Monetary Fund. *Annual Report on Exchange Arrangements and Exchange Restrictions 1986*. Washington D.C.

International Herald Tribune. New York. Daily newspaper.

International Monetary Fund. *International Financial Statistics* (Vol. XLIII, No. 12, Dec. 1990). Washington D.C.

Issing, Otmar. "Notenbanken. II: Verfassung, Ziele, Organisation und Instrumente" (Central Banks. II: Constitution, Objectives, Organization and Instruments). In *Handwoerterbuch der Wirtschaftswissenschaften*, Bd. 5. Stuttgart 1980: 334-349.

Issues & Studies. Taipei, Taiwan. Monthly journal.

Ji Jun. "Shenru tantao jinyibu zuo hao jihe gongzuo" (Thorough Inquiry on How to Further Improve Auditing Work). ZGJR 3/88: 50.

Jia Geng. "Choujin yingen yu yasuo guimo - lun wo guo xuqiu kongzhi de zhuolidian ji zhuanhuan tiaojian" (To Reduce Money Supply and the Volume of Investment - Discussion of the Focal Point and the Preconditions for Change in China's Demand Control). JJYJ 5/88: 10-14.

Jianding. "Jianding buyi de an shisan jie san zhong quanhui de jingshen ban" (To Unswervingly Act in the Spirit of the Third Plenum of the Thirteenth Central Committee). ZGJR 12/88: 4f.

Jiaqiang jilu. "Jiaqiang jiluxing, wubi po 'sanlun'" (To Strengthen Discipline; the '3 Attitudes' Have to Be Destroyed). ZGJR 11/88: 7-9.

Jin Jiandong. "Woguo de zhongyang yinhang ji qi zai hongguan jingji guanli zhong de zuoyong" (China's Central Bank and its Functions in Macroeconomic Management). In Liu Hongru 1986: 35-50.

"Woguo zhongyang yinhang huobi zhengce de mubiao xuanze he shixian shouduan" (The Selection of Targets for China's Monetary and Banking Policy and Their Implementation). ZGJR 11/86: 16-19.

Jin Weihong. "Jianli yige kexue de jinrong hongguan tiaokong tixi" (To Establish a Scientific Financial Macroeconomic Control Structure). ZGJR 9/90: 34-37.

Jin zuida. "Jin zuida nuli guanche luoshi wending jinrong de ge xiang cuoshi" (To Undertake the Greatest Efforts to Implement All Measures to Stabilize the Financial system). ZGJR 10/86: 16-19.

Jingji cankao. Daily economic newspaper (in Chinese).

Jinrong shibao. Daily financial newspaper (in Chinese).

Jinrong yaowen (Important Financial News). ZGJR 7/90: 56.

Jinrongjuan (Chinese-Chinese dictionary on monetary affairs). Shanghai 1987.

JJYJ. *Jingji Yanjiu* (Economic Research). Beijing. Monthly publication.

King, Frank H.H. *Money and Monetary Policy in China 1845 - 1895.* Cambridge 1965.

Kongzhi. "Kongzhi zongliang, tiaozheng jiegou" (To Control the Volume and to Adjust the Structure). ZGJR 3/88: 4f.

Kraus, Willy. *Wirtschaftliche Entwicklung und sozialer Wandel in der Volksrepublik China* (Economic Development and Social Change in the People's Republic of China). Berlin 1979.

Li Guixian. "Jixu guanche zhixing yi jin fangzhen cujin jingji wending fazhan" (Further Implementation of the Contractionary Policy to Accelerate Steady Economic Development). ZGJR 7/88: 4-8.

"Jiaqiang hongguan tiaokong, zhengdun jinrong zhixu, shenhua jinrong gaige" (To Enhance Macroeconomic Control, Rectify the Financial Order and to Deepen Financial Reform). ZGJR 2/89: 4-9.

"Renzhen guanche wuzhong quanhui jingshen jianchi yi jin de huobi xindai fangzhen" (To Conscientiously Implement the Spirit of the Fifth Plenum of the Central Committee and to Maintain the General Policy of Scarce Currency and Credit). ZGJR 1/90: 4f.

"Zhenfen jingshen, tuanjie xiezuo, nuli wancheng yijiujiuling nian jinrong gongzuo renwu" (To Be Inspired with Spiritual Enthusiasm, to Unite and Cooperate and to Make Great Efforts to Fulfill the Financial Tasks in 1990). ZGJR 2/90: 4-8.

"Jianchi dang de lingdao, zuohao sixiang zhengzhi gongzuo" (To Uphold the Leadership of the Party and to Fulfill the Ideological and Political Tasks Well). ZGJR 3/90: 4f.

"Jianchi 'shuangjin' fangzhen, shishi tiaojie, cujin jingji wending fazhan" (To Uphold the 'Two Contractionary' General Policies, to Adjust in Good Time and to Promote the Steady Economic Development). ZGJR 4/90: 4f.

Li Peng. "Ba shenhua gaige tong zhili, zhengdun jinmi jiehe qilai" (To Closely Connect the Deepening of the Reforms With Control and Rectification). ZGJJTZGG 1/89: 6f.

"Jianchi fangxiang, jianding xinxin, wenbu qianjin" (To Maintain the Direction, Strengthen Confidence and Steadily Advance). ZBJJTZGG 2/89: 6-9.

Li Xingbin and Fan Heying. "Yao zhubu jiejue caizheng ji yinhang wenti" (The Problem of the Finance Ministry Pressuring Banks Must Be Gradually Solved). ZGJR 2/90: 22.

Li Yining. "A preliminary Study of the Adjustment Effects of Monetary Measures on China's Present Macroeconomy." *Social Sciences in China* 4/86: 55-64.

"Women mianlin de shi tizhixing tonghuo pengzhang" (The Inflation We Are Facing Depends on the System). WEH 6 March 1989: 2.

Li Yubing et. al. "Fahui renmin yinhang duanqi daikuan de tiaokong zuoyong" (To Develop the Control Function of the PBC Over Short-Term Credit). ZGJR 7/87: 42-44.

"Jiaqiang renmin yinhang duanqi daikuan he nianduxing daikuan de guanli" (To Strengthen the PBC's Administration of Short-Term and Annual Loans). ZGJR 6/90: 30f.

Li Yunqi et. al. "Guoyou caichan gerenhua: zhongguo jingji gaige qushi yu xuanze - gei zhongguo lingdao ren de jianyishu" (Privatization of State Property: Trends and Choices of the Reform of China's Economic System - a Proposal to the Chinese Leadership). WEH 27 Feb. 1989: 15.

Liang Yingwu. "Tuixing shangye huipiao chengdui tiexian, qingli daikuan tuoqian" (To Promote the Discounting of Commercial Paper Issued by Enterprises and to Sort Out Defaults on Credit). ZGJR 5/86: 11f.

Lin Guobao. "Jinrong hunluan houguo bi tonghuo pengzhang geng kepa" (The Consequences of Financial Chaos Are More Terrifying Than Inflation). WEH 26 Dec. 1988: 13.

Lin Jiken. "Jichu huobi, huobi chengshu he huobi gongying liang" (Monetary Base, Multiplier and Money Supply). JJYJ 6/87: 45-48.

Liu Hongru (Ed.). *Zhongguo jinrong shiye de fazhan he jinrong tizhi gaige* (The Development of Finance in China and the Reform of the Financial System). Beijing 1986.

Liu Hongru. "Lun jianli yi zhongyang yinhang wei zhongxin de shehui zhuyi jinrong tixi — jian tan <yinhang guanli zanxing tiaoli> de banbu he shishi" (Discussion on the Establishment of a Socialist Financial System with a Central Bank in the Center — On the Promulgation and Implementation of the <Provisional Regulations on Bank Administration>). ZGJR 3/86: 7-10.

"Gaishan zhongyang yinhang hongguan kongzhi, wanshan xindai zijin guanli banfa" (To Improve the Central Bank's Macroeconomic Control and to Perfect the Administrative Measures for Credit). ZGJR 11/86: 11-15.

"Zhongguo jinrong tizhi gaige yanjiu" (On China's Financial System). Beijing 1987.

Liu Yiqun. "Gongye qiye kucun jiya weihe jugaobuxia" (Why the Inventories of Industrial Enterprises Cannot Be Reduced from the Present High Level). ZGJR 8/90.

Liu Zhiqiang. "Huobi tongji yu fenxi de jiben kuangjia" (The Basic Framework for Monetary Statistics and Analysis). ZGJR 11/86: 33-35.

Lu Peijian. "Renzhen zuohao lishihui gongzuo chongfen fahui zhongyang yinhang zuoyong" (To Conscientiously Carry Out the Work of the Board of Directors and to Completely Develop the Functions of a Central Bank). ZGJR 3/84: 4f.

"Yijiubawu nian jinrong tizhi gaige de jixiang zhongdian gongzuo" (Some Key Aspects of the Reform of the Financial System in 1985). ZGJR 2/85: 2f.

Lutz, Friedrich A. *Geld und Waehrung* (Money and Currency). Tuebingen 1962: 28-103.

Ma Delun. "Xindai da jiancha riji" (Diary on the Large-Scale Credit Examination). ZGJR 12/88: 28f.

Ma Yongwei. "Guanche shisan da jingshen, shenhua nongcun jinrong tizhi gaige" (To Implement the Spirit of the Thirteenth Party Conference and to Deepen the Reform of the Agricultural Financial System). ZGJR 2/88: 15f.

Mo Ran. "Dui qianghua renmin yinhang hongguan tiaokong jizhi de sikao" (Reflections on Strengthening the Macroeconomic Control Mechanisms of the People's Bank). ZGJR 3/88: 53f.

Neue Zuercher Zeitung. (Swiss daily newspaper.)

Ni Liangtao. "Jiaqiang jinrong hongguan kongzhi de jige wenti" (Some Problems of Strengthening Financial Macroeconomic Control). ZGJR 6/85: 22-25.

Nuli. "Nuli gaohao chouzi rongzi gongzuo, jianjue guanche jinsuo fangzhen" (To Make Great Efforts in the Collection and Circulation of Money and to Resolutely Implement the Contractionary Policy). ZGJR 1/88: 5f.

Obersteller, Christine. *Das Finanz- und Bankensystem der Volksrepublik China — Eine einzel- und gesamtwirtschaftliche Analyse unter besonderer Beruecksichtigung aktueller Reformmassnahmen* (The Financial and Banking System of the People's Republic of China — A Micro- and Macroeconomic Analysis with Special Consideration for Present Reform Measures). Studienreihe der Stiftung Kreditwirtschaft an der Universitaet Hohenheim 1987.

Paraskewopoulos, Spiridon. *Konkunkturkrisen im Sozialismus* (Business Cycles Crisis in Socialist Economies). Stuttgart 1985.

PBC. See People's Bank of China.

PBC Constitution of 1983. See State Council 17 Sept. 1983.

Peebles, Gavin. "Inflation in the People's Republic of China 1950 - 1980." *The Three Banks Review* 142 (6/84): 37-57.

191

Peng Songjian. *Zhongguo caizheng yu jinrong* (China's Finance and Banking). Beijing 1987.

People's Bank of China (PBC).

3/84   "Zhongguo renmin yinhang lishihui di yi ci huiyi zai jing juxing" (The First Meeting of the PBC Board of Directors Has Been Held in Beijing). ZGJR 3/84: 2-4.

4/84   "Guanyu zhongguo renmin yinhang zhuanmen xingshi zhongyang yinhang zhineng de ruogan juti wenti de zanxing guiding" (Temporary Provisions on Some Concrete Problems of the PBC Solely Functioning as a Central Bank). ZGJR 4/84: 12-14.

8 Oct. 1984   (a) "Xindai zijin guanli shixing banfa" (Trial Measures for the Administration of Credit Funds). ZGJR 12/84: 19-21.

8 Oct. 1984   (b) "Zhongguo renmin yinhang xitong xindai zijin guanli de zanxing guiding" (Temporary Provisions on the Administration of PBC Credit). ZGJR 12/84: 29f.

12/84   "Guanyu <xindai zijin guanli shixing banfa> ruogan wenti de jieda" (Explanations on Some Questions About the <Trial Measures for the Administration of Credit Funds>). ZGJR 12/84: 22-24.

16 Feb. 1985   "Zhizhi youxie jiceng yinhang zheng'e xindai yewu, suibian zengshe fenzhi jigou" (To Stop Some Lower Level Bank Branches From Striving for Ever More Credit Business and Arbitrarily Setting up New Sub-Branches). ZGJR 4/85: 11.

4/85   (PBC and Industrial and Commercial Bank of China.) "Guanyu shixing shangye huipiao chengdui, tiexian banfa, qingli tuoqian daikuan de tongzhi" (Circular on the Implementation of Clearing by Using Commercial Paper, on Discounting and on Clearing up Credit Repayment in Arrears). Two parts. ZGJR 8/86: 44-46.

5 July 1985   "Zhongguo renmin yinhang jihe gongzuo zanxing guiding" (Temporary Provisions on the PBC's Internal Auditing). ZGJR 9/85: 34f.

8/85   "Zhongguo renmin yinhang dangzu zhaokai zheng dang hou di yi ci minzhu shenghuo hui" (The PBC Held the First Meeting on Democratic Living Since the Consolidation of the Party). ZGJR 8/85: 7.

9/85   "Duiwai jiekuan you zhongguo renmin yinhang guikou guanli" (Borrowing Abroad is Administered by the PBC). ZGJR 9/85: 38.

10/85   "Guanyu jianshe yinhang shixing <xindai zijin guanli shixing banfa> de buchong guiding" (Supplementary Provisions on the Implementation of the <Trial Measures for the Administration of Credit Funds> for the Construction Bank). ZGJR 10/85: 21f.

11/85   "Zizhu yingyunchu zijin, linghuo tiaoduchu xiaoyi" (To Independently Use Funds and to Flexibly Manage Efficiency). ZGJR 11/85: 28-30.

2/86   (PBC and Industrial and Commercial Bank of China.) "Zhongguo renmin yinhang, zhongguo gongshang yinhang lianhe fachu guanyu baoliu zhongguo renmin yinhang xianzhihang jigou youguan wenti de tongzhi" (Joint PBC and Industrial and Commercial Bank of China Circular on Relevant Questions of Maintaining County Level PBC Branches). ZGJR 2/86: 24.

26 Apr. 1986   "Jinrong xintuo touzi jigou guanli zanxing guiding" (Temporary Provisions on the Administration of Financial Trust and Investment Organizations). ZGJR 9/86: 48-50.

6/86   (PBC Funds Administration Department.) "Guanyu zhixing 'shidai shicun' xindai zijin guanli banfa de jige wenti" (On Some Problems of Implementing the Administrative Measures on Credit Funds Through 'Depositing Credit Funds'). ZGJR 6/86: 27-29.

1/87   (a) "Guanyu wanshan xindai zijin guanli banfa de guiding" (Provisions on the Perfection of the Administrative Measures on Credit Funds). ZGJR 1/87: 27f.

(b) "Zhongguo renmin yinhang dui zhuanye yinhang daikuan guanli zanxing banfa" (Temporary Measures for the Administration of Loans by the PBC to Special Banks). ZGJR 1/87: 29f.

9/87   "Guanyu zuohao xiabannian xindai zijin pingheng gongzuo de tongzhi" (Circular on Balancing Credit Funds Well in the Second Half of the Year). ZGJR 9/87: 4f.

28 Sept. 1987   "Youguan qiye gupiao, zhaiquan ji qita jinrong shichang yewu guanli wenti de tongzhi" (Circular on Relevant Questions of the Administration of Enterprise Stocks, Bonds and Other Financial Market Business). ZGJR 10/87.

12/87   (State Commission for the Reform of the Economic System and PBC.) "Guojia tigaiwei, zhongguo renmin yinhang guanyu shenhua jinrong tizhi gaige shidian de bushu" (State Commission for the Reform of the Economic System and PBC Outline on Deepening Experiments in the Reform of the Financial System). ZGJJTZGG 12/87.

19 Aug. 1988   "Renmin yinhang quanguo fenhang hangzhang huiyi genju guowuyuan jingshen zuochu guanyu jinyibu kongzhi yijiubaba nian huobi toufang he xindaiguimo de guiding" (Provisions by the People's Bank's Nationwide Branch Directors Meeting in the Spirit of the State Council on Further Control of the 1989 Increase in Cash Supply and the Credit Volume). *Jinrong shibao* 19 Aug. 1988.

10/88   "Bawo jinrong xingshi, zuohao wangji xianjin gongying gongzuo" (To Keep a Tight Grip on Finances and to Manage Well the Cash Supply During the Peak Season). ZGJR 10/88: 19f.

11/88   "Zhongguo renmin yinhang dishi fenhang hangzhang gangwei guifan" (Work Norms for the Directors of the PBC's Second Level Branches); "zhongguo renmin yinhang xianzhihang hangzhang gangwei guifan" (Work Norms for the Directors of the PBC's County Level Branches). ZGJR 11/88: 44ff.

14 Nov. 1988   "Zhongguo renmin yinhang diaocha biaoming: Wo guo xintuo jinrong jigou wenti zhongduo" (The PBC Survey Shows: The Problems of China's Financial Trust Organizations are Numerous). WEH 14 Nov. 1988: 6.

4/90   "Zhongguo renmin yinhang zuochu shenru kaizhan xuexi Fan Xinglan, Yang Dalan yingxiong shiji huodong de jueding "(PBC Decision on Thoroughly Launching a Campaign to Study the Heroic Deeds of Fan Xinglan and Yang Dalan). ZGJR 4/90: 10.

People's Bank of China Shanghai. "Diqu renmin yinhang jiaqiang hongguan kongzhi de yixie tansuo" (Some Exploratory Thoughts on the Regional People's Banks Strengthening Macroeconomic Control). ZGJR 2/86: 15-17.

"Diqu zhongyang yinhang ruhe jiaqiang hongguan guanli he linghuo rongtong zijin" (How Regional Central Banks Can Strengthen Macroeconomic Administration and Flexibly Circulate Funds). ZGJR 3/88: 28-30.

People's Bank of China Sichuan. "Renmin yinhang yao geng hao de wei hongguan jingji juece fuwu" (The People's Bank Must Better Serve Macroeconomic Decision-making). ZGJR 5/84: 21-24.

People's Bank of China Taiyuan. "Women shi zenmoyang kaizhan erji fenhang gongzuo de" (How We Can Develop the Work of Second Level Branches). ZGJR 1/86: 20f.

Proposals 1990. "Zhonggong zhongyang guanyu zhiding guomin jingji he shehui fazhan shinian guihua he 'bawu' jihua de jianyi" (Proposals by the CCP Central Committee for the Formulation of the Ten-Year and Eigth Five-Year Plan for National Economic and Social Development). *Jingji cankao* 29 Jan. 1991.

Qiu Qing. "Gaige yinhang xindai zijin guanli tizhi, tuidong yinhang gaige de shenru fazhan" (To Reform the Administrative System of Bank Credit and to Promote the Thorough Development of the Bank Reform). ZGJR 12/84: 9-12.

"Zhongguo renmin yinhang Qiu Qing tongzhi zai gaige jianshe yinhang xindai zijin guanli tizhi huiyi shang de jianghua" (The Speech of Comrade Qiu Qing from the People's Bank of China During the Conference on the Reform of Credit Administration at the Construction Bank). ZGJR 10/85: 16-18.

Ren Junyin. "Jinyibu yindao he shenhua jinrong tizhi gaige de sikao - dui Chongqing shi jinrong tizhi gaige de diaocha" (Reflections on the Further Guidance and Deepening of the Reform of the Financial System - Investigation of the Reform of the Financial System in Chongqing). ZGJR 9/87: 20-22.

"Jinyibu shenhua jinrong tizhi gaige shidian gongzuo de jige wenti" (To Further Explore Some Questions of Experimental Work on the Reform of the Financial System). ZGJR 11/87: 12-14.

Report 1986. "Guanyu diqige wunian jihua de baogao" (Report on the Seventh Five-Year Plan; made on the Fourth Plenum of the Sixth National People's Congress on 25 March 1986). *Beijing Rundschau* 23 (No. 16) 22 April 1986. (Chinese in RMRB 14 April 1986.)

Report 1987. "Yanzhe you zhongguo tese de shehui zhuyi daolu qianjin" (To Advance Along the Road to Socialism with Chinese Characteristics). Report on the Thirteenth Party Conference of the Chinese Communist Party, 25 October 1987. *Beijing Rundschau* 24 (No. 45) 10 Nov. 1987. (Chinese in RMRB 4 Nov. 1987.)

Report 1988. "Zhengfu gongzuo baogao" (Report on the Work of the Government; made on the First Plenum of the Seventh National People's Congress on 25 March 1988). *Beijing Rundschau* 25 (No. 17) 26 April 1988. (Chinese in RMRB 15 April 1988.)

Resolution 1984. "Zhonggong zhongyang guanyu jingji tizhi gaige de jueding" (Resolution of the Central Committee of the Chinese Communist Party on the Reform of the Economic System; passed by the Third Plenum of the Twelfth Central Committee of the Chinese Communist

Party on 20 October 1984). *Beijing Rundschau* 21 (No. 44) 30 October 1984. (Chinese in RMRB 21 October 1984.)

Reynolds, Paul D. *China's International Banking and Financial System*. New York 1982.

RMRB. *Renmin ribao*. Beijing. (People's Daily (newspaper), published by the CCP Central Committee.)

Schritte der Reform. "Die Schritte der Reform muessen beschleunigt werden" (The Steps of Reform Must Be Fastened). *Beijing Rundschau* 24 (No. 35) 1 Sept. 1987.

Shangye jingjijuan (Chinese-Chinese dictionary on economics and trade). Shanghai 1986.

Sheng Mujie. *Zhongyang yinhang xue* (Central Banking). Beijing 1989.

Shenhua. "Shenhua jinrong gaige de zhanlue zhiju" (To Deepen the Formulation of a Finance Reform Strategy). ZGJR 2/88: 29.

Shevel, I. "New Tendencies in the Chinese Credit and Banking System." *Far Eastern Affairs* 3/85: 78-86.

Shi Xiaofeng. "'Zhaiwu lian' de yuanyin he duice" (The Reasons of the 'Debt Chain' and the Counter Policies). ZGJR 4/90: 43.

Song Feng'e. "Jinyibu jiaqiang xindai zijin de hongguan guanli" (To Further Strengthen Macroeconomic Administration of Credit Funds). ZGJR 3/88: 9-12.

"Guanzhu jichu huobi, gaohuo shehui zijin" (To Strictly Control the Monetary Base and to Enliven Social Funds). ZGJR 6/88: 7-9.

"Jianjue guanzhu zhongyang yinhang daikuan, gaohuo xindai zongliang tiaokong" (To Resolutely Control Central Bank Credit and to Enliven the Control of the Credit Volume). ZGJR 11/88: 12-14.

Song Guoqing. "Shuanggui tizhi xia de huobi zhengce" (Monetary Policy Under the Double-Track System). JJYJ 8/88: 18-25.

Song Yingwei. "Jinrong gaige zhong jige zhide zhuyi de wenti" (Some Problems in the Financial Reform Worth Attention). ZGJR 4/87: 26.

South China Morning Post. Hong Kong. Daily newspaper.

State Statistical Bureau. "Zong pingjia: Jingji zhuangkuang xiyou jiaozhi" (General Assessment: The Economic Situation is Both Satisfactory and Worrying). RMRB 19 Jan. 1989: 2.

"Die volkswirtschaftliche und gesellschaftliche Entwicklung 1988" (Statistics for China's National Socio-Economic Development in 1988). *Beijing Rundschau* 26 (No. 10) 7 March 1989.

"Statistics for China's National Socio-Economic Development in 1989." *Beijing Review* 33 (No. 9) 26 Feb. 1990.

"Statistical Communique of the State Statistical Bureau of the People's Republic of China on National Economic and Social Development in 1990." *Beijing Review* 34 (No. 10) 11 March 1991.

State Council (Source: *Guowuyuan gongbao* (State Council Bulletin), if no other source given).

22 Sept. 1980   "Zhongguo yinhang zhangcheng" (Constitution of the Bank of China)

30 May 1981   "Guowuyuan pizhuan zhongguo renmin yinhang guanyu zhongduan qi shebei daikuan gongzuo jingyan jiaoliu Tianjin xianchang hui de qingkuang baogao de tongzhi" (State Council Circular on the PBC Report about the Tianjin Conference on the Experiences with Medium- and Short-Term Loans for the Purchase of Equipment)

23 Dec. 1981   "Guowuyuan pizhuan zhongguo renmin yinhang guanyu tiaozheng yinhang cunkuan, daikuan lilu de bagao de tongzhi" (State Council Circular on the PBC Report About the Adjustment of the Interest Rate on Deposits in and Loans by Banks)

14 July 1982   "Guowuyuan pizhuan zhongguo renmin yinhang guanyu renmin yinhang de zhongyang yinhang zhineng ji qi yu

zhuanye yinhang de guanxi wenti de qingshi de tongzhi"
(State Council Circular on the PBC's Request for
Instructions on the Central Bank Functions of the
People's Bank and Problems in the Relationship with
the Special Banks)

27 Dec. 1982   "Guowuyuan dui zhongguo renmin yinhang < guanyu
chengli zhongguo renmin baoxian gongsi dongshi hui de
baogao > he < zhongguo renmin baoxian gongsi
zhangcheng > gei zhongguo renmin yinhang de pifu"
(State Council Reply to the PBC on the < Report on the
Establishment of a People's Insurance Company of
China Board of Directors > and on the < People's
Insurance Company of China Constitution >

15 June 1983   "Zhonghua renmin gongheguo jinyin guanli tiaoli"
(People's Republic of China Administrative Regulations
for Gold and Silver)

25 June 1983   "Guowuyuan pizhuan zhongguo renmin yinhang guanyu
guoying qiye liudong zijin gai you renmin yinhang
tongyi guanli de baogao de tongzhi" (State Council
Circular on the PBC Report About the Change to
Unified Administration of State Enterprises' Working
Capital by the PBC)

17 Sept. 1983   "Guowuyuan guanyu zhongguo renmin yinhang
zhuanmen xingshi zhongyang yinhang zhineng de
jueding" (State Council Decision on the PBC Solely
Functioning as a Central Bank). Also: "PBC
Constitution of 1983." (English in: Foreign Affairs
Department, People's Bank of China. *The People's
Bank of China, Its Functions and Organizations*.
Beijing, 1984.)

23 Sept. 1983   "Zhonghua renmin gongheguo yijiubasi nian guokuquan
tiaoli" (1984 People's Republic of China Treasury Bond
Regulations)

28 Dec. 1983   "Zhonghua renmin gongheguo jinyin guanli tiaoli
shixing xize" (Rules for Implementation of the

Regulations for Administration of Gold and Silver in the People's Republic of China)

30 May 1984   "Guowuyuan pizhuan zhongguo renmin yinhang guanyu ge zhuanye yinhang fafang gudingzichan daikuan fengong wenti de bagao de tongzhi" (State Council Circular on the PBC Report About the Problem of Division of Labor in Fixed Asset Loans Given by Special Banks)

3 March 1985   "Baoxian qiye guanli zanxing tiaoli" (Temporary Regulations on the Administration of Insurance Companies)

14 March 1985   "Guowuyuan pizhuan zhongguo renmin yinhang guanyu tiaozheng bufen cunkuan, daikuan lilu de baogao de tongzhi" (State Council Circular on the PBC Report About the Adjustment of Some Interest Rates on Deposits and Loans)

8 July 1985   "Guowuyuan pizhuan zhongguo renmin yinhang guanyu tiaozheng chuxu cunkuan lilu he gudingzichan daikuan lilu de baogao de tongzhi" (State Council Circular on the PBC Report About the Adjustment of Interest Rates on Savings Deposits and on Fixed Assets Loans)

7 Oct. 1985   "Zhongguo renmin yinhang, guowuyuan keji lingdao xiaozu bangongshi guanyu jiji kaizhan keji xindai de lianhe tongzhi" (Joint Circular by the PBC and the Office of the State Council Science and Technology Leading Group on the Active Development of Science and Technology Loans)

12 Oct. 1985   "Guowuyuan pizhuan zhongguo renmin yinhang guanyu quanmian kaizhan xindai jiancha de baogao de tongzhi" (State Council Circular on the PBC Report About Comprehensively Launching the Credit Investigation)

7 Jan. 1986   "Yinhang zanxing tiaoli" (Temporary Bank Regulations). Also: "Bank Regulations of 1986."

17 July 1986   "Zhongguo renmin yinhang guanyu fabu < chengshi xinyongshe guanli zanxing guiding > de tongzhi" (PBC Circular on the Promulgation of the < Provisional Provisions for the Administration of Urban Credit Cooperatives >)

27 March 1987   "Qiye zhaiquan guanli zanxing tiaoli" (Temporary Regulations on the Administration of Enterprise Bonds)

7 April 1987   "Guowuyuan fachu yaoqiu gedi jiaqiang gupiao, zhaiquan guanli de tongzhi" (State Council Circular Requesting the Strengthening of the Administration of Stocks and Bonds Nationwide)

17 June 1987   "Guowuyuan pizhun waizhai tongji jiance zanxing guiding" (State Council Approval of the Provisional Provisions for the Statistical Supervision of Foreign Bonds)

25 Nov. 1987   "Quanguo kongzhi shehui jituan goumaili bangongshi, guojiajiwei, guojia jingwei, caizhengbu, zhongguo renmin yinhang, shangyebu, gonganju guanyu weifan kongzhi shehui jituan goumaili guiding de chuli zanxing banfa" (Office for the National Control of the Purchasing Power of Social Institutions, State Planning Commission, State Economic Commission, Finance Ministry, PBC, Trade Ministry and Public Security on the Temporary Measures to Handle Violations of the Provisions for the Control of the Purchasing Power of Social Institutions)

13 Dec. 1987   "Jinrong jigou daikehu banli jiqi he yuanqi waihui maimai guanli guiding" (Administrative Provisions for Spot and Forward Exchange Transactions by Financial Institutions for Their Customers)

31 Dec. 1987   "Caizhengbu, zhongguo renmin yinhang, guoji jiaowei, guojia kewei, wenhuabu, guangbo dianying dianshibu, xinwen chubanshu guanyu jiaqiang bumenjian de xiezuo peihe jinyibu gaohao geren shouru tiaojieshui zhengshou guanli de lianhe tongzhi" (Finance Ministry, PBC, State

Education Commission, State Science Commission, Cultural Ministry, Ministry for Broadcasting, Film and TV and the News Publishing Office Joint Circular on Strengthening Coordination and Cooperation Between Ministries in Order to Handle Well the Collection of the Personal Income Adjustment Tax)

13 Apr. 1988   "Zhonghua renmin gongheguo quanmin suoyouzhi gongye qiye fa" (Law of the People's Republic of China on Industrial Enterprises in State Ownership)

18 Aug. 1988   "Guowuyuan pizhuan zhongguo renmin yinhang < guanyu kongzhi huobi, wending jinrong jixiang cuoshi de baogao > " (State Council Circular on the PBC < Report About Some Measures to Control the Currency and to Stabilize the Financial System >)

22 Aug. 1988   "Guowuyuan bangongting zhuanfa zhongguo renmin yinhang guanyu gaige yinhang jiesuan baogao de tongzhi" (General Office of the State Council Circular on the PBC Report About the Reform of the Bank Clearing System)

3 Sept. 1988   "Zhongguo renmin yinhang guanyu kaiban renminbi changqi baozhi chuxu cunkuan de gonggao" (PBC Announcement on the Beginning of Long-Term Value-Guaranteed Savings Deposits)

8 Sept. 1988   "Zhonghua renmin gongheguo guowuyuan ling xianjin guanli zanxing tiaoli" (People's Republic of China State Council Decree on the Temporary Regulations for the Administration of Cash)

12 Sept. 1988   "Xianjin guanli zanxing tiaoli shishi xize" (Rules for Implementation of the Temporary Regulations for the Administration of Cash)

21 Oct. 1988   "Zhonghua renmin gongheguo shenji tiaoli" (People's Republic of China Auditing Regulations)

27 Apr. 1989   "Guanyu 1988 nian guojia yusuan zhixing qingkuang he 1989 nian guojia yusuan caoan de baogao" (Report on the Implementation of the 1989 Budget and the 1989 Budget Draft)

31 July 1989   "Guowuyuan guanyu faxing 1989 nian baozhi gongzhai de tongzhi" (State Council Circular on the Issuing of 1989 Value-Guaranteed Government Bonds)

27 Apr. 1990   "Guanyu 1989 nian guomin jingji he shehui fazhan jihua zhixing qingkuang yu 1990 nian jihua caoan de baogao" (Report on the Implementation of the National Economic and Social Development Plan in 1989 and the Draft Plan for 1990)

26 June 1990   "Zhonghua renmin gongheguo 1990 nian guokuquan tiaoli" (People's Republic of China Decree on 1990 Treasury Bonds)

Statistical Yearbook 1986. *Statistical Yearbook of China 1986* (in English). Edited by State Statistical Bureau. (Beijing) Hong Kong 1986.

1988 (in Chinese: *Zhongguo tongji nianjian*). Edited by State Statistical Bureau. Beijing 1988.

1989 (in English). Edited by State Statistical Bureau. (Beijing) Hong Kong 1989.

1990 (in Chinese: *Zhongguo tongji nianjian*). Edited by State Statistical Bureau. Beijing 1990.

Tan Yueheng. "Jinrong tizhi gaige zhong de yinhang tixi chongzu wenti" (The Problem of Bank Reorganization Within the Reform of the Financial Structure). *Zhongguo shehui kexueyuan yanjiushengyuan xuebao* 5/87: 22-26.

Tang Gengyao. "Zhongguo de waihui guanli" (China's Foreign Exchange Administration). In Liu Hongru 1986: 51-65.

Tang Yongyi. "Kaiban 'neibu yinhang' tigao zijin shiyong xiaoyi" (To Set up 'Internal Banks' in Order to Increase the Efficiency of the Use of Funds). ZGJR 2/88: 22f.

Taubmann, Wolfgang. "Die Volksrepublik China: Ein wirtschafts- und sozialgeographischer Ueberblick" (The People's Republic of China: An Economic and Socio-Geographic Overview). Landeszentrale fuer politische Bildung Baden-Wuerttemberg: Die Volksrepublik China (in der Reihe: *Der Buerger im Staat*) 37 (Heft 1) 3/87: 3-12.

Tong Dalin. "Zhongguo jingji tizhi gaige shi nian jianshu" (Brief Account of the Ten Years of China's Reform of the Economic System). ZGJJTZGG 2/89: 11-14.

Tong Zengyin. "Jiesuan gaige shiguan zhongda" (Reform of the Clearing System, an Important Matter). ZGJR 1/89: 11f.

Tuchtfeld, Egon. "Wirtschaftssysteme" (Economic Systems). In *Handwoerterbuch der Wirtschaftswissenschaften* Bd. 9., Stuttgart 1982: 326-353.

Vetter, Horst. "Das chinesische Bankenwesen" (The Chinese Banking System). *Die Bank* 9/85: 463-467.

The Wall Street Journal. Princeton. Daily newspaper.

Walters, Carl Emil. *Party-state Relations in the People's Republic of China: The Role of the People's Bank and the Local Party in Economic Management.* Ann Arbor 1982.

Wang Lan. "Wo guo tonghuo pengzhang de yuanyin ji qi duice" (The Reason for Inflation in China and the Counter-Policies). ZGJR 11/88: 18f.

Wang Lijuan. "Guanyu chuxu huapo xianxiang de sikao" (Reflections on the Landslide Phenomenon in Savings Deposits). ZGJR 8/88: 58f and 52.

Wang Xiangpin. "Dangqian zijin shichang pouxi" (Analysis of the Present Money Market). ZGJR 2/88: 38f.

"Shichang 'piruan' tanyuan" (Exploration of the Reasons of the Market 'Slump'). ZGJR 1/90: 28,29,16.

Wang Zhi. "Jinnian huobi faxing neng kongzhizhu ma?" Can This Year's Issuing of Cash be Kept Under Control?). WEH 27 Feb. 1989: 6.

Weber, Max. *Gesammelte Aufsaetze zur Religionssoziologie I* (Collected Essays on the Sociology of Religion I). Tuebingen 1920, 1988. (Especially "Konfuzianismus und Taoismus" ("Confucianism and Daoism"), pp. 276-536.)

Weggel, Oskar. "Geschichte und Gegenwartsbezug" (History and Relevance to Present Times).
> Part 6 "Die grosse Proletarische Kulturrevolution (1966-76): Der Maoismus bring seine Zukunft hinter sich" (The Great Proletarian Cultural Revolution (1966-76): Maoismus Leaves Its Future Behind). C.a. 5/88: 369-406.
> Part 7 "Reformen sind die wahre Revolution! Der Wandel des Zeitgeistes in der nachmaoistischen Epoche (1977ff)" (Reforms Are the True Revolution! Changes in the Spirit of the Times in the Post-Mao Epoch (1977ff)). C.a. 7/88: 526-569.

"Der Wandel in China seit der Kulturrevolution" (The Changes in China Since the Cultural Revolution). In *VR China im Wandel*. Bundeszentrale fuer politische Bildung. Bonn 1988: 78-99.

WEH. *Shijie jingji daobao* (World Economic Herald). Shanghai. (Weekly newspaper with critical contributions on the political and economic situation in the PRC. Publication ended with 4 June 1989.)

Wei Zhenguang. "Zhengque fahui yinhang dui shehui zongxuqiu de tiaojie zuoyong" (Correctly Develop the Regulatory Functions of Banks on Total Social Demand). ZGJR 12/85: 8f.

Wu Jiaxiang. "Ba wushi zhuyi zhexue chedihua" (Make Pragmatism Thorough). WEH 6 Feb. 1989: 14.

Wu Jiesi. *Woguo jinrong tizhi gaige de tansuo* (Exploratory Study of China's Reform of the Financial System). Beijing 1987.

Wu Qincheng. "Ruhe fazhan woguo jinrong shichang" (How to Develop China's Money Market). ZGJR 9/90: 24f.

Wu Xingdong. "Jiekai 'zhaiwu lian' you he liangfang?" (What Is an Effective Strategy to Solve the 'Debt Chain'?). ZGJR 7/90: 4-6.

Wulf, Luc de and Goldsbrough, David. "The Evolving Role of Monetary Policy in China." *International Monetary Fund Staff papers*. Washington D.C. 6/86: 209-242.

Xiandai hanyu cidian (Chinese-Chinese general dictionary). Beijing 1985.

Xie Ping. "Huobi jinsuo zhengce de hongguan xiaoguo" (The Macroeconomic Results of a Contractionary Monetary Policy). ZGJR 1/90: 23-25.

Xinwenbao. Shanghai. Daily newspaper (in Chinese).

Xing Benxiu. "Shichang piruan bu ying guijiu yu baozhi chuxu" (The Market Slump Should Not Be Attributed to the Value-Guaranteed Savings Deposits). ZGJR 6/90: 21.

Xu Jian. "Jianli xinde hongguan jinrong tiaokong jizhi" (To Establish a New Macroeconomic Financial Control Mechanism). WEH 12 Dec. 1988: 7.

Xue Muqiao. "Muqiande huobi zhengce yao yi wending jingji wei zhu" (The Main Objective of the Present Monetary Policy Is the Stabilization of the Economy). ZGJR 1/88: 18f.

Yang Changzeng. "Renmin yinhang fenzhi jigou gongzuo fangfa qianyi" (Simple Proposal on the Work Methods of Branch Institutions of the People's Bank). ZGJR 6/86: 22-24.

Yang Lien-Sheng. *Money and Credit in China: A Short History*. Cambridge 1952.

Yang Peixin. "On Building a Socialist Capital Market in China." *Chinese Economic Studies* XX (No. 2, 1986-87): 67-74. (From: RMRB 7 April 1986.)

"Huigu shinian gaige wo dechu jielun: Zhi neng jianchi gaige cai neng zhizhi tongguo pengzhang" (Conclusions From a Review on Ten Years of Reform: Inflation Can Only Be Controlled by Continuing Reform). WEH 27 March 1989: 14f.

Ye Yixin. "Jinrong shichang; gaige, zai tansuo zhong qianjin — Shenyang shi jinrong tizhi gaige pianduan" (Financial Markets: Reform, Probing Its Way Forward — Short Introduction to Shenyang's Reform of the Financial System). ZGJR 2/88: 35-37.

Yu Haocheng. "Zhongguo xuyao xinquanwei zhuyi?" (Does China Need a New Authoritarianism?). WEH 6 Feb. 1989: 14.

Yu Li et. al. "Wo guo yinhang meiyou biyao shixing cunkuan zhunbeijin zhidu" (There is no Need for China to Have a Minimum Reserve Requirement). *Shaanxi caijing xueyuan xuebao* (Xian) 3/87: 42-46.

Yu Naidong and Wang Liqing. "Shidu tiaodi yinhang cun, daikuan lilu, cujin jingji wending zengzhang" (Appropriately Lower the Interest Rates on Deposits and Credit In Order to Accelerate Steady Economic Growth). ZGJR 6/90: 28f.

Yuan Zhiming. "Jiefang shengchanli xian yao jiefang ren" (Before Liberating Productive Forces Man Has to Be Liberated). WEH 6 Feb. 1989: 15.

ZGJJTZGG. *Zhongguo jingji tizhi gaige* (China's Reform of the Economic System). Beijing. (Monthly Magazine of the Commission for the Reform of the Economic System.)

ZGJR: *Zhongguo jinrong* (China Finance). Beijing. (Monthly magazine published by the PBC). In footnotes "ZGJR + date" as a source refers to the Consolidated Balance Sheet in the copy concerned. "ZGJR + date + page" as a source refers to a single page from which a minor fact has been obtained. In all other cases, the majority, the author is given as as reference.

Zhan Wu. "Wenzhoushi jinrong tizhi gaige de xiaoguo he qishi" (Results and Relevations of the Reform of the Financial System in Wenzhou). RMRB 23 Sept. 1987.

"Jinrong hongguan kongzhi de xiaoguo yu wanshan" (Results and Perfection of Macroeconomic Control Through the Financial System). ZGJR 3/88: 43.

Zhang Dun. "Renmin yinhang diaocha tongji gongzuo de yaoqiu" (Requirements of Survey and Statistical Work by the People's Bank). ZGJR 9/87: 32f.

Zhang Guanghua. "Chengzhang zhong de wo guo waihui tiaojie shichang" (China's Maturing Foreign Exchange Adjustment Market). ZGJR 6/90: 44f.

Zhang Guile et. al. "Tantan woguo yinhang tizhi de gaige" (Reform of China's Banking System). ZGJR 10/83: 23f.

Zhang Huaqiao. "Dui jinrong tizhi gaige shidian juxianxing de sikao" (Reflections on the Limited Meaning of Experiments in the Reform of the Financial System). ZGJR 11/87: 20-22.

Zhang Ning. "Guanyu gufenzhi fazhan de sikao" (Reflections on the Development of a Stock System). WEH 28 Dec. 1988: 2.

Zhang Shaojie et. al. "Rongzi: Xianshi yunxing de jizhi ji qi gaige" (Currency Circulation: Present Mechanisms and Their Reform). JJYJ 11/87; 10-20.

Zhang Xiaojun. "Zhongguo: Fazhan de tizhi huanjing, gaige de genben nanti" (China: The Development Environment and the Basic Difficulties of Reform). WEH 30 Jan. 1989: 10.

"Fenyun zhongshuo xin quanwei zhuyi" (Various Opinions on New Authoritarianism). WEH 13 March 1989: 10.

Zhang Xin. "Xin quanwei zhuyi zui keneng dailai shenmo?" (What Does New Authoritarianism Most Likely Bring About?). WEH 20 March 1988: 13.

Zhang Xiumin. "Jinrong fazhi gongzuo de huigu he muqian de renwu" (Review of the Legal System in Finance and the Present Tasks). ZGJR 6/88: 13-15.

Zhang Xuezhi et. al. "Fazhan hengxiang jingji xuyao hengxiang zijin rongtong" (In Order to Develop a Regionally Interwoven Economy Horizontal Currency Circulation Is Needed). ZGJR 2/88: 24.

Zhang Yongyu et. al. "Chushi fengmang — 1987 nian zhongguo renmin yinhang hongguan tiaokong chengji xianzhu" (First Attempt — The Achievements of the PBC's 1987 Macroeconomic Control Are Remarkable). ZGJR 4/88: 24-28.

Zhao Baowei et. al. "'Gongzhai sicun' touxi" (An Analysis of 'Public Funds As Private Savings'). ZGJR 1/90: 31f.

Zhichi. "Zhichi nongfu chanpin shougou dali zuzhi zijin" (Organize Funds on a Large Scale in Order to Support the Purchase of Agricultural and Sideline Products). ZGJR 9/88: 11f.

Zhou Jun. "Zhongyang yinhang de huobi zhengce yu huobi junheng" (The Monetary Policy of the Central Bank and the Monetary Balance). *Hunan jinrong zhigong daxue xuebao* 4/86: 1-15.

Zhou Zhengqing. "Anzhao 'kongzhi zongliang, tiaozheng jiegou' de fangzhen anpai hao jinnian de xindai jihua" (To Well Organize This Year's Credit Plan in Accordance with the General Policy of 'Control of the Volume, Adjustment of the Structure'). ZGJR 3/88: 6-9.

"Linghuo yunyong huobi zhengce gongju shixian hongguan kongzhi mubiao" (To Flexibly Use the Tool Monetary Policy to Implement Macroeconomic Control Targets). ZGJR 5/88: 23-25.

"Jianding de wancheng qingcang wajian de mubiao" (Staunchly Fulfill the Target of Cleaning Up Stocks). ZGJR 8/88: 6-10.

"Dangqian quanguo jinrong xingshi he zhunbei caiqu de jixiang cuoshi" (Contemporary Shape of Nationwide Finance and Some Measures in Preparation of Implementation). ZGJR 4/90: 6-8.

Zhou Zhishi. "Lishun lilu tixi, fahui tiaojie zuoyong" (To Improve the Interest Rate Structure and to Develop Its Adjustment Functions). ZGJR 12/87: 44f.

"15 chengshi zijin shichang lianluowang zai kaituo fazhan zhong" (A Money Market Liaison Net Between 15 Cities Is Being Developed). ZGJR 1/88: 59f.

INDEX

CORNELL EAST ASIA SERIES

For ordering information, please contact:

Cornell East Asia Series
East Asia Program
Cornell University
140 Uris Hall
Ithaca, NY 14853-7601
USA
(607) 255-6222.

1-93/.6M/BB